The Golden Age of Piracy in China, 1520–1810

The Golden Age of Piracy in China, 1520–1810

A Short History with Documents

Robert J. Antony

ROWMAN & LITTLEFIELD
Lanham • Boulder • New York • London

Published by Rowman & Littlefield
An imprint of The Rowman & Littlefield Publishing Group, Inc.
4501 Forbes Boulevard, Suite 200, Lanham, Maryland 20706
www.rowman.com

86-90 Paul Street, London EC2A 4NE

Copyright © 2022 by The Rowman & Littlefield Publishing Group, Inc.

All rights reserved. No part of this book may be reproduced in any form or by any electronic or mechanical means, including information storage and retrieval systems, without written permission from the publisher, except by a reviewer who may quote passages in a review.

British Library Cataloguing in Publication Information Available

Library of Congress Cataloging-in-Publication Data

Names: Antony, Robert J., author.
Title: The golden age of piracy in China, 1520-1810 : a short history with documents / Robert J. Antony.
Description: Lanham, Maryland : Rowman & Littlefield, [2022] | Includes bibliographical references and index.
Identifiers: LCCN 2021060855 (print) | LCCN 2021060856 (ebook) | ISBN 9781538161524 (cloth) | ISBN 9781538161531 (paperback) | ISBN 9781538161548 (epub)
Subjects: LCSH: Piracy—China—History—16th century. | Piracy—China—History—17th century. | Piracy—China—History—18th century. | Piracy—China—History—16th century—Sources. | Piracy—China—History—17th century—Sources. | Piracy—China—History—18th century—Sources.
Classification: LCC DS735.A2 A68 2022 (print) | LCC DS735.A2 (ebook) | DDC 951—dc23/eng/20211217
LC record available at https://lccn.loc.gov/2021060855
LC ebook record available at https://lccn.loc.gov/2021060856

Contents

Preface vii

PART I: NARRATIVE HISTORY

1 Piracy in China's Maritime World 3
2 Piracy in the Mid-Ming Dynasty (1520–1580) 13
3 Piracy during the Ming-Qing Transition (1620–1684) 23
4 Piracy in the Mid-Qing Dynasty (1775–1810) 33
5 The Significance of Piracy in China's History 45

PART II: DOCUMENTARY EVIDENCE

1 Piracy in the Mid-Ming Dynasty (1520–1580) 55
2 Piracy in the Ming-Qing Transition (1620–1684) 83
3 Piracy in the Mid-Qing Dynasty (1775–1810) 103

Chronology 139
Glossary 143
A Note on Chinese Documentary Evidence 149
References and Additional Readings 153
Index 163

Preface

For fifteen years I lived on what had once been two of the most notorious pirate islands in the Pearl River Delta—Taipa and Hengqin. Today, of course, they have lost most of their past notoriety. The pirate villages and shanties have been replaced with modern high-rise apartment towers, five-star resort hotels, shopping malls, casinos, and amusement parks. Still a few vestiges of their dubious past remain in their seedy backstreet mahjong parlors and crack houses. Nowadays gangsters and gamblers have displaced the pirates who once fervently prayed for divine blessings and protection at the Empress of Heaven (Tianhou) Temple in Cheok Ka Village where I lived on Taipa. It was at this temple where I first heard legends about Zhang Bao, Zheng Yi Sao, and other pirates from Vong Kei, the eighty-year-old temple caretaker, who had heard these stories from his father and grandfather, who likewise were temple caretakers. The stories about pirates, handed down as legends, as recorded memories, and as official documents, are seemingly fathomless and never-ending. In this short book I hope to add a small part to this vast literature by recounting the story of China's golden age of piracy through a brief narrative history together with a sampling of supporting documentary evidence.

I divide the book into two parts. The first part offers a concise overview of the golden age of piracy in China. It has five chapters: first I place piracy in the larger context of China's early modern maritime world, taking a China-centric rather than the more familiar Euro-centric approach. Next I review the three phases or cycles of large-scale piracy during the three centuries when piracy in China was at its peak—in the mid-Ming Dynasty (1520–1580), in the Ming-Qing transition (1620–1684), and in the mid-Qing Dynasty (1775–1810). The first part concludes with a discussion of the significance of piracy in China's history. In building this narrative history of piracy in early modern China, I also introduce some of the broader approaches and themes broached by other scholars.

The main body of the book, in the second part, consists of historical sources about pirates and piracy during the golden age in China. Most of the documents were written by actual participants, either officials or eyewitnesses. As for the pirates themselves, in some cases we do have their testimonies and confessions, which were frequently taken under torture in courts of law and therefore must be used with caution. The documentary evidence consists of a wide range of primary sources, including archival criminal cases and depositions, government reports and proclamations, memoirs of pirate captives and victims, and folklore handed down from generation to generation. I have tried to give a mix of published and unpublished sources, some translated into English for the first time, to provide a rare glimpse into the nature of the mostly unknown world of Asian-based piracy. While the majority of evidence was written in Chinese, I have also included examples of sources written in English, Japanese, Portuguese, and Dutch. I have spent a good bit of effort editing the sources, opting for loose rather than literal translations, to make them more readable and accessible to English-language readers. In compiling the primary documents for this book I have had to be selective, and it is likely that I have left out episodes and figures that some readers would have wanted to be included.

These primary sources provide windows into the murky world of piracy in China between the sixteenth and nineteenth centuries. While most of the written evidence had been prepared for a relatively small literate public in China or elsewhere around the world, for the majority of people living in the past who could not read, they learned about pirates from the stories told by their parents and elders, balladeers and playwrights, street criers and public executioners. Many of these oral tales have been handed down until today. To better understand piracy it is important to examine as many different sources as possible. The study of piracy demands multiple perspectives. I let the sources speak for themselves and allow readers to make their own conclusions about the pirates and piracy introduced in this book.

Because many of the names and terms used in this study may be unfamiliar to readers I have included a glossary and chronology, as well as extensive explanatory footnotes throughout the text. Besides footnotes, in the documentary evidence my comments are added to the original sources in brackets. I also have listed in the glossary and index the Chinese characters for special terms and the names of people and places, and for those interested in digging further into the Chinese sources, there is a note on the documentary evidence on Chinese piracy. The references section includes not only the works I have cited but also a list of suggested further readings. I have also included four maps, two tables, and fourteen illustrations, including seven facsimiles of original Chinese documents. Additional resources, including Chinese documents, maps, and illustrations, can be found on the book's webpage under the "Features" tab at https://rowman.com/ISBN/9781538161548/The-Golden-Age-of-Piracy-in-China.

Let me end this preface with my heartfelt thanks to all my friends, students, and colleagues who have helped me in one way or another over the past several decades in my understandings of Chinese history and culture. There are always too many individuals to name, and I apologize to those who I have missed, but I must mention the following accomplices who have enlightened me about pirates and history and have helped me in locating and explaining various sources—Wei Qingyuan, Qin Baoqi, Zhuang Jifa, Ye Xianen, Li Qingxin, Liu Ping, Zheng Guangnan, Akira Matsuura, Dian Murray, Paul Van Dyke, James Watson, Angela Schottenhammer, Hang Xing, Joseph Lee, Hyunhee Park, Fumihiko Kobayashi, Nancy Park, and Vincent Ho, as well as my students Ma Guang, Susan Schopp, Wong Wei Chin, Patrick Connolly, Chen Bin, Xue Qianhui, Kuang Meihua, Liang Xiuqing, Huang Meiling, Li Huishi, He Xingyin, and Liu Jiaqi. I would like to acknowledge the staffs and researchers at the First Historical Archives in Beijing, National Palace Museum in Taibei, Zhejiang Provincial Archives, Guangdong Provincial Library, Fu Sinian Library at Academia Sinica in Taiwan, Harvard-Yenching Library, and East Asian Library at Princeton University for all their help with the documentary evidence for this book. Most of this book was written between 2019 and 2021, during the coronavirus pandemic, while I was a visiting scholar at the School of Historical Studies at the Institute for Advanced Studies in Princeton and an associate in research at Harvard University's Fairbank Center for Chinese Studies. I am indebted to both institutions for their academic support and the intellectual camaraderie of their members. I especially want to thank Marcia Tucker, librarian at the Historical Studies–Social Science Library at the Institute for Advanced Study for her indefatigable efforts in getting books and articles to me during the pandemic. I also want to thank Susan McEachern, Katelyn Turner, Haley White, and the anonymous readers at Rowman & Littlefield for their valuable guidance and advice. Finally, and most importantly, I wish to thank my wife and life partner Lanshin for her tireless encouragement and help in completing this project. I dedicate this book to her.

Part I

NARRATIVE HISTORY

Chapter One

Piracy in China's Maritime World

For centuries piracy has captured the imagination of writers and readers alike. Described as daring adventurers, heroic rebels, or bloodthirsty villains, pirates in fact and fiction continue to fascinate people of all ages. Our appetite for stories about pirates seems unquenchable. There are hundreds of books, cartoons, songs, television dramas, and movies produced about pirates every year. Yet pirates are not only fascinating, they are also thought provoking and important. Although often dismissed in the past by scholars as historically insignificant, in reality, pirates have played key roles in the development of modern society. Piracy has always been intricately linked to issues of social and economic dislocation, maritime security, and national sovereignty. Today piracy costs legitimate commerce and businesses billions of dollars each year, including money spent for ransom payments, private security deterrence, and deployment of naval forces, not to mention the toll in human lives and lost property. Conversely, piracy has also stimulated and sustained a vast shadow economy and a vibrant subculture.

While much has been written about pirates in Western society, rigorous scholarly research on piracy in China is only beginning to appear. In reconstructing the history of piracy we encounter several problems, not the least of which is the lack of reliable primary sources. Because of the nature of their work, pirates necessarily left few records. To do so would have been risky. They did not want to draw attention to themselves from officials. Sometimes pirates went to extremes to remain anonymous, even murdering entire crews of ships that they attacked in order to eliminate any witnesses. What we know about pirates, therefore, comes chiefly from their enemies and victims. As the documents are intrinsically biased, obscure, and fragmentary, it is necessary to use many different types of sources and in multiple languages.

Another problem is explaining what piracy meant in its Chinese context. Piracy has always been a fluid, malleable concept with multiple layers of meaning relative to time, place, and culture. Are our contemporary Western definitions of piracy the same as those in China both today and in the past? How, for example, do we distinguish piracy from war, privateering, and smuggling? While European rulers attempted to make precise legal distinctions between these different phenomena, in China piracy and smuggling were often viewed as categorically the same, and Chinese rulers had no concept of privateering as used by Western states. For much of the Ming and early Qing dynasties (roughly sixteenth and seventeenth centuries), recurrent sea bans prohibited or severely restricted private maritime trade. Merchants who disregarded the regulations were criminalized and for the most part treated no differently than pirates. During the chaos and anarchy of the Ming-Qing transition (1620–1684), piracy and warfare became greatly confused—pirates became soldiers and soldiers became pirates. During times of war, Western governments sanctioned private vessels as privateers, which could legally attack and plunder enemy shipping. Privateering has been described by some scholars as a form of legalized piracy. But in China neither the Ming nor Qing governments sanctioned or legitimized any form of private maritime raiding; what Europeans called privateering to Chinese officials was simply piracy. In late imperial China laws made little distinction between bandits on land and on sea. Piracy consisted of various crimes—robbery, kidnapping, murder, extortion, rape, sedition, and rebellion—that could take place on seas, rivers, and coasts (Ptak 1998; Antony 2014c, 114).

Although some pirates were politically motivated, fundamentally piracy was an economic endeavor that involved lots of buying and selling. Most people became or helped pirates to earn money. Unlike merchants and smugglers, however, pirates traded in stolen goods obtained through predation and violence. Except for food, weapons, and other necessities, pirates sold or bartered most of their booty in black markets and even legitimate ports. Booty mostly consisted not of gold and silver but rather of various amounts of copper coins and items of daily life (Doc. 28). While small, ad hoc gangs typically split up the loot soon after heists, the larger, more permanent gangs usually put most of the spoils into a common fund, either kept aboard ship or stockpiled on shore in their lairs. Gang members would later sell the loot and share the profits in equitable portions (Docs. 31, 33, 40).

People have always reacted to piracy in many different ways. For most officials and land-based elites in China, pirates represented an exotic and dangerous "other." Many Chinese regarded the high seas as a lawless space beyond the pale of civilization. Official documents frequently labeled pirates as *haifei* or *yangfei* (terms meaning sea bandits), in which the root of the suffix *fei* in Chinese was an absolute negative that denied individuals their humanity and consequently their right to exist. In late imperial China piracy was a serious crime linked to treason and punishable by death. Chinese imperial states, like European states, viewed their wars against piracy as conflicts between civilization and barbarism. Yet in some areas and for some people, pirates were neither criminals nor shadowy figures. While official discourses treated pirates as criminals and traitors, in Ming popular fiction and unofficial histories they were often treated as romantic adventurers and patriotic heroes (Wang 2021; Doc. 7). Sometimes their presence and activities were well known, even encouraged and approved by local communities. In coastal South China, many villagers and fisherfolk collaborated with pirates as fences, suppliers, and arms dealers, and actually had cordial relations with the outlaws (Docs. 3, 5, 19, 40). In Fujian province, for instance, people considered the pirate-adventurer Zheng Zhilong as an upright, benevolent man because he aided the poor and provided many people with jobs. His son, Zheng Chenggong (better known in the West as Koxinga), was even eulogized as a deity in Taiwan after his death in 1662 (Croizier 1977). Other pirates were likewise celebrated as heroes and sometimes as deities by local communities.

China's water world was one of shared social, economic, and cultural activities and of patterns not easily defined and delimited by ethnic differences or by national boundaries. Chinese pirate ships were veritable melting pots where one could find men, women, and children of diverse social, cultural, ethnic, and national backgrounds. It was not unusual for pirate gangs to have crews consisting of Chinese, Japanese, and Southeast Asians and at times even Europeans, Americans, and Africans (Docs. 1, 5, 14). Crews were a motley assortment, not only of scalawags and misfits but also of ordinary sailors and fisherfolk who routinely alternated between licit and illicit pursuits in making a living. Pirate ships also had crews of both men and women. For many Chinese, pirating was literally a family business. Unlike the situation in the West, where there were taboos against females on pirate ships, in South China women were not only accepted as shipmates but also often played important organizational and leadership roles in pirate gangs, as were the cases of Cai Qian Ma and Zheng Yi Sao in the late eighteenth and early nineteenth centuries (Docs. 30, 40).

Although piracy reached a peak in the West in the late seventeenth and early eighteenth centuries, in the waters around China the "golden age of piracy" stretched for nearly three centuries from the mid-sixteenth to early nineteenth centuries. Over those years there was an unprecedented surge in Chinese piracy unsurpassed in size and scope anywhere else in the world. China's golden age of piracy evolved in three great waves. First, roughly between 1520 and 1580, there was a tremendous rise in piracy all along China's southern coast from Zhejiang province to Hainan Island, as well as to the waters around Japan, Korea, and Southeast Asia. This was the age of the so-called dwarf bandits (*wokou* in Chinese, *wakō* in Japanese, and *waegu* in Korean), who actually can best be described as ethnically mixed groups of merchants, smugglers, and pirates.[1] They were followed by bands of rebels, merchants, and pirates during the chaotic Ming-Qing dynastic transition between 1620 and 1684. During this cycle piracy was symptomatic of the political anarchy, economic instability, and social dislocations of the era. Many of the "sea rebels" (*haikou* or *haini*) combined commerce with piracy and insurgency. Next came a short but intense period of piracy, between 1775 and 1810, characterized by large, well-organized leagues of "ocean bandits" (*yangfei*). Chinese piracy had reached a crescendo during the third wave, when tens of thousands of poor fisherfolk and sailors engaged in piracy as a means of survival. For more than half of those 290 years between 1520 and 1810, pirates were a pervasive force in China's maritime world. While in the West the heyday of piracy began to decline in the early eighteenth century, it was reaching unparalleled heights in Asian waters. Never before in history had piracy been so strong and enduring; while in the West at its peak the pirate population never exceeded six thousand individuals, in China during each of the three waves the numbers of pirates reached several tens of thousands.

During China's golden age of piracy most of the action took place along the South China coast and across the vast South China Sea (map 1.1). China's coastline is one of the longest in the world, stretching for approximately 9,000 miles from the Yellow Sea in the far northeast to the Gulf of Tonkin in the far southwest. The littoral, especially of Guangdong, Fujian, and Zhejiang provinces, is interspersed with countless bays, mangrove swamps, and islands, which provided shelter to pirates and dissidents seeking to remain outside the gaze of the state and long arm of the law. Buffered between the Pacific and Indian oceans, the South China Sea encompasses roughly 1,400,000 square miles from China in the north to Indonesia and Borneo in the south. Taiwan and the Philippines border the east, with the Malay peninsula, Thailand, Cambodia, and Vietnam on the west. Even before the appearance of European explorers and traders in the sixteenth century, it was and has since remained one of the busiest shipping zones in the world. This huge expanse of water, with its countless islands and harbors, also provided not only mariners and merchants but also pirates and smugglers with jobs and livelihoods for centuries. In fact, piracy has played an integral role in shaping the history of maritime Asia.

---

1. Like the term *pirate*, in China the meaning of *wokou* has been in constant motion, shifting from Japanese seaborne raiders in the sixteenth century to invading Japanese soldiers during World War II in the twentieth century.

Piracy in China's Maritime World 7

Map 1.1. The South China Maritime World.
Source: created by Robert Antony.

Maritime trade was the lifeblood of this region. By the early sixteenth century numerous sea lanes crisscrossed the entire South China Sea linking China, Japan, and Korea to the Philippines, Vietnam (Annan), Thailand (Siam), Sumatra, and Java. Even after the arrival of Europeans in the sixteenth century, the entire region continued to be dominated by Asians and intraregional trading networks into the nineteenth century. When Europeans built their settlements around the rim of the South China Sea they did so in places along well-established Chinese trunk routes to Southeast Asia. There already existed an intricate mélange of interconnected markets that linked the smaller ports, harbors, and fishing villages to the larger entrepôts of Canton, Chaozhou, Amoy, Nagasaki, Manila, Bangkok, Malacca, and Batavia. By the late seventeenth century sea lanes connected these larger trading marts with one another and with the global markets in Europe and the Americas (Reid 1996; Blussé 1999; Antony 2017).

Not only did legitimate shippers use the sea lanes to carry on trade, but so too did those individuals who wished to subvert the system and trade outside the state's gaze. Piracy inescapably became entangled in the development of the early modern market economy and global commercialization. As licit trade increased so too did illicit trade, and the two were intimately connected. Although pirates engaged in a different sort of business from that of legitimate merchants, they were nonetheless also important in the expansion of China's maritime economy. During the sixteenth and early seventeenth centuries, because of the repeated bans of successive Chinese governments on maritime trade, it became difficult to distinguish between trader, smuggler, and pirate (Docs. 8, 20, 23). For much of the Ming period, piracy and smuggling necessarily became the most common and profitable form of commerce. In the early and mid-Qing periods, because legitimate markets could never keep pace with consumer demands, clandestine trade inevitably expanded to take up the slack.

Piracy actually stimulated the development of new markets and ports in China, many of which were established specifically to handle the growing contraband trade. To survive pirates needed support from people on land as well as friendly ports where they could outfit their ships, recruit new crews, and sell their booty. One such place was the Portuguese enclave of Macau. Since its founding in the sixteenth century Macau served as a friendly port of call for pirates, smugglers, and dissidents of all sorts. It was described as "the wickedest city in Asia" and the "Tripoli of the Orient"—an international rendezvous for desperadoes and misfits. In the early nineteenth century a Swedish resident named Anders Ljungstedt depicted the city as the ideal hiding place for thieves, gamblers, and vagabonds because "the jurisdiction is divided [between Portugal and China], and the tenor of the laws variously applied" (Ljungstedt 1836, 108). The many gambling parlors, opium dens, and seedy inns of its Inner Harbor served as natural meeting places where pirates socialized, got drunk, caroused with prostitutes, brawled, and made plans for new ventures. Not surprisingly, the pirate chieftain Zhang Bao made Macau the headquarters for his extortion operations, where he set up a "tax bureau" to collect ransom payments and protection fees. One of his accomplices was a local man named Zhou Feixiong, who was a notorious doctor, conjuror, and petty thief. He later received a minor office in Macau for helping to negotiate the surrender of Zhang Bao and Zheng Yi Sao in 1810 (Doc. 40).

Jiangping (or Giang Binh in Vietnamese) was one of Asia's most notorious black markets between 1780 and 1802, when it was razed by Vietnamese troops fighting Tay Son rebels. Located on the Sino-Vietnamese border in the Gulf of Tonkin, the town was surrounded in the south by countless small islands and sandy shoals and in the north by rugged mountains and dense forests, which made Jiangping nearly impossible to reach except by boat. It was situated along a major sailing route connecting northern Vietnam and southern China, and nearby were the ports of Hepu, Qinzhou, and Dongxing in China and Mong Cai and Pho Hien in northern Vietnam. Jiangping was a typical border town and black market, famous for its China Bazaar, where almost anything imaginable was sold. The town was a gathering place for laborers, sailors, fisherfolk, and traders from South China, Vietnam, and other areas of Southeast Asia, and many residents and sojourners specialized in handling stolen goods and provisioning the pirates based on adjacent islands. For over twenty years this black market served as an integral node in the vibrant shadow economy that traversed the South China Sea, connecting an

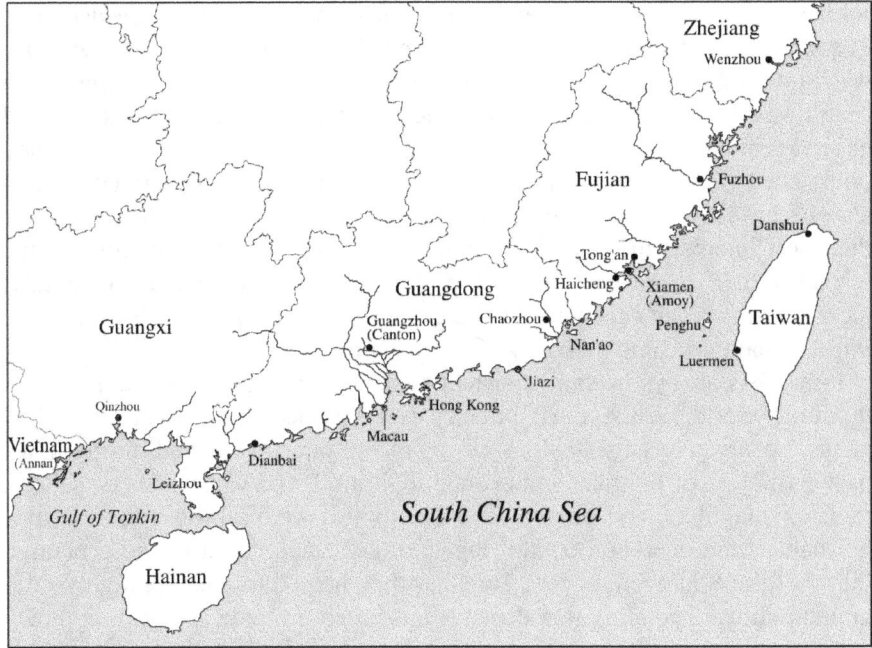

Map 1.2. The South China Coast.
Source: created by Robert Antony.

extensive network of both licit and illicit markets (Docs. 27, 28). Today, as in the past, fishing and smuggling remain as major sectors of the local economy (Antony 2010b).

There also existed a persistent shifting between legitimate and clandestine ports, as the cases of Yuegang and Amoy (Xiamen) in Fujian province demonstrate. At first, Yuegang developed as a prosperous smuggling port in the fifteenth century to offset the official port at Quanzhou. Then in 1567 the government changed the name Yuegang to Haicheng and recognized the port as an administrative seat. Afterward pirates and smugglers moved elsewhere to do business, in particular to Amoy, which in the late sixteenth century became a meeting place for Chinese and foreign smugglers and pirates (map 1.2). For much of the seventeenth century Amoy served as a major base of operations for the Zheng family's maritime empire. In 1684, after the downfall of the Zheng regime in Taiwan, the Qing court recognized Amoy as a legitimate port and the clandestine trade once again moved elsewhere (Docs. 5, 16, 19). Most of the illicit ports, however, were never as large and successful as Yuegang and Amoy; instead, they remained small and anonymous and therefore unrecorded in history.

A key factor in the success of piracy was the support that pirates received from coastal residents, including fishers, sailors, merchants, gentry families, soldiers, and officials. Whenever pirates lost that support piracy declined. The situation in South China in the eighteenth and early nineteenth centuries was quite different from what it had been in the sixteenth and seventeenth centuries, when many sea merchants, local gentry, and even officials opposed government sea bans and supported pirates. In Fujian, for example, piracy diminished greatly over the latter part of the eighteenth century in large measure because wealthy and influential coastal families decided that it was in their best interests to support the new Qing government and oppose piracy (Calanca 2010). Likewise, during the first decade of the nineteenth century, local merchants and gentry in Guangdong organized militia to help bolster the imperial navy to combat pirates (Antony 2006).

Piracy has always been a persistent and inherent feature of South China's maritime world. While most piracies were perpetrated by small, ad hoc gangs, upsurges in large-scale, well-organized piracy occurred during times of dynastic crisis, political and economic turmoil, and wars. Fishers, sailors, traders, smugglers, and pirates, whose activities were all too often indistinguishable from one another, knit together the social, cultural, and economic fabric of the South China Sea. Together they helped to create a highly integrated political economy that depended as much on trade as it did on piracy and smuggling. Denizens of this water world shared in a collective culture of their own making, a distinct culture of survival and resistance that stood in marked contrast to the terra-centered culture on land.

After 1810 huge pirate leagues never reappeared in China, but piracy has stubbornly persisted in Asian waters. Although in recent years there has been a marked resurgence in piracy across the globe, it has seldom reached the high levels of violence and predation of the past. Along the South China coast petty ad hoc gangs of pirates have incessantly formed and reformed as they have for centuries, mostly engaging in plundering and extorting small, poorly armed native fishing and commercial vessels. Today piracy appears in many of the same areas and for many of the same reasons—most notably poverty and weak states—that it thrived in hundreds of years ago. The largest numbers of piracies in recent years, as in the past, take place in Asian waters. As a recurring cyclical phenomenon, the piracy of today is inseparably connected with the piracy of the past.

Chapter Two

Piracy in the Mid-Ming Dynasty (1520–1580)

The golden age of piracy in China began in the middle of the Ming dynasty during the reign of the Jiajing emperor (r. 1522–1566). Beginning in the 1520s, China witnessed a steady growth in the number of piracies along the coast. Within two decades numerous small gangs of pirates had expanded into larger, better-organized fleets. Reaching its zenith in the 1550s, at a time when the Ming navy and coastal defense forces were in decline (roughly by 20 percent of their early Ming levels) and the dynasty was facing a serious threat on the northern frontier from resurgent Mongol armies under Altan Khan (1507–1582), pirates severely challenged imperial authority in South China's maritime world. At the height of their power they even threatened the major cities of Nanjing, Suzhou, and Hangzhou. This was also a time of civil war in Japan when sailors and masterless samurai (*ronin*) took to the sea as raiders. Characterized by Ming officials as "dwarf bandits" (*wokou*),[1] a term used disparagingly for Japanese pirates, they actually included virtually all pirates and sea peoples operating along the coast of China. *Wokou* gangs were composed of disparate crews of Japanese, Chinese, Southeast Asian, European, and African renegades and rovers, but most of these pirates (perhaps 80 percent) were Chinese. As used in Ming sources, *wokou* signified Japanese sea raiders, uncertified tributary envoys, Chinese maritime smugglers and private merchants, captives and slaves, and sometimes overseas Chinese (Shapinsky 2016, 40–41; Wang 2021, 5, 109–13). Using armored sailing junks and swift galleys they plundered shipping and pillaged ports from

---

1. Although mention of *wokou* raids on the China coast date back to the late thirteenth century in the Yuan dynasty, they only became a major problem in the mid-sixteenth century. By and large, important differences between the *wokou* activities of the Mongol and Ming periods were that in the former case Japanese constituted the majority of pirates and they mostly raided the Korean coast, and in the latter case the pirates were multinational in composition and they mostly raided the Chinese coast.

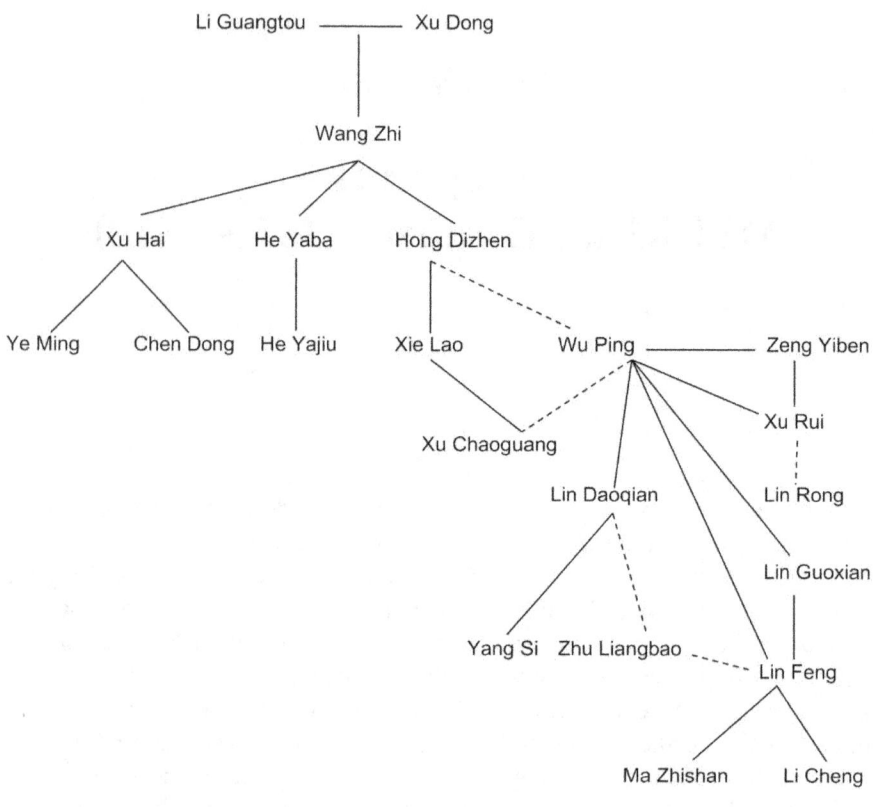

Figure 2.1. Affiliations between Major Pirate Leaders in South China, 1540–1580.
Source: created by Robert Antony.

China to Java (Doc. 1). Figure 2.1 outlines the major pirate leaders and their affiliations in South China between 1540 and 1580.

The upsurge in piracy in the 1520s resulted largely from the Jiajing emperor's determination to rigidly enforce existing sea bans and to enact tough new ones. The imperial court outlawed all private overseas trade and instead hopelessly attempted to restrict maritime commerce within the narrow confines of the tributary system.[2] Anyone caught building large ocean-going

---

2. The tributary system, as a historical term, is a modern Western label for a set of highly regulated, ritualized exchanges that occurred between China's imperial court and leaders of other Asian states. The tribute givers came from polities that were autonomous in the management of their day-to-day affairs but acknowledged, at least in theory, the authority of the Chinese emperor. Besides its political function, the tributary system also served as an important conduit for international trade. It reached its apex during the Ming dynasty.

junks, trading with foreigners, traveling abroad without authorization, or colluding with smugglers were to be treated as pirates and when caught faced execution. Instead of curbing illegal activities, however, the bans actually encouraged them. Because tribute missions were infrequent and the amounts of imports and exports severely limited, they satisfied neither Chinese nor foreign merchants. As a result illicit trade quickly expanded up and down the coast to meet the growing demands and increasingly more people came to depend on illicit trade for their livelihoods. Piracy became the most vivid expression of opposition to official maritime policies and the most important means for conducting seaborne trade (Docs. 2, 5).

In effect the Ming government's enforcement of the sea bans criminalized large segments of the maritime population. Gradually all segments of coastal society, from fishers and sailors to merchants and gentry, became involved in illegal activities (Docs. 4, 8). As one official, Zheng Ruozeng, succinctly put it: "Pirates and merchants are all the same people—when markets are open pirates become merchants and when markets are closed merchants become pirates" (Jiang and Fang 1993, 263). A striking feature of Chinese piracy in this era was the fact that many powerful leaders, including Xu Dong, Wang Zhi, Hong Dizhen, and Xu Hai, all had merchant backgrounds. These merchant-pirates mixed trade with smuggling and pillaging, organized large fleets of warships, and established bases on China's offshore islands, in Japan, and in Southeast Asia. Many pirate gangs seemed invincible because they received protection from influential families and local officials, as well as financial backing from local merchants and gentry elites (Docs. 2, 5, 6).

Because the Ming sea bans were unenforceable, an extensive clandestine trade developed along the coast of South China in the early sixteenth century that involved Chinese, Japanese, Southeast Asian, and Portuguese smugglers and pirates. The sea bans gave merchants little choice but to conduct their activities covertly on offshore islands, such as Nan'ao, Wuyu, Damao, and Shuangyu (Doc. 5). In fact, for more than twenty years, between 1524 and 1548, Shuangyu, which is situated off the Zhejiang coast near the city of Ningbo, served as the major international smuggling emporium and the center of *wokou* activities. At first, in the 1520s, Shuangyu merely operated as a seasonal trading outpost, where Chinese, Japanese, and Portuguese smugglers built temporary shanties to house themselves and to store their goods during the trading season. In the late 1530s, after several Chinese smuggler-pirates, such as Li Guangtou (Baldy Li), began to guide foreign merchants from Southeast Asia to Shuangyu to trade, the island quickly developed into a permanent, year-round trading mart. On Shuangyu and other island strongholds pirates and merchants traded silks, brocades, pearls, copper, porcelains, spices, Japanese swords, firearms, and various foreign items from such places as Patani, Malabar, Europe, and Japan.

Around this time the Xu brothers (Xu Song, Xu Dong, Xu Nan, and Xu Zi), accompanied by Portuguese and Southeast Asian traders, moved their smuggling headquarters from the Malay Peninsula to Shuangyu and Damao islands. After several mergers with smaller outlaw groups, by 1542 the Xu brothers' syndicate had become the most powerful merchant-pirate bloc on the South China coast. Under their direction, Shuangyu became the hub of an intricate and sophisticated clandestine trading network active in the markets in southeastern China in Fujian, Guangdong, and the Ming southern capital in Nanjing, as well as in Japan, Southeast Asia, and, through the Portuguese, even in Europe. The leader of the Xu brothers' syndicate was Xu Dong (or Xu Er), the second brother. By the 1540s he had become the most powerful merchant-pirate on the South China coast. Originally a sea merchant who had been arrested for smuggling, he escaped from jail around 1526 and fled to Patani and then Malacca, where he married a local woman and began to build up his fortune through smuggling and piracy. Later he joined forces with *wokou* bands in Japan to continue his clandestine activities from Shuangyu Island. Together with Li Guangtou and other pirates, in the early 1540s, Xu's armed merchant fleets plundered coastal villages and towns in Fujian and Zhejiang, while at the same time he conducted a brisk unlawful trade with Japanese merchants in the port city of Hakata in Kyushu (Chin 2010).

In response to the rapid expansion of smuggling and piracy the Ming government dispatched soldiers and warships (figure 2.2) to eradicate the emporiums on Shuangyu and other islands. To oversee the antipiracy operations, in 1547 the Jiajing emperor appointed Zhu Wan (1494–1550) as the new Grand Coordinator of Coastal Defense in Zhejiang and Fujian provinces, the areas most affected by piracy (Doc. 4). After arriving at his new post, he discovered that pirates, Portuguese and Japanese traders, and powerful local gentry families actively collaborated with one another in smuggling and pirate enterprises (Doc. 5). He immediately set into motion a series of new measures to enforce the sea bans to eliminate the pirate trade and he carried out several vigorous military campaigns against pirates. By effectively deploying available troops against illegal trading centers in both provinces, within a year his policies began to show results in disrupting the infrastructure of the contraband trade. Most significantly Zhu Wan completely destroyed the *wokou* entrepôt on Shuangyu Island in 1548. In the next year in a key naval battle his forces defeated and captured the pirate boss Li Goutou (Dog Head Li) and ninety-six followers, who Zhu summarily executed. Unsurprisingly Zhu Wan's policies were unpopular among the prominent coastal families and many local officials who had vested interests in maintaining the status quo. Ultimately they succeeded in having the emperor impeach Zhu Wan, who in disgrace committed suicide in 1550 (Higgins 1981, 10–13, 139–41). In the af-

Piracy in the Mid-Ming Dynasty (1520–1580) 17

Figure 2.2. Ming Dynasty War Junk.

termath of Zhu Wan's campaigns, several pirate leaders, including Xu Dong, fled overseas to Southeast Asia and Japan. The government later replaced Zhu Wan with another competent and somewhat more successful official named Hu Zongxian (1512–1565), who introduced measures to win over local gentry and merchant support to combat pirates (Hucker 1971; Fitzpatrick 1979, 12–13, 20–23; Doc. 8).

After Xu Dong fled China, one of his lieutenants, Wang Zhi (d. 1560), assumed leadership of the pirate syndicate (Docs. 6, 7). Originally a wealthy salt merchant from Huizhou in Anhui province, he had been forced to become a smuggler and pirate because of the Ming bans on overseas trade. During the 1550s he commanded a huge, well-armed merchant fleet that operated from bases in Kyushu in Japan and Shuangyu in China. In particular, he became active in the illicit gun and gunpowder trade between Japan, Southeast Asia, and China, and as several historians have noted he was instrumental in the diffusion of European weaponry into Japan (So 1975, 148; Petrucci 2010; Chonlaworn 2017, 190–91). Wang, who had a reputation as a shrewd businessman and benevolent protector, enjoyed support from the local populations in the areas in which he traded in Japan and China. To protect his interests, he engaged Japanese thugs and warrior-pirates as security guards on his ships, which had come under increasing attacks from both Chinese pirates and government forces. As his enterprises expanded, Wang sold protection to other Chinese merchants as well as to Japanese and Portuguese traders. Although foremost a businessman, nonetheless, Wang never hesitated to use his fighters to attack and plunder rivals. In response, other Chinese merchants and smugglers likewise armed themselves and the situation quickly spiraled out of control. By 1555 powerful *wokou* gangs in hundreds of ships and numbering more than a thousand individuals armed with guns were regularly plundering the southeastern coast of China. Later, in 1557, Wang surrendered to Ming officials expecting to receive an imperial pardon, but after languishing in prison for more than a year the throne decided to execute him.

Another pirate boss, Wu Ping, had operated clandestine trading enterprises for more than twenty years before fleeing to Vietnam (or Annan as it was known in those days) in 1565. At that time he commanded a fleet of about a hundred pirate ships, which were active along the coasts of Fujian and northeastern Guangdong. As his primary base of operations, Wu Ping chose Nan'ao, an island strategically located along the major north-south trading route and whose administration was split between the provincial jurisdictions of Fujian and Guangdong. On the island he built a stockade where he settled his family and amassed provisions, armaments, and booty. After being driven off Nan'ao Island, Wu Ping fled to Vietnam but after that there are differing stories about his fate (Chen Chunsheng 2010; Doc. 9).

Like many other pirate leaders Wu Ping ran a close-knit family organization, which included brothers, uncles, cousins, and even his younger sister, who was later deified by local fishers on Nan'ao Island as the Goddess for Protecting Treasure. It is uncertain, however, if Wu Ping's sister ever existed as a real person. Nonetheless, today her statue stands on a tiny outcropping appropriately dubbed "Treasure Island," which is a place of worship for fisherfolk and nearby residents in Guangdong and Fujian (Doc. 10).

Two of Wu Ping's associates, Lin Daoqian and Zeng Yiben, both benefited from Wu's departure to Vietnam by expanding their own gangs out of the latter's dismantled organization. Lin Daoqian had organized a huge trading cartel that extended from Fujian and Guangdong to Taiwan, the Philippines, and Siam (Thailand). In 1566, in collusion with *wokou* bands, he plundered the port of his hometown Zhaoan, and in 1571 he joined forces with several local pirates for a raid that took them as far south as the Pearl River Delta and gateway to Canton. In 1573 Lin fled first to Luzon and later to Patani, where he lived for several more years as a merchant and pirate. Zeng Yiben was also active in Fujian and Guangdong between 1564 and 1569. Collaborating with *wokou* gangs, in 1567 he attacked the Chaozhou coast and in 1568 he even threatened Canton. In the next year, however, naval campaigns drove him to the Leizhou area of western Guangdong, where he was arrested and promptly executed (*Haikang xianzhi* 1938, 539–40).

Not only were many Chinese, Japanese, and Southeast Asians engaged in piracy and smuggling in South China in the sixteenth century, but so too were many unscrupulous Europeans. When the Portuguese first sailed into the South China Sea they came as traders and adventurers, and many acted no different than pirates. From bases in Southeast Asia they traded clandestinely with Chinese and Japanese pirates and smugglers on Shuangyu and other islands. Later in 1557, on the pretext of defending the region against Chinese pirates, the Portuguese established a foothold on the tiny Macau peninsula, which they subsequently held until 1997. Whenever it was to their advantage, Portuguese attacked Chinese and Japanese pirates who disturbed their trade. Yet at other times, it was to their advantage to act as pirates, robbing rival ships, pillaging villages, and kidnapping people to sell as slaves. Some Chinese even believed that the Portuguese were vicious and immoral people who abducted children to devour as food (Doc. 11). During this age of empire building and commercial rivalry, in fact, trade and piracy were often indistinguishable, and several European governments maintained tolerant attitudes toward piracy (usually under the rubric of privateering), viewing it as an important auxiliary to their naval forces and to legitimate trade. Limitless opportunities in Asia for riches, either through trade or pillage, attracted European renegades and adventurers to the region. They had few scruples about violating Ming sea bans. In fact, around this same time, several Portuguese fortune hunters were arrested, tried, and executed as pirates in Fujian province. In the eyes of most Chinese officials, such explorers as Mendes Pinto were simply rapacious pirates (Pelúcia 2010). Still other Chinese, such as Lin

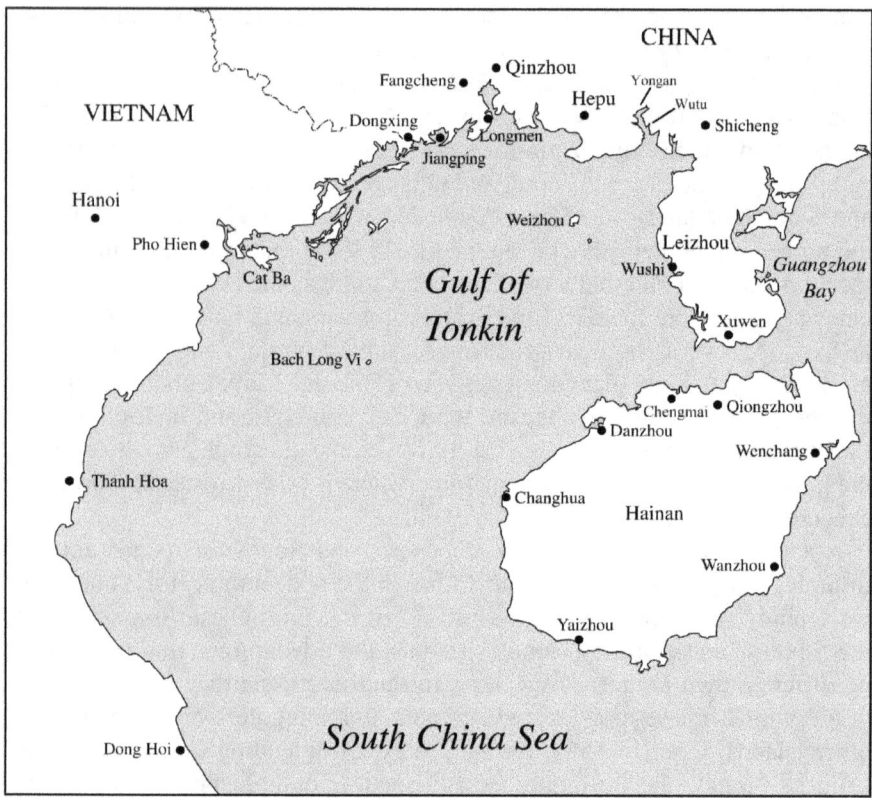

Map 2.1. The Gulf of Tonkin.
Source: created by Robert Antony.

Xiyuan, considered the Portuguese as peaceful traders who opposed piracy (Doc. 12). The Portuguese themselves claimed that they collaborated with the Ming navy to suppress pirates, actions that led the Chinese government to grant them settlement at Macau (Doc. 13).

Besides the *wokou* pirates, who operated along the southeastern coasts of China mainly in Zhejiang and Fujian, there was another breed of pirates in the Gulf of Tonkin that Ming officials labeled as "pearl thieves" (*zhuzei*). Although they normally operated in small gangs, nonetheless they were well organized and at times even expanded into formidable forces that effectively defied the authorities. In the Ming period the government monopolized the pearl industry and strictly regulated its collection and distribution, much to the disadvantage of the pearl divers who found it increasingly difficult to earn a living. There were therefore frequent reports throughout the sixteenth century of pearl thieves operating from Weizhou and other islands near the pearl beds in the gulf. These thieves were mostly poor Dan or Tanka fisherfolk from China and Vietnam who clandestinely harvested and sold pearls to merchants in Qinzhou, Hepu, Mong Cai, and Pho Hien (map 2.1). The largest and most significant episode involving pearl thieves occurred in the late 1570s when two notorious pirates, Su Guansheng and Zhou Caixiong, gathered a force of more than a thousand Dan pearl gatherers and fishers to rob pearl beds, ships, villages, and government installations throughout the gulf region. In 1581 soldiers captured and executed Su and more than four hundred followers, but Zhou apparently escaped and was never heard from again (Antony 2014a, 105–7; Doc. 14).

Erratic pirate raids continued along the South China coast into the early seventeenth century, but by the 1580s the number of incidents dramatically decreased. After the Jiajing emperor died in 1567, his successors slowly and cautiously began to open up overseas trade with Southeast Asia, but not with Japan.[3] Gradually as military officers and troops became accustomed to warfare they developed new techniques and strategies for defeating the pirates. Among these new leaders Qi Jiguang (1528–1588) stands out; he helped to revitalize Ming armed forces, constructed new warships equipped with firearms and cannons, and was one of the first commanders to organize an elite corps of musketeers trained in the volley technique, which proved effective in fighting pirates (Sim 2017). As a result several major pirate leaders were killed in battle, as were thousands of rank-and-file pirates; many more pirates surrendered to the state or fled to Southeast Asia. In addition, the political reunification of Japan under the Tokugawa Shogunate (1600–1868) in the latter part of the sixteenth century did much to curtail Japanese piracy in the whole region. In 1574 a Ming naval fleet chased the last of the *wokou* pirates all the way to the Philippines, and in 1581 the pearl thieves had been soundly defeated in the Gulf of Tonkin. As China's economy finally stabilized in the last decades of the sixteenth century, piracy diminished for a time. Markets reopened and pirates once again became merchants.

---

3. Actually, although the Ming court relaxed its bans on maritime trade after 1567, nevertheless, in 1572, 1592, 1626, and 1628 it reissued several prohibitions that continued to restrict trade.

Chapter Three

Piracy during the Ming-Qing Transition (1620–1684)

The next wave of large-scale piracy surged forth during the Ming-Qing transition between 1620 and 1684, following a lull of forty years. At the height of the dynastic wars, in the 1640s to 1660s, piracy reached a peak. Often labeled in official accounts as "sea rebels" (*haikou* or *haini*), the pirate upsurge was symptomatic of the general crisis in China that accompanied the change of dynasties. Because of the economic and political anarchy of this period, it was impossible to make clear distinctions between piracy, rebellion, and trade. Taking advantage of the instability, members of the Zheng family of Fujian constructed a maritime empire in the South China Sea based on combinations of trade, piracy, and political intrigue. Other pirates joined bandits and rebels to attack markets and walled cities, while European traders, who continued to receive support from their governments, also took advantage of the turmoil in China to pillage ports and merchant ships (Andrade and Hang 2016).

The piracy of this period resulted from a combination of adverse political, military, economic, and ecological factors. By the start of the seventeenth century, the relative stability and prosperity of the previous several decades had been abruptly shattered. Internally, corruption, factionalism, and fiscal bankruptcy crippled the Ming government. Externally, Manchu incursions on the northeastern frontier challenged Ming sovereignty and forced the government to commit large amounts of money and troops to defend its borders, thereby weakening its military presence along the coast. After 1626 the Ming government at various times again issued prohibitions on overseas trade. At the same time, the Chinese economy stagnated and then declined, as foreign trade came to a standstill and prices climbed sharply. Social disorders increased as the military and economic crisis deepened; there followed numerous tenant and worker revolts, food riots, and bandit disturbances throughout the southern provinces. For several decades Fujian and Guangdong found themselves at the center of fighting, pillaging, and devastation. One eyewitness named Chen Shunxi noted in his diary in 1679 that in his home area of Wuchuan in southwestern Guangdong, soldiers, village militia, bandits, and pirates were everywhere fighting one another and indiscriminately looting towns and villages (Chen Shunxi 2010, 45). Dispossessed by one side or another, people did not have time to recuperate before soldiers or pirates came back to raid again.

In addition to the previously mentioned problems, beginning around 1600 and continuing for several decades, a series of floods, droughts, typhoons, and earthquakes ravaged Fujian and Guangdong provinces, leaving destitute untold numbers of people who turned to banditry and piracy for survival. In 1626, coastal Fujian suffered a severe famine (Doc. 16). Several years later in Haicheng County, a drought and crop failures caused the cost of rice to shoot up to 150 taels silver per picul (roughly 132 lbs.), and when people ran out of grasses, roots, and leaves to eat, in desperation they ate human flesh. We have this vivid firsthand description of the hopelessness: "In their desperate search for food, nothing was left but human flesh. Fathers and sons ate one another, and those who had not ended up in the stewpot died of diseases or hunger. [Others] drowned or hung themselves. . . . Everyday thousands died. The bodies piled up and the stink could be smelled for several *li* away" (Calanca 2010, 90). During those years the conditions in Guangdong were no better. There were famines nearly every year between 1642 and 1665. As the cost of food increased tremendously, bandits and pirates appeared everywhere. Conditions deteriorated so much that in Xin'an County, in the economically advanced Pearl River Delta, there were reports that men and women were sold for a peck (about 13 lbs.) of rice, and human corpses were butchered for food (Ng 1983, 103). Under such horrific conditions piracy escalated out of control everywhere along the southern littoral.

At the same time, Europeans aggressively waged wars with one another around the globe, and in the process they also plundered Asian ships and ports. By the seventeenth century, the Dutch had replaced the Portuguese and Spanish as the dominant Western power in Asia, and like their predecessors they sometimes combined trade with plunder. In Asia the Dutch government was represented by the Dutch East India Company (or VOC),[1] which operated as an immense privateering enterprise empowered to wage war. In fact, proceeds from the company's privateering ventures were a vital component

---

1. The Dutch East India Company or Vereenigde Oostindische Compagnie (VOC) was a trading company founded in the Dutch Republic in 1602 to expand and protect that country's trade in Asia, as well as to assist in the Dutch war of independence from Spain. The company prospered through most of the seventeenth century as the instrument of the powerful Dutch commercial empire centered in the East Indies (today Indonesia). The company was dissolved in 1799.

of its overall income in the early seventeenth century (Andrade 2004, 417, 423). The main objectives of the Dutch were to destroy rival European shipping and to disrupt the Chinese junk trade with Spanish-controlled Manila. Encouraged by their home governments, Dutch adventurers took advantage of the political vacuum in China to plunder Chinese junks and occasionally even coastal settlements. The smaller poorly armed junks provided easy prey for these Western predators. In 1622 the Dutch attacked Macau, but having failed to take the city, afterward seized the Pescadores (Penghu Islands), looting and burning villages and kidnapping hundreds of people to sell as slaves. Many kidnapped victims, however, died before being sold. In 1624 the Dutch occupied Taiwan, and from this base conducted trade and piratical-privateering expeditions until Zheng Chenggong (Koxinga) expelled them in 1662 (Andrade 2011). The presence of European freebooters in the South China Sea contributed further to destabilizing the coast, not only because they intercepted ships trading with China, Japan, and Southeast Asia but also because they supplied weapons to pirates and fenced their booty. Therefore, the pirates never lacked the money, supplies, and weapons necessary for carrying on their activities (Cheng 2013, 32–33).

Events of the first half of the seventeenth century, in many respects, represented continuations of unresolved issues of the previous century. As in the earlier period of *wokou* disturbances, the most skillful pirates generally associated with smuggling syndicates that conducted trade throughout the South China Sea. For example, in the 1620s, more than ten pirate-merchant fleets operated, competed, and coexisted in the waters of southeastern China. Among these pirate bosses were Li Dan, Liu Xiang, Cui Zhi, and Yan Zhenquan (Docs. 15, 16). They alternated plundering one another and merchant ships with business ventures in Nan'ao, Penghu, Taiwan, Macau, Japan, and the Philippines. However, unlike the earlier *wokou* period, the large-scale piracy of the early seventeenth century focused on plundering ships at sea and less on inland settlements. Also different from the earlier wave of piracy, with the fall of the Ming dynasty in 1644, in many cases piracy took on a political dimension with Ming loyalism. The major pirate leaders who operated along the South China coast between the 1620s and 1670s are presented in table 3.1.

Beginning in the 1620s, the Zheng family, first under Zheng Zhilong (1604–1661), and then under his son Zheng Chenggong (1624–1662) and grandson Zheng Jing (1642–1681), began building a sizable maritime empire that within twenty years came to dominate trade in the South China Sea (Carioti 1996; Cheng 2013; Hang 2016). Zheng Zhilong, who began his career as a merchant, smuggler, and pirate in southern Fujian, displayed remarkable organizational skills and an uncanny knack for manipulating officials. For a time he lived in Macau, where he converted to Christianity (baptized as

Table 3.1. Major Pirate Leaders in South China, 1622–1677

Year	*Pirate Leaders*	*Home Area*	*Comments*
1620–1622	Cui Zhi and Lin Qilao	Fujian	active in Fujian, Taiwan, and Guangdong; collaborated with the Dutch
1622–1625	Yan Zhenquan (Yan Siqi) and Li Dan (Captain China)	Fujian	Pirate-merchants active in Japan and Taiwan
1626	Zheng Zhilong (Nicolas Gaspard), Zheng Zhihu	Fujian	active in Fujian, Taiwan, Guangdong, Japan, and Southeast Asia; collaborated with the Dutch
1626	Yang Lu (Yang Liu), Yang Ce (Yang Qi)	Fujian	
1628	Zhou Laosan		
1629	Li Zhiqi		
1629	Li Kuiji	Fujian	former lieutenant under Zheng Zhilong who turned against his former boss
1630	Zhong Bin		
1632	Liu Xiang (Jan Glaew)	Fujian	pirate and main rival of Zheng Zhilong; defeated in 1635
1639–1640	Gu Rong, Lu Da, Liao Er, Zhang Wuxiaozi		
1645	Zhou Hezhi (Zhou Cuizhi)	Fujian	
1645	Zheng Chenggong (Koxinga)	Fujian (born in Japan)	pirate-rebel active in Fujian, Taiwan, Guangdong, Zhejiang, Japan and Southeast Asia
1645	Su Cheng, Su Li	Guangdong	smugglers, pirates and rebels in Chaozhou area
1646	Gao Zhen, Lin Fang, Huang Xin, Mai Mingrang, Ye Yuanju, Li Houxi, Liang Dijiao	Guangdong	
1647	Yang Hang	Fujian	
1650	Huang Hairu, Chen Bin	Guangdong	
1650	Deng Yao, Chen Shangchuan	Guangdong	mostly active in Gulf of Tonkin
1651	Wang Ji	Guangdong	
1656	Guo Zilong, Huang Yuan	Fujian	local pirates, plundered Yunxiao area
1659	Gao Chen, Xu Sheng	Fujian	local pirates, plundered Yunxiao area
1662	Zheng Jing	Fujian	son of Zheng Chenggong
1662	Zhou Yu, Li Rong	Guangdong	Dan fishermen turned pirates and rebels
1662	Yang Yandi (Yang Er), Yang San, Xian Biao	Guangdong	mostly active in Gulf of Tonkin
1669	Qiu Hui (Chou Hong Rou)	Guangdong	Dan fisherman turned pirate
1677	Cai Yin, Wang Ding, Ou Jiu	Fujian	

Nicholas Gaspard);[2] later he went to Manila, Hirado, and Taiwan. Following the deaths in 1625 of his two compatriots, Li Dan (so-called Captain China) and Yan Zhenquan (or Yan Siqi), he struck out on his own as a full-fledged pirate, and around this time also began to collaborate with the Dutch as their privateer, engaged to plunder Chinese junks trading with Manila. Over the next year Zheng Zhilong captured ten Chinese ships with cargos valued at more than 20,000 taels of silver, which he shared with his VOC backers in Taiwan in return for their support and protection. In 1626 he launched raids on the Fujian coast, taking several walled cities in Quanzhou and Zhangzhou prefectures. Two years later his forces captured the port city of Amoy and severely crippled the Ming navy in several battles. By then he had gained popular support from merchants, gentry, and villagers along the Fujian coast who saw him as a seaborne Robin Hood who robbed the rich and fed the poor. This image of the noble pirate helped him recruit several thousand poor peasants and fisherfolk during the severe famines and hardships that hit the province in the 1620s (Blussé 1990; Andrade 2004, 428–31; Docs. 16, 17).

Unable to militarily defeat him, in 1628 the Ming emperor pardoned Zheng Zhilong and soon afterward appointed him as a "patrolling commander" in the imperial navy in Fujian and ordered him to clear the seas of pirates. Zheng's situation had completely changed. While collaborating with the Dutch in Taiwan he plundered the seas as a privateer, that is, as a private citizen with a Dutch commission or license to plunder enemy shipping. His attacks on ships were legitimized under European laws, but because the Ming government did not recognize such laws, for Chinese officials Zheng's actions were simply piracy. After surrendering to the Ming, however, his status changed from that of private citizen to naval officer commissioned by the government to eradicate piracy. This gave him the chance to exterminate his rivals legitimately and systematically, most notably his major rival Liu Xiang, who Zheng defeated off the Leizhou peninsula in 1635. His fleet even inflicted a major naval defeat on the Dutch after they tried to support his adversaries.

By the 1630s, with official recognition, Zheng Zhilong dominated the lucrative Fujian-Taiwan trade network from strongholds on Amoy and neighboring islands, and after defeating Liu Xiang, his ships sailed freely throughout the East and South China Seas from Japan to Batavia. In 1640 he was appointed as the "regional commander" of the Fujian military. At his home fortress near Amoy he surrounded himself with an elite bodyguard of three hundred to six hundred African musketeers, who dressed in European uniforms and trained in Dutch drilling techniques. Official reports claimed that no ships could sail without his permission. He levied protection fees on merchant junks and fishing fleets, and he plundered those vessels that had

---

2. Zheng Zhilong also went by the name Nicholas Iquan.

refused to pay (Doc. 18). Reportedly, too, many high-ranking officials in Fujian and even in the imperial court were on his payroll (Cheng 2013, 44–47, 73–75; Hang 2016, 51–57, 87–88). By the 1640s he had eliminated all of his rivals and had become so formidable that he was like "a whale swallowing up the sea" (*Ming Qing shiliao wubian* 1972, 7b). From humble beginnings as a petty trader Zheng's career had evolved from smuggler to pirate to privateer to naval officer—yet despite his many hats his piratical behavior had changed little over the years. Zheng had become one of the most powerful and wealthiest men in China.

With the fall of the Ming dynasty in 1644, Zheng Zhilong wavered for another two years before finally surrendering to the Manchu conquerors. Unfortunately for Zheng, he misjudged the Qing ruler who placed him under house arrest in Beijing until 1661, when he was finally executed. Many of his clansmen, including his son, Zheng Chenggong, however, continued to resist the Qing in the name of Ming loyalism (Doc. 19). Although his supporters did not view him as a pirate, Qing officials, Dutch statesmen and merchants, and his many victims continued to label him as such. Some in England, however, called him a king. Perhaps we should call him a "political pirate," someone who opposed the Manchus on ideological grounds yet at the same time continued to use piratical methods to maintain power and acquire wealth. Taking advantage of the political turmoil, he expanded his power base in South China and by 1651 he controlled the Zheng family organization and its expanding seaborne empire. For the next ten years his fleets monopolized shipping in Fujian, Guangdong, Taiwan, the Philippines, and much of Southeast Asia. Zheng financed his huge maritime conglomerate through trade, robbery, and extortion. At the peak of his power he commanded naval and land forces of no fewer than one hundred thousand warriors, many of whom were trained in Western military techniques and equipped with modern armaments. In April 1661, after failing to take Nanjing, he crossed over with twenty thousand troops and four hundred warships to Dutch-held Taiwan where he laid siege to the VOC's headquarters at Fort Zeelandia and forced the garrison to surrender on February 1, 1662. This was one of the few European colonies to have ever fallen to an Asian military force (Andrade 2011). After his unexpected death half a year later, his son Zheng Jing seized power and gradually over the next twenty years transformed Taiwan into an independent Chinese state that challenged Qing legitimacy on the mainland (Hang 2016, 155–62).

In consolidating his control over the Zheng maritime empire, Zheng Jing bolstered his navy by allying with several pirate groups in Fujian and Guangdong. One of the most colorful pirate leaders was Qiu Hui, who had the curious nickname of "Stinky Red Meat" (Chou Hong Rou) and was based on the small island of Dahao off the Chaozhou coast. Qiu was originally a Dan fisherman with a reputation for ruthlessness and violence. His gang plundered towns and villagers all across the Guangdong coast, kidnapping people for ransom money and to sell in Taiwan. He abducted young girls, in particular, to offer as wives to Zheng's soldiers in Taiwan. Zheng Jing also made pacts with Xian Biao, Yang Yandi, and Chen Shangchuan, pirate leaders based on Longmen Island in the Gulf of Tonkin. After Zheng Jing's death in the winter of 1681, Taiwan fell to the Qing two years later (Hang 2016, 165–66, 226, 233).

In the meantime, after the Ming dynasty collapsed in the 1640s, anarchy quickly spread everywhere and piracy escalated out of control. The new Manchu rulers responded with even harsher sea bans than their Ming predecessors. Imperial decrees commanded officials in coastal areas to burn all boats, to prohibit the construction of large sea junks, and to bar the purchase of foreign-made vessels. Chinese merchants were also prohibited from setting out to sea under pain of death (Doc. 20). Still unable to curb piracy, beginning in 1661, the government adopted a scorched earth policy, what historians have called the Great Clearance, forcing residents along the coast to relocate inland at a distance of roughly ten to twenty miles. All houses and property within that no-man's zone were destroyed and anyone caught trying to return to the coast was beheaded. Soldiers erected trenches, walls, barriers, guardposts, and watchtowers to make sure the evacuation zone remained clear of people (Doc. 21). As a result of this policy, an estimated 5.3 million hectares (*mu*) of land remained unproductive for more than twenty years (Ho 2011, 2013).

Such draconian measures did not destroy the pirates but rather devastated the maritime communities that depended on the sea for their livelihood. In fact, the stringent Qing policies and protracted fighting totally disrupted the flow of trade, which during these years moved away from China to Taiwan, Macau, and to other trading ports across Asia. Those policies also drove many people into open rebellion (Calanca 2010, 91; Doc. 22). In Fujian coastal villagers raised makeshift armies in defiance of Qing policies. As one eyewitness recalled, "Farmers and fishermen all claimed to be military commanders, accepting seals and titles from Regent Lu [a Ming imperial pretender], and even country women passed themselves off as monks to receive investiture and gather soldiers" (Ho 2011, 186). In Guangdong two brothers, Su Cheng and Su Li, who had been smugglers, organized a fleet of pirates whose stated purpose was the establishment of a new dynasty. Although some displaced farmers had joined their cause, most of their followers were fishers, smugglers, and pirates. Before its collapse in 1664, the Su organization controlled a three-hundred-mile stretch of coastline between Haifeng and Chaozhou. Farther south in the area around Canton, between 1662 and 1664, Zhou Yu and Li Rong led bands of displaced Dan fishers in a pirate uprising that shook the economic core of the province (Antony 2003, 33–34; Doc. 23).

Along the Sino-Vietnamese border in the Gulf of Tonkin, other Ming loyalists and pirates, such as Deng Yao, Chen Shangchuan, Xian Biao, and Yang Yandi, continued to resist the Manchus and engage in acts of piracy for nearly twenty years from 1660 to 1681 (Doc. 24). The most famous and dreaded of the gulf pirates was Yang Yandi (or Yang Er), who in his lifetime was portrayed both as a righteous hero and a brutal villain (Doc. 25). He and his younger brother, Yang San, began their piratical careers in the 1640s or 1650s as small-time, local pirates, but later joined up with a more formidable gang led by two brothers, Wang Zhihan and Wang Zhijian, operating from bases on the Leizhou peninsula. Afterward they joined the Ming resistance against the Manchus in western Guangdong with another pirate-rebel leader named Deng Yao, until he was defeated in 1661. Yang Yandi then fled to Vietnam where he received protection and support from a local strongman and later, probably around 1666, he went to Taiwan where he joined the Zheng regime, reportedly receiving an official position as a regional commander. In 1677 he left Taiwan with some seventy ships and several thousand followers to return to the Gulf of Tonkin, where they occupied Longmen Island as their lair. Because Longmen was the gateway to the walled city of Qinzhou, the pirates were able to control all trade and communications by sea to this important administrative and commercial center. During this time Yang and other pirates continued to provide convoy service for Zheng Jing's trading ships bound for Southeast Asia. Raiding and fighting continued intermittently until 1682, when Qing forces drove Yang and other pirates from their stronghold. Yang retreated with roughly three thousand followers to the area on the Cambodian-Vietnamese border, finally settling at My Tho (near present-day Saigon). In 1687 or 1688 a subordinate murdered Yang Yandi (Doc. 26). Although Yang and other gulf pirates joined the pro-Ming forces in resistance against the Manchus, it is likely that they were motivated less by Ming loyalism than by survival instincts during the chaotic dynastic wars when society was so much in disarray (Antony 2014b; Hang 2017).

Between 1680 and 1730, attitudes and public policies toward piracy and trade had changed dramatically in both China and the West. In 1684, just a year after the Qing military had crushed the remnants of the Zheng forces in Taiwan and had finally secured control over all of China, the Kangxi emperor (r. 1662–1722) rescinded most of the sea bans. Convinced that national security depended on the prosperity and stability of the southern coastal provinces, the imperial court legalized the overseas junk trade and opened up several ports to foreign commerce.[3] An interconnected network of customs

---

3. However, in 1715 there was a new ban on fishing boats carrying weapons and in 1717 a short-lived ban on trade with Southeast Asia. In 1757 Canton became the single legal trading port for Western merchants; this so-called Canton System lasted until China's defeat in the First Opium War in 1842.

offices, subcounty yamens, and military posts were established, or reestablished, all along the southern littoral, and the civil officials and military officers who manned these posts had the specific tasks of regulating trade and eliminating piracy and smuggling. In the 1720s the Qing government also began enacting a series of laws to protect private property and trade, including harsh new laws against piracy. At the same time, the state attempted to incorporate maritime society and culture more fully into the imperial system, for instance, by elevating the status of the state-recognized sea deity, Mazu, with the title Empress of Heaven (Tianhou). The new measures brought stability and prosperity to coastal South China and piracy declined. Thereafter, most Chinese sea merchants, who now had a vested interest in maintaining the existing system, became bulwarks of support in pirate suppression. It was also about the same time that Western merchants began putting pressure on their home governments to suppress piracy and officials responded by passing tough antipiracy laws and by building navies to protect their merchant ships on the high seas. Western piracy soon waned in Asia as it did elsewhere around the globe. For the next sixty years the seas around China remained relatively calm (Antony 2003, 165).

Chapter Four

Piracy in the Mid-Qing Dynasty (1775–1810)

The last great pirate wave, in the late eighteenth and early nineteenth centuries, was an age of indigenous piracy across Asia. Beginning about 1775 and accelerating between 1790 and 1810, several competing pirate leagues, which were composed of self-contained fleets, plagued the South China Sea. Although throughout those years petty gangs of local pirates continued to operate in coastal waters, they were overshadowed by the larger, well-organized fleets of "ocean bandits" (*yangdao*) (Docs. 27, 28). Once again South China's littoral had slipped away from the control of the imperial government into the hands of huge pirate leagues (Murray 1987; Antony 2003). Unlike the previous two waves of piracy, during the third wave there were noticeably fewer cases of piracy and privateering sponsored by Western governments in China's waters.[1]

The intensification of piracy along the South China coast at that time resulted from several factors. A combination of changing socioeconomic conditions—especially China's population explosion and the increased trade in Southeast Asia and the West—were among the most important underlying causes. The expansion and prosperity of commerce in the entire region acted as a catalyst for maritime predation among the poverty-stricken fisherfolk and sailors living in southern China. Paradoxically this was an "age of prosperity," but one in which wealth was unevenly distributed (Kuhn 1990, 30–48). Despite the flourishing economy, population pressure intensified competition and kept wages low for most seafarers. It is hardly surprising that the majority of pirates in this era were common sailors, fishers, and hired laborers who engaged in occasional piracy in order to survive in an increasingly harsh

---

1. The most serious case involved the infamous Captain John McClary who operated as a British privateer in the South China Sea in 1781–1782 but was labeled a pirate by his fellow countrymen after he plundered a cargo junk owned by the Hong merchant Chowgua.

and competitive world. Piracy arose not because of a general immiseration of society but rather because of the strains that prosperity had placed on the more marginal elements of Chinese society. In short, contradictions inherent in maritime society created conditions of conflict, violence, and predation. Piracy remained an endemic and integral part of maritime society and culture and was a logical outcome of early modern China's burgeoning economy (Antony 2003, 54–81).

Socioeconomic factors were not the only reasons for the upsurge in Chinese piracy. There were also important military and ecological causes. Poor sailors and fisherfolk took advantage of the weakened state when Qing military forces were diverted elsewhere to fight various insurgencies—the Tay Son Rebellion in Vietnam (1771–1802); the Lin Shuangwen Rebellion in Taiwan (1787–1788); the Miao Uprising in Sichuan, Hubei, and Guizhou (1795); and the White Lotus Rebellion in central China (1795–1804)—to join or form pirate gangs. As with the rise of piracy in the previous cycle, in the late eighteenth and early nineteenth centuries, South China experienced an unusually large number of natural disasters that destroyed crops, created severe food shortages, and threw countless numbers of people out of work. The years from 1790 to 1850 were particularly active ones for typhoons along the South China coast. Between 1775 and 1810, there were twenty-nine years of famines, the most severe ones occurring in 1778, 1786–1789, 1795–1796, and 1809–1810. In Zhangpu on the southern Fujian coast in 1795, for example, the cost of rice increased from double to ten times the normal amount, which in real terms meant that a peck of rice equaled anywhere from five months' to two years' wages for common sailors. During the height of the pirate disturbances between 1802 and 1810, the Pearl River Delta experienced food shortages every year except 1807 (Antony 2003, 37–38).

Other factors in the rise of piracy were more immediate. Particularly important to the growth and development of large-scale piracy was the external patronage of the Tay Son rebels in Vietnam.[2] Although not the cause in the upsurge in piracy, the Vietnamese rebellion did significantly contribute to its expansion and organization. Finally, internally the emergence of talented and charismatic leaders among the pirates assured the organizational cohesion necessary for the expansion of piracy.

In the 1780s and 1790s, after Tay Son rebels in Vietnam began to support raids into Chinese waters, opportunistic piracy gradually gave way to more

---

2. Before 1802 China referred to Vietnam as Annan. The Tay Son Rebellion was a massive peasant uprising led by three brothers that started in southern Vietnam in 1771. In 1778, with the rebels in control of much of central and southern Vietnam, the reigning Le emperor requested help from the Qing emperor, who subsequently dispatched a military expedition to quell the uprising. But when the rebels defeated the Chinese army the Qianlong emperor quickly negotiated a settlement and recognized the new Tay Son regime. By 1802, however, the rebellion had been crushed.

professional, large-scale piracy. The rebels, who needed both money and fighters for their cause, actively recruited Chinese pirates, guaranteed them safe harbors, supplied them with ships and weapons, and rewarded them with official ranks and titles so they would engage in maritime raiding as a means of obtaining revenue. Tay Son sponsorship offered pirates a semblance of legitimacy and respectability, transforming them from being mere robbers and outlaws into lawful naval forces. The Qing government, however, continued to view them as pirates and their ranks and titles as bogus.

Between 1780 and 1802 many Chinese fishers and sailors from Guangdong and Fujian became pirates under the Tay Son banner. Chen Tianbao, one of the earliest pirate chiefs, began his career as a poor fisherman before joining the Tay Son rebels. Between 1784 and 1797, he quickly rose up the ranks to brigade general, to military governor, and then to "virtuous marquis," becoming one of the most important officials in the rebel camp, with the authority to recruit and grant titles to other pirates. One of his recruits, Mo Guanfu (d. 1801), also became a brigade general and in 1796 Tay Son leaders designated him as the "King of the Eastern Sea" (Doc. 28). Because of their Vietnamese sponsorship Chinese officials labeled these bands "foreign pirates" (*yifei*), though in fact most gang members were Chinese. Following the seasonal monsoons, pirate fleets set out every spring and summer from bases along the Sino-Vietnamese border in the vicinity of Jiangping for Chinese waters along the coast from Guangdong to Zhejiang and returned each autumn laden with booty that they shared with their Tay Son patrons (Murray 1987, 35–56; Antony 2014c). In 1797 officials estimated that the pirates had hundreds of large warships and as many as ten thousand followers. This was at a time when the Qing navy had fewer than half as many ships and combatants (*Gongzhongdang*, dated 29th day, 12th lunar month, 1st year Jiaqing reign [January 26, 1797]).

Although the pirates had scored great successes in Chinese waters, by 1801 Tay Son power had waned. As the rebel defeat became imminent, thousands of pirates surrendered to Qing officials in return for pardons (including Chen Tianbao). Vietnamese troops also apprehended large numbers of pirates and turned them over to Chinese authorities for execution (including Mo Guanfu). The next year supporters of the Vietnamese king had retaken Hanoi, captured the Tay Son leader, razed the black market at Jiangping, and sent the remaining pirates fleeing back to China (Antony 1994). At first, the pirates were in disarray and fighting among themselves, but over the next two years several capable chiefs—particularly Cai Qian (d. 1809), Zhu Fen (d. 1809), and Zheng Yi (d. 1807)—began reorganizing the pirates into huge leagues of "ocean bandits." Figure 4.1 depicts the major pirate leaders in Guangdong and Fujian and their affiliations between 1795 and 1810.

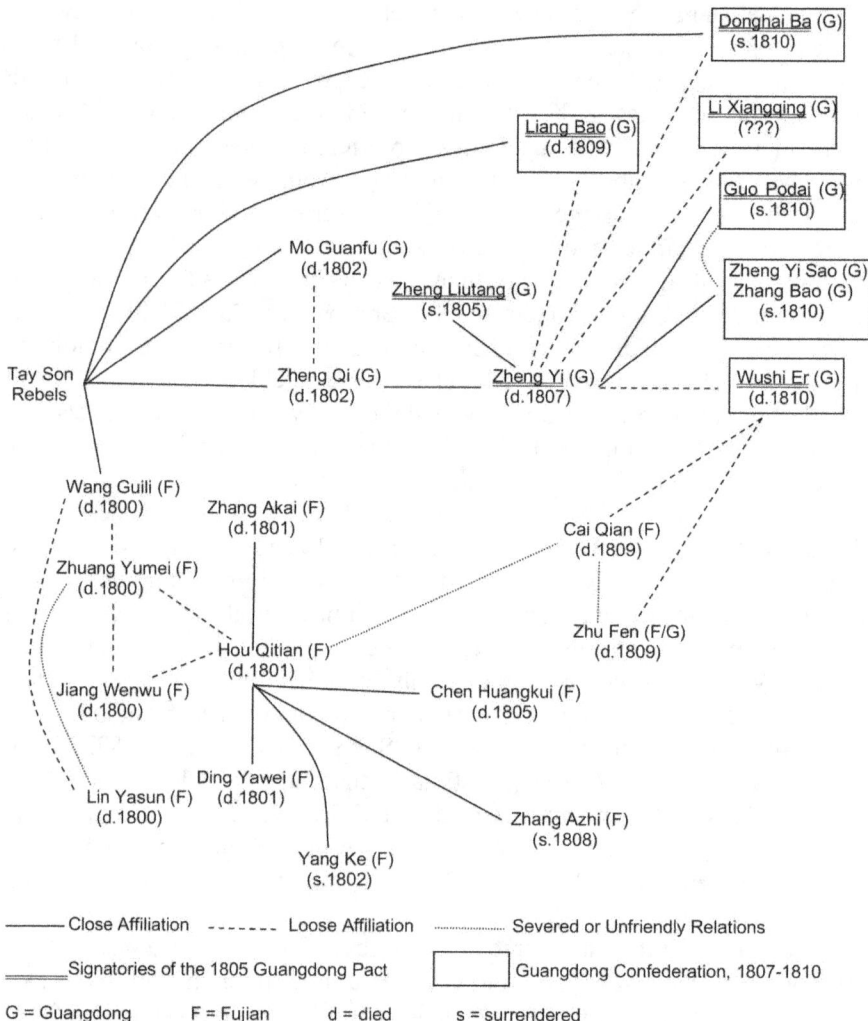

Figure 4.1. Affiliations between Major Pirate Leaders in South China, 1795-1810.
Source: created by Robert Antony.

From bases in southern Fujian, between 1800 and 1804, Cai Qian slowly arose to dominate the entire region between Taiwan and Zhejiang. Born about 1761 into a poor family in Tong'an County, Fujian, near the entrepôt of Amoy, he became an orphan as a child. It was said that he was skilled in martial arts, undoubtedly a requisite for survival in the rough-and-tumble world of sailor towns. In his youth he traveled around Fujian from port to port working intermittently as a hired laborer, peddler, cotton bower, and net mender for local fishermen. In the early 1790s, when he was in his thirties, he became a pirate, and by 1800 commanded a band consisting of roughly a hundred vessels (Doc. 29).

His wife, known to us only as Matron Cai Qian (Cai Qian Ma), played an important role in his rise to power. She had a reputation as a dockside doxy before Cai Qian purchased her from a barber for a large sum of money. Aboard ship she proved to be a skillful and resourceful leader and a cunning and fierce fighter. According to one account, she even commanded her own vessels with crews of "women warriors" (Doc. 30). Although there are conflicting accounts, she likely died in 1804 in battle with the Qing navy off the coast of Taiwan.

As Cai Qian's power increased so did his activities and ambitions. His organization grew larger and more powerful through a formalized protection racket that had connections with secret societies on shore. At the height of his strength, between 1805 and 1806, he made repeated attacks on Taiwan, intent on occupying the island as his base. At that time he commanded more than five thousand pirates. Receiving support from bandits on the island, Cai Qian launched raids along the west coast at Zhanghua, Luermen, and Donggang. With apparent popular support, he proclaimed himself the "Majestic Warrior King Who Subdues the Sea" as a preliminary to establishing his own kingdom on the island. His forces, however, were defeated in 1806 in a series of battles with the Qing navy and local militias. Forced to abandon thousands of comrades in Taiwan he secretly slipped back to Fujian. After purchasing new ships and supplies, he continued for the next several years with forays around Taiwan, Fujian, and Zhejiang, constantly being harassed by the imperial navy. Over the next several years provincial leaders imposed a strict embargo that severed Cai's support on land. In desperation he fled to Vietnam to recuperate, but after returning to China he died in a naval battle in October 1809. Without their gallant leader the remnants of his tattered organization soon scattered (Wei 1979; Chang 1983).

Zhu Fen was another Fujian pirate who occasionally cooperated with Cai Qian, but at other times was his bitter rival. Zhu was a native of Zhangzhou, in southern Fujian, and although his family was well-to-do, as a youth he preferred to associate with rascals and misfits.[3] As a young man, he was described as a local bully with connections to several pirate chiefs. To avoid arrest after being reported to officials by his fellow villagers, Zhu, with his wife and family, fled to sea to become pirates. By 1800 he commanded a fleet of several tens of ships, calling himself the "King of the Southern Seas." In 1804, after breaking off an alliance with Cai Qian, Zhu plundered the areas

---

3. It is no coincidence that Cai Qian and Zhu Fen were rivals. The people of Quanzhou and Zhangzhou had a long history of armed feuds with one another.

around Amoy and Quemoy (Jinmen Island), and in the next year he attacked shipping around Zhaoan and Yunxiao (both in Fujian), in conjunction with Wushi Er's fleet from western Guangdong. Between 1805 and 1808, Zhu remained most active in the waters around Fujian, Taiwan, and northeastern Guangdong. At the height of power he probably had four thousand followers and more than a hundred ships. In early 1809, in a naval battle in Guangdong, he was mortally wounded, and soon afterward most of his followers surrendered to the Qing government (*Xiamen zhi* 1961, 675–76).

Meanwhile, farther to the south in Guangdong province, once the Tay Son rebels had been defeated in 1802, a pirate chief named Zheng Yi, who came from a long line of Cantonese pirates, began reorganizing the disparate gangs into a huge confederation. In 1805 he led seven of the most powerful pirate leaders, including Guo Podai, Wushi Er, and Donghai Ba, in signing a pact intended to impose law and order over the unruly gangs (Doc. 31). The reinvigorated pirates established new bases along Guangdong's coast and outer islands, as well as inside the core Pearl River estuary near the provincial capital of Canton. From their strongholds they extended their hegemony over most of the fishing and coastal trade, as well as over many villages and market towns, through a formal protection racket based on extortion, bribery, and terrorism. Pirates easily found unscrupulous men like Zhou Feixiong in Macau and Li Chongyu in Jiazi (a port in Guangdong) who willingly aided them with provisions, weapons, and information and handled their ransom payments and protection fees (Docs. 32, 40). Even the state-licensed salt trade had fallen victim to the pirates, whose junks had to purchase "safe conduct passes" at two hundred dollars per vessel. The ransom and sale of captives was also a major source of pirate income (Antony 2010a; Doc. 38). So bold were the pirates that they increasingly attacked Western vessels (table 4.1). In 1806, for instance, pirates plundered a passage boat and kidnapped John Turner, the chief officer of the merchant ship *John Jay*.[4] Pirates held him prisoner for five months, only releasing him after a ransom of $6,000 was paid (Turner 1814).

By 1806 the pirates, not the imperial navy, had military superiority at sea. For the most part Qing warships were antiquated and cumbersome, and they were significantly fewer in number and greatly inferior to many of the swifter and heavily armed pirate warships. Although Fujian and Guangdong both had official quotas of 130 to 150 naval vessels these numbers were rarely met. Ships destroyed by storms or pirates were infrequently replaced while others were in constant disrepair. After Nayancheng (1764–1833) arrived in Canton as the new governor-general in 1805, he reported to the throne that there were fewer than twenty thousand naval personnel and only eighty-three warships

---

4. In some accounts the name of the ship is given as the *Tay*.

Table 4.1. Pirate Attacks on Foreigners and Foreign Ships, 1793–1810

Date (mm/yyyy)	Place	Particulars	Consequences
—/1793	near Macau	pirates attacked the Portuguese ship *Flore do Mar*	all but four crew members killed
—/1796	near Macau	a Portuguese ship plundered by pirates	pirates killed all non-Chinese onboard
—/1796	near Macau	pirates attacked British ship *Kennett*	most of the crew killed
—/1800	Whampoa	pirates attempted to board British schooner *Providence*	repulsed by schooner's crew
—/1804	Taipa	pirates occupied Taipa anchorage and threaten Macau	reduced Macau to two-day supply of rice
10/1804	near Lintin	pirates disrupted communications between Lintin and Macau	difficulties supplying foreign ships anchored at Lintin
—/1805	near Macau	pirates captured Portuguese brig returning from Manila	several crew held captive for over a year
08/1805	near Macau	chop boat belonging to Dobell and Biddle plundered by pirates	both men barely escaped but all their belongings taken
12/1806	near Macau	John Turner and five Lascars captured by pirates and held for five months	ransom valued at $6,000 paid to pirates
02/1807	Macau	pirates attempted to land and attack Guia fort	repulsed by Macau soldiers
—/1808	near Macau	pirates attacked launch of the British ship *Dover*	ship escaped with little damage
—/1808	near Macau	pirates captured American schooner *Pilgrim* on route from Manila	eight to nine crewmen held captive for several months
02/1809	near Cheunpi	an officer and two sailors of the *Royal George* in the ship's yawl attacked by pirates	
02/1809	near Macau	pirates captured Portuguese-flagged brig	pirates refitted brig for pirating; in September the brig was retaken
08/1809	near Macau	pirates attacked American ship *Atahualpa*	
09/1809	near Macau	pirates captured Richard Glasspoole and six sailors from the *Marquis of Ely*	ransom of $4,200 and supplies paid to pirates
09/1809	mouth of Pearl River	pirates blockaded three Siamese tribute junks	
09/1809	near Macau	pirates captured brig belonging to Portuguese governor of Timor	
01/1810	near Whampoa	pirates attacked a small foreign boat	three chests carried away; boat's crew thrown overboard; one Lascar drowned

in service. Four years later, damage and destruction left the Guangdong navy with fewer than seventy seaworthy warships. At the same time the pirates, who numbered in the tens of thousands, had hundreds of ships, some with crews of as many as a hundred sailors (Docs. 33, 36). While naval cannons had shot weighing only one catty (roughly 1.3 lbs.), pirates had heavier shot of fourteen catties (about 18 lbs.) (Wei 2006, 97–102; Antony 1994, 21). About this same time, Captain Francis Austin of the H.M.S. *St. Albans* assessed Chinese naval armaments: "At present their breastwork is too low, their guns not capable of being pointed but by moving the vessel, and so ill-cast and mounted as to be evidently unsafe to fire" (Murray 1979, 372). In battle after battle pirates outmaneuvered and outgunned the navy.

In 1807 Zheng Yi died in a storm at sea. The leadership passed into the hands of his widow, Zheng Yi Sao (1775?–1844) and the young and charismatic Zhang Bao (1783?–1822).[5] Under their combined leadership Guangdong pirates reached the apex of power. Zheng Yi Sao, who had been a prostitute on one of Canton's floating brothels before she married Zheng Yi in 1801, played a key role in helping her husband consolidate his dominance over the burgeoning pirate league. When her husband suddenly died she maneuvered quickly to assure support from her deceased husband's family in her own bid for power (Murray 1981; Doc. 40). In taking command she was assisted by the twenty-one-year-old Zhang Bao, her husband's adopted son and now her lover. There is little doubt, however, that Zheng Yi Sao was the real boss. As one contemporary observer noted: "Zhang Bao . . . obeyed Zheng Yi Sao's orders and consulted her on all things before acting" (Wen 1842, 2a).

Zhang Bao had joined the pirates when he was fifteen, after being kidnapped by Zheng Yi's gang. The young lad quickly came to the attention of the chief, who adopted him into the Zheng family after a homosexual liaison, a common method of initiating adolescents into a gang as well as a means of male bonding (Murray 1992). In a short time, Zhang Bao was given command of his own vessel where he ably demonstrated his skills in both seamanship and piracy. Within weeks of Zheng Yi's death, he was at the side of Zheng Yi Sao, sharing her boudoir and all the power (Antony 2003, 48–51). By that time the confederation had stabilized at six large, self-sustaining fleets, each flying a separate colored banner; the pirates numbered anywhere from forty thousand to sixty thousand individuals. Zheng Yi Sao and Zhang Bao led the largest and most powerful Red Banner Fleet, consisting of more than twenty thousand pirates and several hundred warships (Doc. 33). In figure 4.2 the

---

5. In English language sources Zheng Yi Sao is known variously as Cheng I Sao, Ching Shih, Shih Yang, Shi Xianggu, and Shih Heang Koo; Zhang Bao is known variously as Cheung Po, Zhang Baozai, and Cheung Po Tsai.

Figure 4.2. The Pirate Zhang Bao.

charismatic Zhang Bao, seated aboard his junk with two attendants, is portrayed in an early nineteenth century book illustration.

Wushi Er, a signatory to the 1805 pirate pact and member of the Guangdong confederation, led the largest and most powerful Blue Banner fleet in the Gulf of Tonkin. In many ways, he was an archetypical professional pirate—one of the earliest to join the Tay Son Rebellion in the 1790s and the last major pirate to be defeated by the Qing in 1810. Born Mai Youjin in the small fishing village of Wushi on the west coast of the Leizhou peninsular around 1765, he began his criminal career in his teens as a petty thief and blackmailer in several ports around the gulf. After being abducted by a gang of pirates, Wushi Er later claimed to have been coerced to participate with them in their raids in the waters of western Guangdong and northern Vietnam. Sometime in the 1790s he joined the Tay Son cause and was soon afterward appointed as a brigade general. In 1797 he commanded a band of roughly a hundred men and received a new title from the Tay Son ruler as the "Vice Admiral Who Pacifies the Sea," and a few years later he was again promoted as the "King Who Pacifies the Waves." After the Tay Son collapsed in 1802, he returned to Chinese waters, establishing bases on the Leizhou peninsula and Weizhou Island (Doc 34). By 1805 Qing officials reported that he had become the most formidable pirate in the Gulf of Tonkin with a fleet of eighty to ninety war junks. He oversaw a vast criminal network that centered on the gulf region but also had branches in northeastern Guangdong and southeastern Fujian. Each year his ships took in profits of several thousands of taels silver from plunder, ransoms, and extortion, making it necessary for him to employ a small bureaucracy of scribes to write blackmail letters and to keep accounts of the booty, as well as of weapons and provisions. By 1809 his Blue Banner fleet was divided into eight squadrons, organized around a central core of family members, including his elder brother and several cousins. At that time he commanded more than a hundred ships and some three thousand to five thousand pirates (Antony 2003, 92–93).

The Guangdong pirates were at the height of their power in 1809, yet within a year they utterly collapsed. Having repeatedly defeated the imperial navy, the pirates had virtual control over the Guangdong coast and even many inland villages and towns. That summer, following a series of devastating natural disasters that brought on a severe famine, pirates swarmed deep into the Pearl River Delta, penetrating within a few miles of Canton itself in search of food and plunder (Docs. 37, 38). Once again a number of Western vessels came under pirate attack, and in September, Richard Glasspoole and six fellow crewmen from the *Marquis of Ely* were kidnapped for ransom. Unable to stop the pirates militarily, the Jiaqing emperor (r. 1796–1820) initiated an appeasement policy, coaxing pirates to surrender in exchange for pardons and rewards. Almost immediately pirates began to petition to surrender, culminating with the surrenders in April 1810 of Zhang Bao and Zheng Yi Sao with more than 17,000 followers, including 5,000 women and children, together with roughly 280 junks and some 12,000 firearms (Docs. 39, 40). The government quickly rewarded Zhang Bao with a naval commission and sent him to fight the remaining pirates in western Guangdong, particularly the powerful fleets commanded by Wushi Er and Donghai Ba. Once they were defeated further resistance quickly crumbled (Antony 2003, 51–52).

Later the emperor transferred Zhang Bao to the Pescadores where he became a regiment commander. He died there of natural causes in 1822, still a young man in his thirties. After his death, Zheng Yi Sao relocated first to Macau and then to Canton, accompanied by their son. Her efforts to make him a successful military officer failed, and in the end she outlived even him, dying quietly in Canton in 1844, likely in her late sixties, as the operator of a gambling hall (Murray 1987, 148–50).

Between 1809 and 1810 roughly forty thousand pirates and family members had surrendered to the authorities in Guangdong. What was their fate? Governor-General Bailing (1748–1816) quickly implemented measures to first feed and then resettle them and to make sure that they would not slip back to their old ways (though many did). While most leaders were placed in the military, the vast majority of rank-and-file pirates were relocated in various areas throughout the province, but mostly far away from the coast. Women and children, who had been abducted by pirates, were sent back to their homes. Once resettled these former pirates were put under the watchful care of village elders and local constables, who had the responsibility to assure their good conduct and help them find honest work. Not everyone who surrendered, however, was automatically pardoned. Among Zheng Yi Sao's followers, for example, 245 of the most notorious offenders were tried and punished: 95 were beheaded, 79 were banished to other provinces, and 71 were sentenced to penal servitude. By the end of 1810, for all practical purposes, the golden age of piracy in China had come to an end, though piracy never completely disappeared in the region (Antony 2006).

Chapter Five

The Significance of Piracy in China's History

Although not too long ago few China scholars considered piracy as a serious subject for study, today China's maritime history has become one of the hottest topics of research, including the long overdue study of piracy (Connolly and Antony 2017). This change came about for many reasons, not the least of which is the amazing success of Disney's multimillion-dollar blockbuster series *Pirates of the Caribbean*, which has even expanded its scope to include pirates of the South China Sea. The recent upsurge in piracy in Southeast Asia, especially around the Malacca Strait and Indonesia, as well as in Somalia, has further contributed to the new interest in piracy in China and around the world. But why is piracy important as a topic of research?

To begin with, the study of pirates is significant for what it can tell us about the lives of ordinary people. Piracy, in fact, had become a regular and integral component in the lifecycles of many mariners in the sixteenth to nineteenth centuries. Although some pirate chieftains, particularly during the mid-Ming and Ming-Qing transition, had merchant backgrounds, nonetheless, the vast majority of rank-and-file Chinese pirates came from the underclass of laboring poor; they were mostly sailors and fisherfolk (roughly 70 percent in the early nineteenth century). Typically they were single males who lacked regular employment and were constantly in debt. Piracy too was a young man's profession. Most pirates were in their twenties; few were over forty. For many individuals poverty drove them to commit crimes as a way to survive. For others piracy offered opportunities for adventure and freedom, as well as a chance to become rich and perhaps famous. Some individuals said they became pirates because of the oppression of government officials and soldiers (Docs. 7, 33, 39). As elsewhere around the world, a number of Chinese pirates, such as Zheng Chenggong, Yang Yandi, Zhang Bao, and Wushi Er, have become folk heroes, while others have even become deified, including Zheng Chenggong and the sister of Wu Ping (Doc. 10).

Seafarers were a highly mobile workforce, moving around from port to port taking whatever jobs were available. Piracy provided a rational and practical alternative or supplement to inadequate employment and low wages. When times were hard and jobs were scarce many sailors and fishers took work aboard pirate ships as they would aboard other ships. In some cases, piracy was a contractual agreement whereby individuals agreed to sign on a pirate ship for a stipulated amount of time, typically for eight to nine months. Although there were many full-time professional pirates, particularly among the leaders, for most people who took to pirating it was a part-time job. The majority of gang members were occasional, amateur pirates (Docs. 27, 33). Piracy therefore had an important function in providing work, even on a casual basis, for countless numbers of people who could not be fully absorbed into the regular, legitimate labor market.

Among Chinese pirates, there also were significant numbers of women. Because many women made their homes aboard ship and worked alongside their menfolk, it was not unusual to find females among the pirates. Even women captives often willingly joined pirate gangs. Many women, in fact, married into the pirate profession and freely lived and died as outlaws. Aboard ship, most pirates abided by their conjugal vows, with husbands and wives remaining faithful to one another (with the apparent exception of Cai Qian's wife) (Docs. 30, 33, 36). In the early nineteenth century, several female pirates even became powerful chieftains, such as Cai Qian Ma and Zheng Yi Sao, both of whom commanded formidable pirate fleets (Docs. 30, 40). These and other female pirates were able to survive in a man's world by proving themselves as capable as men in battle and in their duties as sailors. In many cases women pirates actually bested their male counterparts. Women were not merely tolerated by their male shipmates but were actually able to exercise leadership roles aboard ships.

Female pirates represented the most radical departure from China's traditional society and customs, defying accepted notions of womanhood and breaking with established codes of female propriety, virtue, and passivity. Unlike their counterparts on Western ships, Chinese female pirates did not have to disguise themselves as men. They lived and worked openly as women aboard ships. From the perspective of the Chinese state, such women who behaved like men perverted the social order and normal gender relationships, turning Confucian orthodoxy on its head. Indeed, they challenged the patriarchal hierarchy upon which both the state and society rested. For seafaring women, piracy presented opportunities to escape from poverty and the rigid restraints placed on females. It gave them the chance for adventure and freedom unheard of for most women on land.

Whenever piracy flourished, so too did the shadow economy, providing tens of thousands of additional jobs to coastal residents. Like the pirates themselves, most of the individuals who traded with them were fishers, sailors, and petty entrepreneurs (like Li Chongyu), who engaged in both licit and illicit enterprises to earn a living. In many instances extra money gained from clandestine activities provided an important, even major, part of their overall income. Because tens of thousands of people on both sea and shore came to depend on piracy either directly or indirectly for their livelihoods, it became a self-sustaining enterprise and a significant feature in China's early modern history. Piracy was also important because it allowed marginalized fisherfolk, sailors, and petty entrepreneurs, who had otherwise been excluded, to participate in the wider commercial economy.

While piracy undermined legitimate trade and profits, it nevertheless had important positive economic consequences. For the most part, pirates did not want to destroy the existing economy but rather to gain a more equitable share in it. As the growth of legitimate commerce promoted the development of new ports, so too did the pirates' illicit trade. Numerous ports and black markets sprung up along China's coast and in Taiwan, Japan, and Southeast Asia to handle the trade in stolen goods and to service pirate ships and crews. They became the "spaces between," virtual no-man's lands or zones of international contact that governments tolerated and allowed to flourish for shares of the spoils. They were places of opportunity for anyone willing to take risks outside the law (Laver 2016). The port of Hirado in Japan in the seventeenth century was one such place; so was the frontier town of Jiangping on the Sino-Vietnamese border. In the late eighteenth century Jiangping was a good example of a port that catered to pirates, smugglers, and traders of all nations. Black markets, such as Jiangping and Hirado, fostered important shadow economies that existed alongside and in competition with lawful trade centers. In such places the lines separating legitimate trade, smuggling, and piracy were blurred and constantly shifting.

The contraband trade also tended to perpetuate piracy. Once pirates generated supplies of goods for sale at discount prices, buyers were attracted to black markets that arose to handle the trade in booty. Large amounts of money and goods flowed in and out of black markets, all of which were outside the control of the state. The establishment of clandestine markets to specifically handle stolen merchandise was also a clear indication of weaknesses in the structure of regular, lawful markets. Pirates therefore made important contributions to the growth of trade and the reallocation of local capital (Antony 2010a).

At the height of their power huge pirate leagues gained firm holds over many coastal villages and port towns, as well as over shipping and fishing enterprises, through the systematic use of terror, bribery, and extortion. During such times all vessels operating along China's coast were liable to pirate attack unless they bought safe conduct passes. To avoid attack, owners of merchant and fishing junks paid protection fees to the pirates, who in turn issued passports guaranteeing impunity to the purchaser (Doc. 18). In the early nineteenth century pirates had virtual control over the state-monopolized salt trade, and even Western merchants paid "tribute" to pirates to protect their ships. The extortion system was highly institutionalized with registration certificates, account books, full-time bookkeepers, and collection bureaus. Extortion was not only a major form of pirate income but also the most direct and effective way that pirates exercised hegemony over an area (Docs. 18, 38). Pirates, who were able to penetrate the structure of local society through the establishment of protection rackets, actually constituted a level of control over maritime society that operated independently of and in many instances even overshadowed that of the government and local elites, making them significant and pervasive forces in littoral society (Antony 2003, 118–19; MacKay 2013).

What is more, pirates built strongholds not only on remote islands (such as Weizhou) but in and around key commercial and political hubs such as Canton, Macau, Chaozhou, and Amoy. In the Pearl River Delta not far from Canton, for example, Chinese pirates over several centuries maintained bases on Taipa, Coloane, Hengqin, and Lantao islands—areas that Western traders called the Ladrones or Pirate Islands (map 5.1). There they openly careened and refitted their ships and defiantly set up their headquarters to conspire with soldiers and officials who were on the take. The close proximity of pirate lairs to economic and political centers was clear indication of just how deeply piracy had penetrated Chinese society.

Piracy was an act of violence and often great terror. For pirates, in most instances, violence was rational, calculated, and purposeful. They deliberately constructed reputations for brutality and destructiveness in efforts to minimize resistance and maximize profits. Pirates brutally flogged captives to elicit information, usually about where they hid valuables, and they inhumanly dismembered and disemboweled soldiers and officials who attempted to arrest them. They also tortured and murdered foreigners as a form of reprisal. However horrifying and repulsive, pirate cruelty must be judged in the context of the times and in relation to official behavior. For Chinese pirates, the image of a brutal, oppressive state was heightened by the bloody executions of hundreds, sometimes thousands, of people along the South China coast each year. Pirates mimicked the example of officials. It was an age of

Map 5.1. Canton, Macau, and the Pearl River Delta.
Source: created by Robert Antony.

awful brutality in which the conscious use of violence and terror, both by officials and by pirates, constituted a recognizable display of awesome power and authority over the weak and powerless (Antony 2012; Docs. 9, 25, 38).

Chinese pirates drew upon a remarkable array of cultural and religious backgrounds. Chinese officials and Westerners alike viewed pirates as being very superstitious—they would do nothing without first consulting their gods (Doc. 38). Yet pirates, like other seafarers, took oracles and omens seriously. During voyages fishers, sailors, and pirates made daily offerings to the gods of the wind and sea, as well as to Mazu or other protective deities. Whenever they sailed past well-known temples, crews would make offerings aboard ship or go ashore to worship in the temple. Zhang Bao built a shrine on his largest ship—described as a floating pagoda—so he and his subordinates could easily seek protection and advice from their gods. Chieftains, such as Zheng Zhilong and Zhang Bao, even manipulated religious beliefs to enhance their own positions and legitimacy. During their lifetimes a rich folklore developed around both men asserting that they enjoyed special divine protection and had supernatural powers to perform miracles (Docs. 16, 35). Zhang Bao, for instance, claimed a special relationship with a little-known sea goddess with the odd name Third Old Lady (Sanpo) (Doc. 35). Officials considered Sanpo a false god whose adherents practiced exorcistic rituals and spirit possession, activities that the state considered unorthodox and licentious. Perhaps because her adherents believed that she willingly answered the prayers of anyone who venerated and sacrificed to her, pirates were fervently devoted to Sanpo (Antony 2003, 150–61).

Forged out of hardship, prejudice, and poverty, pirates created a transgressive culture based on violence, crime, and vice and characterized by excessive profanity, intoxication, gambling, and brawling. In marked opposition to the dominant culture on land, poor sailors, fisherfolk, and pirates devised their own unique lifestyles, habits, and standards of behavior for survival. Pirates formed self-regulating "escape societies" with their own laws that governed the redistribution of looted wealth and aimed to keep order over normally unruly outlaws (Docs. 31, 40). Shuangyu Island provided one such escape society that operated outside the law as an important international black market and pirate stronghold for several decades in the sixteenth century. During the Ming period Taiwan, which the state had never formally claimed, became an ideal nonstate space for pirates. Later and even more successful, Zheng Chenggong and Zheng Jing ruled Taiwan for twenty years as an autonomous state with its own military forces, government bureaucracy, and laws. The politico-cultural world of pirates was important because it challenged the mainstream Confucian model of governance and offered a potential alternative for China's poor and disenfranchised (Antony 2003, 139–50; MacKay 2013, 557–65).

Piracy also was important for what it reveals about state and empire building in the early modern world, especially the interactions of pirates, smugglers, and privateers with European and Asian political powers. In the mid-Ming period, encouraged by their home governments, Portuguese merchants in Asia routinely utilized overly aggressive trade practices that appeared little different from piracy, at least to Chinese officials and their victims. During the chaos of the Ming-Qing dynastic wars, European powers willingly used their own and Chinese privateers to further their economic interests in Asia and around the world. The Dutch East India Company actually operated the largest and best-financed privateering enterprise in the seventeenth century, collaborating with such Chinese pirates as Zheng Zhilong. In the late eighteenth century, in Vietnam Tay Son rebels recruited Chinese pirates as critical sources of naval manpower and of revenue from booty. Put simply, piracy in its many forms played a key role in maritime imperial expansion and nation building.

To conclude, reading about pirates is not only interesting but important. Their histories inform us about both official and popular attitudes toward crime and violence. The very scale of piracy during its golden age in China between the sixteenth and early nineteenth centuries made it a significant factor in the historical development of China. There were not only tens of thousands of sailors and fishers who became pirates but at least as many and likely even more people on shore who aided and supported pirates, thus affecting a significant portion of the maritime population. Both directly and indirectly, piracy had a great impact on the social, economic, and cultural developments of the South China Sea in the early modern period.

Today the number of piracy cases is decreasing in China's waters; nonetheless, several areas in Southeast Asia, especially around Indonesia and the Malacca Strait, remain pirate "hot-spots." Although governments have been working diligently to suppress piracy, pirates persist in legends, folklore, movies, and songs. Often ignoring the facts, novelists, journalists, tour guides, and even some scholars have used and misused pirates in many interesting ways. In China, as in the West, pirates have been depicted variously as bloodthirsty villains, treacherous rogues, sword-fighting heroes, champions of the poor, and avengers against injustice. The irony of this, of course, is that a society that has worked hard to eliminate piracy over the past several centuries has continued to immortalize pirates as colorful folk heroes.

Part II

DOCUMENTARY EVIDENCE

1. Piracy in the Mid-Ming Dynasty (1520–1580)

DOC. 1. SATO SHINEN'S DESCRIPTION OF
JAPANESE PIRATES, EARLY TO MID-SIXTEENTH CENTURY

*In the 1520s pirate raids along the China coast began to increase (figure 6.1). Although most of the so-called dwarf bandits (*wokou*) were Chinese, nonetheless they were often joined by Japanese pirates, adventurers, and masterless samurai warriors. The following excerpt, purportedly written by a Japanese pirate, succinctly describes the escalation of piracy on China's coast as well as illustrates the broad scope of pirate activities both in China and Southeast Asia at that time. It is also interesting to note that the author mentions the adoption of guns, which had only been introduced into Japan a short time earlier—according to some scholars by the Chinese pirate Wang Zhi.*

During the Eisho and Taiei eras [1504–1527] several warriors . . . from islands . . . off the coast of Iyo banded together and crossed the ocean to foreign lands, where they operated as pirates and became wealthy. Murakami Zusho, the lord of Noshima, was selected as their leader. The pirates pillaged coastal towns and seized all kinds of things, making themselves rich. They operated along the coast of China . . . and among the islands of the southeast as far as the Philippines, Borneo, and Bali. For several years they continued these forays. . . . In time *ronin* [masterless samurai], fishermen, scoundrels, and others from the Kyushu-Shikoku area joined the pirate bands, and gradually their size increased from eight to nine hundred to more than a thousand men. Consequently, all the islands of the southwestern seas were harassed by pirates. Even Ming China feared them, and as a result sent out her huge armies [to drive them away]. China also strengthened its coastal defenses. It was at this time that the pirates came to be known as *wakō*.[1] . . .

Iida Koichiro of Oshima in the province of Iyo and Kitaura Kanjuro of Momojima in the province of Bingo[2] were the first [pirate leaders] to sail to foreign lands, pillage the coastal villages, steal property, and enrich their families. It is said that at first the two leaders had only fifty or sixty men under them, but with each raid their profits mounted considerably and, as a result, the bands became larger and more powerful.

In foreign countries soldiers were drawn up to guard the coast against our raids. Consequently, we increased our military strength. If we could not destroy the armies guarding the coast, we could gain no profit. Therefore, before setting sail we made complete preparations for engaging such armies in battle. In regard to these preparations, Wu and Song[3] had a large number of guns and it became necessary to take proper countermeasures. Toward the end of the Tembun era [c. 1554] we adopted the use of guns, which increased our military strength and enlarged the size of the pirate bands. In 1555 the number of men in the seven groups [of *wakō* raiders] reached a total of more than a thousand. Each ship was loaded with 700 *koku*[4] of rice. There were eight or nine main vessels, the best of which were called *hagaibune*.[5] . . . In 1563 our seven bands totaling 1,300 men attacked Pinghai[6] in Ming China. . . . We had one hundred and thirty-seven vessels of various sizes. . . . The total number of pirates of all classes reached the figure of 1,352 men, plus sixty fishermen and the like who made up the crew. Of the above, two or three hundred Chinese pirates had joined our ranks.

Source: *Sato Shinen no shuki* [Memoirs of Sato Shinen]. Translation adapted by the author from Brown 1951, 28–29.

DOC. 2. ZHENG XIAO'S COMPLAINT ABOUT SMUGGLING IN HIS HOMETOWN, 1530

Although few contemporary private writings recorded smuggling activities, the biography of Zheng Xiao (1499–1566), written by his son, revealed that

---

1. In fact, the term *wakō* in Japanese or *wokou* in Chinese had been in use in China since the thirteenth century as a designation for bands of Japanese sea marauders.
2. Both Iyo and Bingo provinces, on Japan's Inland Sea, had been hotbeds of piracy since the twelfth century.
3. The names Wu and Song refer to today's Jiangsu and Zhejiang provinces in South China.
4. One *koku* was equivalent to about five bushels.
5. These warships were massive floating fortresses protected with armor plating and equipped with cannons and muskets.
6. In the Ming dynasty, Pinghai was a fortified guardpost on the coast of Xinghua prefecture in Fujian province.

1. Piracy in the Mid-Ming Dynasty (1520–1580)

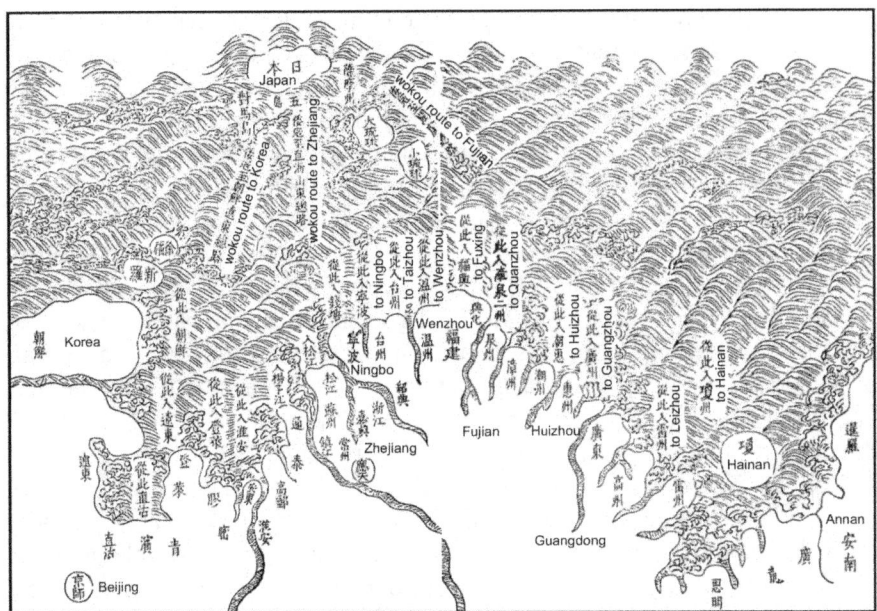

Figure 6.1. Ming Dynasty Map of Japanese Wokou Sailing Routes to China, c. 1520s.

in 1530 there were foreign ships at Haiyan harbor in Zhejiang province, but only a few local notables considered smuggling a serious problem that challenged Ming sovereignty and could lead to piracy. For many people, however, smuggling had become a way of life and an important source of income. Because of his insistent complaints about smuggling activities, which involved his neighbors and local officials, Zheng Xiao was severely criticized and even ostracized in his home community.

In the 9th lunar month [of 1530] the two commanders of the garrison post said that there were foreign ships at sea laden with cargos of many rare goods. It was said that anyone who invested two hundred piculs[7] of rice, could get a profit three times as much within a day. My father said that this [situation] posed a menace to the region and he would not take part in it. He tried to dissuade them [i.e., his fellow villagers], but in vain. My father then reported this to the magistrate, Xia Jun, and the local military commander, Cui Ding,[8] and asked them to deploy troops for the defense [against the foreign ships]. They turned a deaf ear.

---

7. One picul (*dan* in Chinese) is equivalent to about 132.3 lbs.
8. Xia Jun was magistrate from 1530 to 1533, and at that time Cui Ding was local commander in charge of defense against the *wokou*.

My father therefore wrote to the vice commissioner for naval affairs: "Of both the eastern and western sections of Zhejiang, the largest part borders on the sea. In recent years since the defection of Song Suqing[9] to the foreigners[10] [that is, Japanese], the prefectures of Ningbo and Wenzhou in eastern Zhejiang have been subject to the evil influences of treacherous merchants who have connections inside and outside [China], have killed and wounded our officers and troops, and have burned and plundered our villages and market towns. Haiyan is located in an isolated area in western Zhejiang. Previously there have never been [disloyal] guides, so fortunately there has never been any fighting. Recently the defense of Ningbo and Wenzhou had been secured and there were no opportunities for the pirates to do as they pleased. But all of a sudden, this year on the 22nd day of the 9th lunar month [October 12, 1530], a huge ship with seven masts came to the southeastern shore of our district with foreign goods for sale. Their ship was unusually long and wide and on its side was a several storied building which looked like a city wall with battlements, and was well equipped with spears, swords, cannons, rockets, bows, and other weapons.[11] More than a thousand local people gathered seeking to make a profit and vying with one another to the point of almost starting a riot. The men aboard [the ship] said that they were Wo [Japanese], boasted of their prosperity, and induced our innocent people [to trade with them]. Some people have said that it is not necessary to forbid communications between Chinese and foreigners for the purpose of making money. How about Song Suqing who, not long ago, was not a foreigner and how about the recent ships from Zhangzhou, [in which case] the people on board all became traitors. . . . If we do not stop it [that is, communication and trade with foreigners] now, I am afraid that in the future when we have gotten used to it, we would not know how to defend [ourselves] and they would not fear us. Then it would be too late to regret if our city gates had to be closed in the daytime [due to a siege]!" . . . Because they had been investigated, the two commanders had come to hate my father. Even the scholar-gentry in our village also thought my father to be too meddlesome.

Source: Zheng Lüchun 1569, 1:24b–26a. Translation adapted by the author from So 1975, 47–48.

---

9. Song Suqing, known in Japan as Sō Sokyo, originally was a native of Ningbo. Considered a traitor in China because of his close connections with Japan, he was a notorious smuggler and in 1523 became a Japanese envoy who was involved in the disputed tributary mission to Ningbo, which erupted into a riot and pillaging of the city. Some scholars cite this incident as the start of escalated *wokou* piracy in China. Later, Song was arrested and died in a Chinese jail.

10. The author uses the Chinese character *yi*, which can be translated as foreigners or as barbarians. In this context *yi* refers to the Japanese.

11. This ship was likely a *hagaibune*, as described by Sato Shinen in Doc. 1.

DOC. 3. COLLUSION BETWEEN CHINESE, FOREIGNERS, AND PIRATES, 1534

In the Ming dynasty, as in other periods, there was a close connection between smuggling and piracy. Once the imperial court enacted strict prohibitions on maritime trade, smuggling and piracy became the most common avenues by which Chinese, Japanese, Southeast Asian, and European merchants conducted business with one another. The sea bans made outlaws out of merchants and forced them to conduct trade clandestinely outside the gaze of the state. Also because of its illegality, it was easy for smuggling to turn violent and rapacious and to slip into piracy. Because imperial officials were not pleased with the local handling of smugglers, the court sent special investigators of their own. One entry in the Veritable Records, dated September 26, 1534, reported:

To begin with, in the counties bordering on the sea in Zhili [that is, the regions around Nanjing], Fujian, and Zhejiang, disloyal people often went out to sea in violation of the prohibition and then sneaked back through our coastal borders to do trade so as to earn profits. . . . It happened that such traitorous people like Lin Yu and others, along with fifty or so of their ships, had continually come to the region around Songmen[12] [to trade]. They resisted the government troops and as a result there were casualties. Later they were arrested. When their ships were examined, their cargoes were all contraband. According to the reports from Commander Yang Huai and others some pirates [also] had been captured. Further investigation showed that [in fact the people captured] were disloyal merchants, but many had already died in jail from torture. The regional inspector punished with death four of those who had resisted officials and banished the rest to our frontier for unlawfully passing through our [coastal] border.

The emperor's edict replied: The pirates have privately employed large vessels to deal in foreign goods resulting in the death of many people and bringing troubles to our land. How could it be that only four men were accorded severe punishment? . . . If the law is that lax, troubles will certainly increase in the future. Send supervising officials from the [central government's] judicial offices there, where they are to work jointly with the regional inspector to have all the criminals investigated in detail and report back their findings for imperial decision. As for the officials involved, they should be reported and dealt with after this matter is settled.

Source: *Ming Shizong Shilu* 2005, 166:7b. Translation by the author.

---

12. Songmen was an isolated minor port town in Zhejiang province located between the larger ports of Wenzhou and Taizhou.

DOC. 4. IMPERIAL EDICT INSTRUCTING ZHU WAN ABOUT HIS DUTIES AS THE GRAND COORDINATOR OF COASTAL DEFENSE, 1547

On July 24, 1547, the Jiajing emperor promoted Zhu Wan to the post of grand coordinator of Zhejiang with concurrent control over the defense of Fujian's coastal areas. Here is the imperial edict that dispatched Zhu Wan to his new post as well as the imperial instructions. This document provides us with an unusual opportunity to know the emperor's precise instructions to the new grand coordinator. The edict refers briefly yet clearly to the major problems Zhu Wan was expected to address, particularly Chinese collusion with foreigners and piracy. It not only mentioned the collaboration of powerful coastal families but also acknowledged failings of local officials who were unable to deal effectively with the problem of piracy. Furthermore, the edict outlined certain parameters of action, yet still left a great deal of personal discretion to Zhu Wan, particularly in the realm of antipirate defense actions. In keeping with the censorial functions of his post, the edict also placed a great deal of emphasis on surveillance over and rectification of local officials. The major emphasis of these instructions was not on any specific military plan or campaign but rather on enforcement of existing laws, strengthening of defenses, purification of the bureaucracy, and effective coordination of strategy and all other activities within the two provinces.

To the Junior Vice Censor-in-Chief Zhu Wan: In Zhejiang there are seacoasts and strategic hills, including Ningbo which is the port that the Wo foreigners [that is, Japanese] enter [China] to bring tribute. . . . In recent years in Fujian, in such places as Zhangzhou and Quanzhou prefectures, wealthy and influential people, who utilize the conveniences of dealing with foreigners at sea, have seized the chance to attack and plunder the coastal military and civilian [populations]. They clandestinely cooperate with foreigners to carry out rebellion. Such places as Ningbo and Shaoxing [in Zhejiang] are also the same. There are civilian and military officials who have charge over these places, but they neglect their duties. Moreover, [because] the size of Zhejiang is quite large and [officials] have a great deal of tax collection and litigation to administer, their duties and workloads are several times greater than in other provinces. Furthermore, there has been no grand coordinator to supervise and coordinate the duties of local officials in this area. This is because of shortcomings in the [administrative] system.

Now, I [the Jiajing emperor] specially command you [Zhu Wan] to go to the above mentioned areas to be the grand coordinator of Zhejiang and concurrently oversee the Fujian coastal circuits of Fuzhou, Fuxing, Jianning, Zhangzhou, and Quanzhou, and to manage coastal military affairs. Your headquarters will be in Hangzhou, the capital of Zhejiang. In general, your duties are to closely supervise the work of local subordinate officials, collect taxes, inspect and train troops, repair city walls and moats, as well as to prevent corruption and keep law and order among the military and civilian population. If local bandits and pirates rise up or if some Wo [Japanese] exploit the tributary [system] to make trouble along our coasts, you should immediately dispatch government officers to those areas as needed. At the same time you must send a memorial informing me of the matter. For other important issues, however, you must first prepare a memorial and request my permission. On the whole, you should plan strategy and consult with the Investigating Censor[13] to deliberate and decide what action to follow. Should it be necessary to deploy troops and if the seal-holders of the three provincial offices[14] are able to carry out your plans, then you are free to mobilize and deploy them. You may freely commission and transfer civil officials of the fifth degree and below and military officials of the fourth degree and below.[15] If any of them do not obey your orders, then you should proceed with investigations and arrests. If those interrogated should be impeached then so be it. If a matter concerns military issues, you are permitted to use military law to adjudicate it.

In those places in Fujian, such as Zhangzhou and Quanzhou Prefectures, where piracy is rampant, if there are reports of pirates you should personally go there to inspect and then devise a plan to eliminate them. If among the [top] provincial officials, as well as [the officers in charge of] each guard unit, prefecture, subprefecture, and county in Zhejiang . . . and in Fujian, there are any personnel who are honest, hardworking, and capable in the performance of their duties, and have already passed the civil service examination, then you can promote them or reward them based on your own discretion. If there are any greedy, cruel, incapable, or thoughtless officials maltreating the military and civilian population and violating military law, then you should immediately make arrests and interrogations, and then dismiss and punish them [if found guilty]. You should impeach [those guilty] according to the facts in order to create peace and harmony among the local military and civilian population.

In my instructions I have recorded what is proper. As for those who do not do their utmost, they nonetheless must obey you and comply with your proper decisions. When your memorials arrive, we will decide for you as fast as the wind. . . . Yours is an important trust, to act with justice and defend honesty,

---

13. Censors or inspectors were routinely dispatched by the imperial court to observe all governmental activities and report to the throne any illegalities and irregularities in the provinces.

14. The top officials in the provincial administrative, surveillance, and military commissions.

15. In imperial China, all civil and military officials were classified according to numbered ranks or degrees. Normally, only the emperor had the privilege of appointing officials, but in this extraordinary case the emperor allowed Zhu Wan to make appointments so as to put an end to the pirate crisis.

to devote your entire mind to it, and to do your utmost. You must make sure that the thieves [that is, pirates] are stopped, the people are at peace, and the land is tranquil in order to sustain the dynasty. Yours is an important appointment, but if someone settles on a perverse plan and brings harm to the lives of people, the blame for this will fall on you.[16]

Source: Zhu Wan 1587, 1:6b–8a. Translation by Lanshin Chang and the author.

DOC. 5. ZHU WAN'S MEMORIALS ON LOCAL COLLABORATORS AND SMUGGLER-PIRATES, 1548

After having received his appointment certificate in September 1547, Zhu Wan left for Fujian the next month in order to investigate the hotbed of piratical troubles, and after a thorough enquiry he reported his findings to the throne. In a lengthy memorial dated February 5, 1548, he described the widespread nature of smuggling and piracy, the blatant collusion between pirates and influential families and the lax, decadent attitude of military officers and civilian officials on the coast.

In the 1st lunar month of the year [1547], a certain pirate snatched the daughter of a good family on Wuzhou [Island][17] and announced that he would marry her. In a place about ten *li* away [roughly three miles], he set up a high opera stage and publicly arranged theatrical performances for his enjoyment. Also in the 8th lunar month, the Portuguese sailed their ships one after another into the interior [harbors] where they unloaded their goods. Afterward they openly careened two ships at Duanyuzhou for repairs. . . .

In another case, a metropolitan graduate (*jinshi*)[18] in Tong'an County [in Fujian] named Xu Fu had been staying at home to take care of his aged parents. Previously pirates abducted one of his younger sisters. Because a marital alliance was formed between them, as a consequence his family has become quite rich. Again take the case of Lin Xiyuan, a former vice commissioner who had been dismissed from office on account of his poor performance record. Presuming upon his ability, he acts recklessly and stirs up trouble over small matters. Whenever a superior official comes to office he sends him a volume or two of his writings containing slanderous biographies of previous officials. According to him, he is doing this in order to show that he is not

---

16. In fact, local notables along the coast did severely criticize Zhu Wan for exceeding his authority, causing the emperor to impeach him, resulting in his suicide in January 1550.
17. Wuzhou was the ancient name for Jinmen or Quemoy.
18. A civil service degree of a successful candidate of the imperial examination; this was the highest and final degree in imperial China, equivalent to a PhD degree today.

corrupt like them; but in fact, he is giving the [new] official notice that he has a hold on him. Hence, those officials serving the area fear and hate him but can do nothing about him. . . . Without authorization he has accepted litigation cases from the people and resorted to the use of torture in investigation. Also without authorization, he has put up official notices infringing on government prerogatives, and he has built large ships claiming that he uses them as ferry boats, but [in fact] he uses them to transport pirate booty and contrabands. According to the information we have received, he has two ships in the eighth precinct in Yuegang, one in the ninth precinct, one in Wuguan Village in Gaopu, and one in Liuwudian.[19] Owing to the fact that the officials in the region fear him, it is not known how many other [ships and friendly ports] that have not been reported.

In another memorial, dated July 1, 1548, Zhu Wan recorded the deposition of an arrested pirate named Chen Rui (figure 6.2).

The apprehended pirate Chen Rui confessed that in the 25th year of Emperor Jiajing [1546] he, Zhao Qi and Jin Shijie, from Bifei borough in Shanyin [a county in Zhejiang], and Bai Yongan, a retainer of the Guard Commander of Shaoxing [in Zhejiang], all four of them, in the 7th lunar month [1545] went to Shuangyu Island and boarded a ship owned by Fang Sanqiao, a native of Huizhou [in Anhui province]. In the 12th lunar month last year [January 1546] they sailed to Japan but the ship was wrecked beyond repair in a storm. This year Fang Sanqiao hired a Japanese ship and on the 8th day of the 4th lunar month [May 7, 1546], they set sail and on the 19th day [May 18] arrived at Wushamen [in Zhejiang]. On the 21st day [May 20], in the waters at Xiaoshun they captured a boat from the Wangjia postal station and another boat from the Wusha River, after which they sailed to Dafotou [Big Head Buddha] in the waters near Maotou. On the 23rd day [May 22] a sailor by the name of Wang Wenyi sailed the [captured] Wangjia boat to go ashore to look for supplies; [another sailor] Wang San went to the Ninghai area to buy ten piculs of rice and five large kegs of liquor, which he brought back aboard ship. On the 2nd day of the 5th lunar month [May 30], Chen Rui went ashore on an [unnamed] island and was caught by a patrol.

At the time on board the Japanese ship there were only twenty Japanese, as well as Japanese swords, Japanese bows, two kegs of gunpowder, four or five small iron Portuguese cannons, four or five bird-beaked guns,[20] all of

---

19. Yuegang was one of the most notorious friendly ports and black markets in Fujian before the Ming government legitimized it by making it an administrative center in 1567 and changing the name to Haicheng. The other two places were small clandestine ports in Fujian in the sixteenth century. See also Doc. 12.

20. These guns were arquebuses or harquebuses, a type of portable matchlock gun invented in Europe during the 1400s.

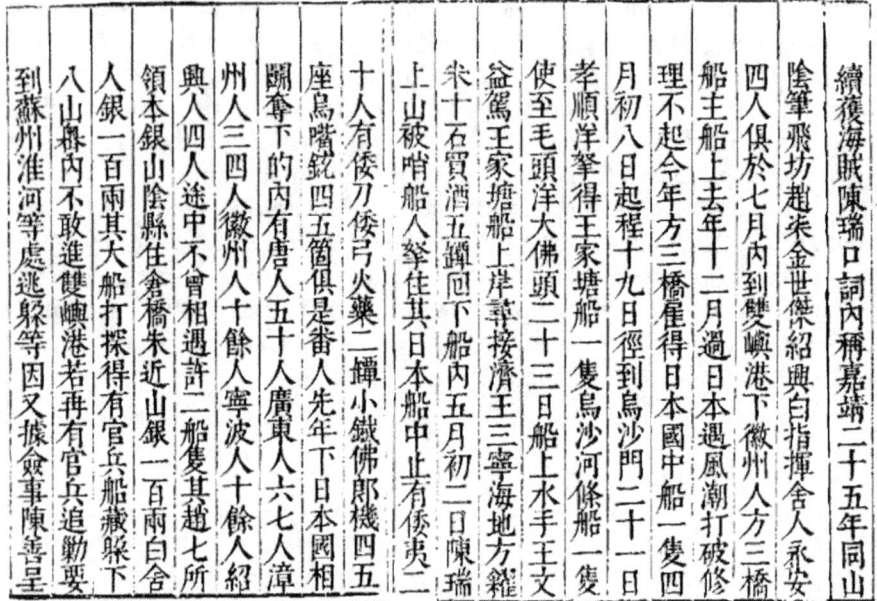

Figure 6.2. The Deposition of Chen Rui, 1548.

which had been obtained by those foreigners in a fight in Japan the previous year. Among the people aboard were fifty Chinese. Of these six or seven were natives of Guangdong, three or four natives of Zhangzhou [in Fujian], more than ten natives of Huizhou [in Anhui], more than ten natives of Ningbo, and four natives of Shaoxing [both in Zhejiang]. On the way they did not meet Xu Er's [that is, Xu Dong's] ships. Zhao Qi had [on his person] one hundred taels of silver that belonged to Zhu Jinshan, who lived in Cangqiao in Shanyin County. Retainer Bai [Yongan] had one hundred taels. The large ship, after learning that officials and soldiers had stationed themselves inside Bashan Bay for an ambush, did not dare go to the harbor on Shuangyu Island. [Instead] had the officials and soldiers chased after them, they [had planned to] sail to places such as Suzhou and the Huai River to hide.

Source: Zhu Wan 1587, 2:19a–b and 2:58b–59b. Translation by Lanshin Chang and the author.

DOC. 6. OFFICIAL ACCOUNT ON
ILLEGAL TRADE ON THE ZHEJIANG COAST, 1549

In this official account in the Veritable Records, dated July 28, 1549, the compilers note the key roles that Wang Zhi, Xu Hai, and other Chinese merchant-pirates played in the escalation of piracy along the South China coast. Their successes, however, would have been impossible without the overt help of powerful and wealthy local families on shore. But as the following report makes clear, colluding with outlaws could lead to violence and treachery. The compilers also correctly point out that, although Japanese did participate in wokou *raids, nonetheless the majority of pirates were Chinese.*

As we understand, the affairs of the coast originated from our disloyal traders Wang Zhi, Xu Hai, and others who often went out to sea unlawfully, carrying Chinese money and commodities and dealing with foreign traders.[21] All this was sponsored by the Xie family of Yuyao [in Zhejiang]. After some time, however, the Xie family withheld some payments, and those disloyal people pressed them for it. Figuring out that they had owed too much to repay, the Xie family threatened them by saying that they would inform the authorities on them. Being resentful and afraid, those disloyal men gathered their followers and the foreign traders together and plundered the Xie family at night. They set fire to the living quarters, killed several men and women, and plundered recklessly before they fled. Fearfully and hurriedly, the magistrate reported to his superiors, saying that the Wo [Japanese] pirates had come to pillage. Grand Coordinator [Zhu] Wan issued orders to have the robbers arrested at once. [He] also ordered that those coastal people who had cooperated with foreigners should come forward to confess their guilt and to inform on one another. Consequently, the people were thrown into a panic; they informed on each other and falsely accused the innocent. For fear that the government troops would search for and arrest them, the treacherous elements thereupon allied themselves with the island foreigners[22] and the notorious pirates at sea.

Taking advantage of the seasonal winds and tides, they went ashore to plunder everywhere. They often assumed the name of *wokou*, but in fact genuine Wo [Japanese] were few. At that time the coast had been at peace for a long time and people were not accustomed to warfare. As soon as they heard about the arrival of pirates, the people all fled like birds or quadrupeds leaving behind empty houses. When government forces fought the pirates, the troops, overawed by their reputation, buckled and ran away. [The trouble]

---

21. The compilers use the term *fan*, having a generic meaning of foreigners, and in this case apparently referring to Southeast Asians.

22. In this case the compilers use the term *daoyi* or "island foreigners," referring to the Japanese.

spread to Fujian waters and the regions between Zhejiang and Zhi[li] [that is, the region around Nanjing]. Troops were deployed, taxes were increased, the whole country was disturbed, and the imperial court was kept busy and worried. It was like this for six or seven years. Only after the resources of the southeast were nearly exhausted were [the *wokou*] barely overcome. The origins of all these troubles, indeed, began with such trivial affairs.

Source: *Ming Shizong Shilu* 2005, 350:2a–b. Translation by the author.

DOC. 7. THE NOBLE PIRATE WANG ZHI IN MING VERNACULAR FICTION

Wang Zhi was one of the leading merchant-pirates in the 1550s, controlling a huge maritime cartel that stretched from Japan to Southeast Asia. Although depicted in official documents as a traitor and vicious criminal, popular fiction and folklore often portrayed him as a noble and righteous pirate, someone sympathetic toward the common people and always seeking social justice. The following excerpt comes from an anthology of short stories about West Lake in Hangzhou first published in 1623 by Zhou Qingyuan. Appearing during the boom in commercial publishing in the late Ming, the story about Wang Zhi is important because it offers us an alternative view of pirates, one normally not found in official writings, but one that illuminates authentic personal feelings about why individuals became outlaws.

Wang Zhi said one day, "Now it is the world of officials and the rich. This is not our world. When we are wronged, where shall we go to complain? Besides, muddle-headed and corrupt officials are numerous. Honest officials pitying commoners are few. . . . They [dishonest officials] have received countless favor from the court and enjoy generous salary and benefits. They continuously receive bribes and are not good people. They harm people, preventing justice being served. Therefore, the bandit heroes of Mount Liang[23] exclusively kill corrupt officials. Why don't we migrate overseas and be carefree and happy?"[24]

Source: Zhou Qingyuan, *Xihu erji* [Second Collection from the West Lake], translated in Wang 2021, 170–71.

---

23. The well-known mountain lair of the 108 bandit-heroes who opposed corrupt officials of the late Northern Song dynasty (960–1126), and whose story has been retold in the novel *Suihu Zhuan* (*Water Margin*). See also Doc. 39 for comparison.

24. In fact, Wang Zhi and other merchant-pirates, due to the Ming sea bans, did move their bases of operations overseas to Japan and Southeast Asia. Later they also established bases on China's offshore islands, such as Shuangyu.

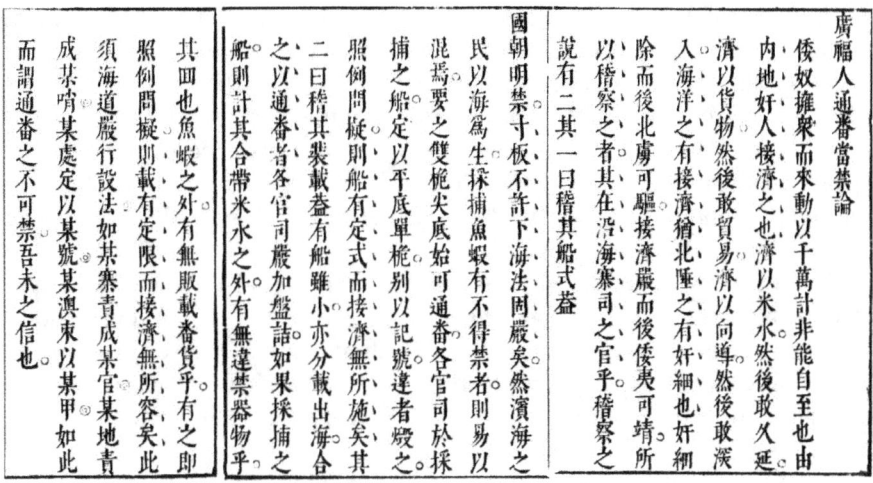

Figure 6.3. Hu Zongxian's Proposal Concerning Guangdong and Fujian, c. 1559.

DOC. 8. HU ZONGXIAN'S PROPOSAL FOR STOPPING THE PEOPLE OF GUANGDONG AND FUJIAN FROM COLLABORATING WITH JAPANESE PIRATES, C. 1559

Hu Zongxian (1512–1565), who was a leading official in Zhejiang and Fujian in the late 1550s, effectively employed alternating annihilation and appeasement policies in dealing with several powerful pirate leaders, including Wang Zhi. In fact, Hu sent personal envoys to Japan to coax Wang Zhi into surrendering in return for a pardon and promises of a military commission. In the end, however, Wang Zhi was executed in early 1560 after languishing in jail for more than a year. Although Hu favored a policy to discourage the local coastal population from aiding the pirates by reinstating maritime trade to help refurbish the coastal economies, the emperor preferred continuation of rigid sea bans and the prosecution of an aggressive war against pirates. Thanks in large measure to Hu's capable administration, by 1559 the wokou *disturbances in Zhejiang had subsided but had moved farther south to Fujian and Guangdong. In Hu's proposal he argued that the best way to stop piracy was to stop the collusion between coastal inhabitants and the Japanese pirates (figure 6.3).*

The reason why tens of thousands of Japanese lackeys[25] can invade our coastal area is not because they know the sea lanes and are familiar with our

---

25. The expression Hu uses is *Wonu* (literally Japanese dwarf slaves), a term of belittlement and subordination indicating the perceived inferior status of Japan vis-à-vis China; in this context Hu is referring to the Japanese pirates.

coast, so that they know how to come here on their own. Rather, it is because our people have connections with them. Our people provide those Japanese lackeys with rice and water, and therefore they dare to stay longer after they invade our lands. [Because our people] provide them with goods, [those lackeys] dare to come here to do business. [Because our people] guide them, [those lackeys] even venture further inland. . . . Therefore, if we can eliminate the supplies and connections [to those lackeys], then there will no longer be Japanese [invading] our shores. . . .

How can this be achieved? Inspections! Our coastal military posts must inspect the boats and the goods carried on the boats. . . . First, our national policy prohibits sailing overseas—not an inch of plank is allowed to go to sea. The law is clear and rigid. However, because the people along the coast depend on fishing to make a living they cannot follow the law. [But] it is not easy to discern who are and are not the real fishers. . . . [To do so] coastal officials must require fishers to use [small] boats with single masts and flat bottoms.[26] Fishing boats must also display special marks and numbers [on their hulls] for the officials to check.[27] If the boats are not registered and have not abided by the size stated in the regulation, [officials] should confiscate and burn the boats and punish the owners according to the law. . . . Second, [officials must] inspect the goods that are carried on boats. Although the boats are small, they are still able to deliver large amounts of goods by separating them into several small loads to trade with the foreigners. Therefore, the local authorities need to strictly inspect the boats. As for fishing boats [when they leave port], officials must count how much rice and water they carry. Also, officials need to check if there are any prohibited goods. When the boats return [to port, officials] must check their catch of fish and shrimp. Should there be any foreign goods, then officials should follow the law to punish [the lawbreakers]. . . .

To be successful it is absolutely necessary that coastal officials strictly implement these [two] regulations. We must designate officials to take charge of the coastal guardposts, assign local military patrols to watch each place [along the coast, and] organize local mutual responsibility units to closely oversee bays and harbors.[28] In this way, I do not believe we will have any illegal trading [with the Japanese lackeys].

Source: Hu Zongxian 1621, 5a–6a. Translation by the author.

---

26. Flat bottom boats, such as the so-called sand junks, were not suitable for sailing on the high seas, and thus were limited to coastal areas, where theoretically they would have been easier to regulate.

27. All boats, whether for fishing or commerce, were required to register their vessels with their local port authorities, which then issued them licenses.

28. The mutual responsibility system, known in Chinese as *baojia*, was a community watch whereby villagers were jointly accountable for the activities, especially criminal behavior, of their neighbors.

DOC. 9. THE GREAT PIRATE WU PING, 1565–1566

Wu Ping was one of the most renowned pirates of the 1560s. Born into a poor servile family in Zhaoan, a county in Fujian on the border with Guangdong, as a child he tended sheep and later in his teens ran off to sea to seek his fortune and fame. He was adopted into a pirate family when he married the daughter of Lin Guoxian, a pirate boss from Raoping County in Guangdong. Wu Ping was most active in the 1560s along the ill-defined border area separating Fujian and Guangdong. In fact, he made Nan'ao Island his base, building a stockade on the island and settling his family there.[29] In 1565 Qi Jiguang and Yu Dayou led land and naval forces, which drove Wu Ping and the pirates from the island. Together with a staunch group of followers, however, Wu Ping escaped to Vietnam, chased by the Ming navy, but it is unclear what happened to him after that. Many legends have appeared over the centuries speculating Wu Ping's plight. What follows are excerpts about Wu Ping taken from several sources. We begin with a short biographical sketch found in the Gazetteer of Zhaoan County.

The great pirate Wu Ping, who was born in Sidu [in Zhaoan County], was short but robust and clever. In his youth he was a poor shepherd boy skilled at marshaling flocks of sheep. His peers listened to him and followed what he said. Everyone thought he was different. Because of his servile status he ran away to become a thief, first robbing his master. While his master had treated him kindly, the wife was cruel. Wu Ping therefore ordered his thugs to take his master's wife, strip off her clothes, and tie jugs of water to her nipples. [Next] he forced her to grind rice, thereby causing the swaying of the jugs to give great pain to her nipples. Wu Ping took great pleasure [in hurting and humiliating her]. . . . [After that] he became a pirate. [At the time] other pirates, such as Xu Chaoguang, Lin Daoqian, and Zeng Yiben, were not only powerful but also farsighted; they recognized Wu Ping's potential [and invited him to join them]. . . . As the pirates became increasingly stronger they were able to battle our navy. Afterward when our imperial forces chased Wu Ping overseas, his followers scattered or joined other gangs.

The following three reports are taken from the Shizong Veritable Records, dated 1565 and 1566. These official reports start with Wu Ping at the height of his power, operating from bases on the islands of Nan'ao and Wuyu, on the Fujian-Guangdong border, his battles with the Ming military forces commanded by Qi Jiguang and Yu Dayou, and his subsequent retreat to Vietnam.

---

29. Until today there is a village on Nan'ao Island named Wu Ping's Stockade.

September 7, 1565. The great Guangdong pirate Wu Ping,[30] who commands some 400 vessels, comes and goes from [bases on] Nan'ao and Wuyu.[31] [Hearing that Wu Ping] plotted to plunder Fujian, Squadron Leader Zhu Ji and Vice Squadron Leader Wang Hao led their soldiers to attack him on the high seas. But in a surprise attack [Wu Ping] surrounded their ships . . . and overwhelmed [Zhu] Ji and [Wang] Hao, killing both men.

February 17, 1566. Originally early in the 10th lunar month of 1565, naval forces encircled the pirate Wu Ping at Nan'ao. [Qi] Jiguang deployed land forces and [Yu] Dayou deployed the navy to attack Wu Ping, who was critically defeated. Wu Ping barely escaped, fleeing to Phoenix Mountain in Raoping County [Guangdong]. The remnants of his gangs [afterward] rejoined him and Wu Ping regained his strength. At the time [Qi] Jiguang continued to attack the remaining pirates on Nan'ao, while [Yu] Dayou sent forth his naval forces . . . to search for [Wu] Ping, but to no avail. [Wu] Ping then hastened to [the port of] Zhanglin, where he plundered civilian ships and subsequently set out to sea.

May 9, 1566. The government troops of Fujian and Guangdong pursued and attacked the pirate Wu Ping in the Bay of Wanqiao Mountain in Annan, where he was soundly defeated. Previously, after being defeated at the battle of Black Pig Sea (Wuzhuyang) in Yangjiang [County], [Wu] Ping fled to Annan. The Military Superintendent and Vice Minister Wu Guifang requested the Wanning Pacification Office in Annan to mount an expedition against him,[32] and he [Wu Guifang] also sent the Assistant Regional Commander Tang Kekuan and Regional Military Commissioner Fu Yingjia with a naval force to join with them. They attacked [Wu] Ping in a pincer movement below Wanqiao Mountain. That evening a great wind arose and our forces used fire [boats?] to attack, torching the ship that [Wu] Ping commanded. His forces were completely defeated. Countless numbers of pirates drowned at sea, while our troops captured and beheaded a total of 398 pirates.

What happened to Wu Ping at the Battle of Wanqiao Mountain? Because his body was never found, soon afterward several different stories emerged concerning his plight. Some tales claim he drowned at sea, while others say he remained in Vietnam where he died of old age. Other popular stories are retold here.

According to the old *Gazetteer of Zhaoan County*, it said that [Qi] Jiguang chased Wu Ping to the seas of Wan'an in Jiaozhi [Vietnam]. Some

---

30. This is a mistake; Wu Ping hailed from Fujian not Guangdong.
31. Wuyu was a small island located just inside the Fujian border.
32. Because Annan (Vietnam) was a tributary state to the Ming dynasty and therefore under its suzerainty, high-ranking Chinese officials believed that they had the right to request help from Vietnamese officials to suppress pirates in Vietnamese waters.

say that [Wu] Ping changed his name and tramped about the rivers and lakes (*jianghu*).³³ Someone [said he] personally saw [Wu] Ping in Jiangzhe³⁴ dressed like a wealthy merchant flaunting about in fine clothes. He said that Wu Ping had burned and scarred his face to change his appearance, so no one could recognize him. He then returned to his old hideouts to collect his treasure and after that he disappeared. No one knows where he went. According to the old *Gazetteer of Chaozhou Prefecture*, it said that Wu Ping escaped to sea, where on an unknown island he died [of old age] like an ancient withered tree. Alas, there is no one story.

Sources: *Zhaoan xianzhi* 1694, 7:36b–37a; Matsuura Akira and Bian Tengkui 2009, 44–45; and *Nan'ao zhi* 1841, 8:35a–b. Translation by Lanshin Chang and the author.

DOC. 10. THE LEGEND OF WU PING'S SISTER

Over the years many stories and legends have developed about Wu Ping and his sister, such as the one here told to the author while doing fieldwork on Nan'ao Island in 2005. Although there is no solid evidence that she existed in real life, nonetheless people venerate her as a goddess of wealth and a local warrior protector deity. In this legend, well known among the islanders, Wu Ping kills his younger sister to spawn her magical powers, which he believed could safeguard him and his buried treasure. The following story comes from the author's fieldnotes.

We don't know the name of Wu Ping's sister. People just called her Wu Ping's Sister or Miss Wu. She was his younger sister. Later on, after she died, people living along the coast and on Nan'ao Island began to worship her as a goddess of wealth. Nowadays, however, many [Chinese] people know Wu Ping, but don't remember his sister.

Today on Nan'ao Island there is a stone statue of Wu Ping's sister located on a small outcropping along the coast that locals refer to as Treasure Island. The statue is an image of a young fisherwoman seated on a simple throne. She is holding a double-edge sword³⁵ in her left hand, and in her right hand is a silver ingot. By her side is a stack of silver ingots and a pot for burning sticks

---

33. In Chinese the term *jianghu*, which literally means "rivers and lakes," is difficult to translate into English. It is used as a metaphor for the unruly worlds of martial artists, knights-errant, wanderers, outlaws, and other free spirits living outside the reach of the government.
34. The area of Jiangxi and Zhejiang provinces in southern China.
35. In China the double-edge sword is not only a military weapon but also is used by Daoist priests and other local religious practitioners in conducting exorcist rituals to ward off evil influences and demons that bring illness or cause harm to communities.

Figure 6.4. The Sister of Wu Ping.

of incense. Whenever people visit her, they rub their hands on her right hand, the one holding the silver, in hopes that some of her wealth will also rub off on them. People have rubbed her hand and ingot so often that now they have turned shiny black (figure 6.4).

According to local lore, Wu Ping occupied Nan'ao Island as his lair. He built a fortified stronghold where he settled his family and stockpiled weapons and other provisions in preparation for attack. Over several years on the island he had accumulated lots of gold and silver, which he stored in eighteen large ceramic urns that he buried in secret in eighteen places all over the island. After he had been on Nan'ao Island for some time, the Ming court deployed a formidable armada under General Qi Jiguang, with more than four thousand soldiers—some islanders told me as many as ten thousand soldiers—to annihilate the pirates. In the fierce battles that ensued, with no place to hide and unable to escape, Wu Ping sensed his impending defeat and certain death. Fearing above all else that his young sister would fall into the hands of soldiers and likely be ravaged and slain by them, he instead killed her, chopping her into eighteen pieces and burying her with his treasure. According to tradition, this was a form of witchery to ensure that his sister would watch over and protect his treasure.[36] That very night, soldiers surrounded Wu Ping's compound, but he mysteriously escaped and was nowhere to be found. Villagers told me that Wu Ping's sister had worked her magic to save him.

Soldiers and villagers scoured the island looking for Wu Ping's treasure, but it was never found. Once, however, an elderly villager told me that when he was a child his great uncle recounted a story he had heard from his father about Wu Ping's buried treasure. One day a long time ago, he said, some villagers discovered a cave in the hills near Wu Ping's stockade and inside was an urn filled with gold and silver doubloons, which they tried to take home. However, the villagers got lost and couldn't find their way out of the cave. Only after they dropped the treasure they had taken were they able to find their way out of the cave, so they returned home empty-handed. Later they could not remember the location of the cave. That is why Miss Wu is worshipped as the Goddess for Protecting Treasure.

Source: Oral interviews recorded by the author on Nan'ao Island in July 2005.

---

36. Many Chinese believe that people who meet untimely violent deaths become vengeful ghosts who remain at their death site to wreak havoc on anyone approaching them; thus the corollary that murdered family members would not hesitate to use violence against intruders to protect family valuables.

DOC. 11. CHINESE VIEWS OF THE PORTUGUESE IN THE SIXTEENTH CENTURY

Many Chinese categorized the Portuguese as evil people, who by their very nature were depraved, unruly, and predatory. The fact that Portuguese merchants carried swords when they conducted business only reinforced such Chinese views. Indeed, their violent, uncontrollable behavior earned them the reputation as ruffians and pirates. Some of the earliest images that Chinese had of the Portuguese were that they were deceitful kidnappers who "seized children for food." Although undoubtedly exaggerated, the following Ming dynasty account from the sixteenth century was recorded by the seventeenth-century scholar Gu Yanwu as evidence of their complete lack of moral standards.

So they [the Portuguese] secretly sought to purchase [kidnapped] children of above ten years of age to eat. Each child was purchased at 100 cash. This caused the evil youths in Guangdong to hasten to kidnap children and the number of children eaten was uncountable. The method [of preparing the child] was to first boil up some soup in a large iron pan and place the child, who was locked up inside an iron cage, into the pan. After being steamed to sweat, the child was taken out and his skin peeled with an iron scrubbing-brush. The child, still alive, would now be killed and having been disemboweled, steamed to eat.

Source: Gu Yanwu, *Tianxia junguo libing shu* [Book of benefits and faults of the empire's local administration]. Translation adapted by the author from Fok 1987, 145.

DOC. 12. LIN XIYUAN'S LETTER LAUDING PORTUGUESE AID IN SUPPRESSING PIRACY, C. 1549

Included in the collection of Lin Xiyuan's writings is a letter he wrote to an official by the name of Weng Can, an assistant prefect stationed at one of the strategic points in southern Fujian, who was also involved in an incident over the Chinese and Portuguese smugglers on the coast. Lin, who had been a court official and one of Zhu Wan's main opponents, actually became wealthy after building a fleet of ships that traded with Southeast Asia and the Portuguese (see Doc. 5). In the letter, although Lin emphatically denied that he had had any connection with the Portuguese traders, he felt it was not right to attack them because they had not invaded China nor had they massacred any Chinese. On the contrary, the Portuguese had helped in suppressing the pirates. This is what he wrote:

When the Folangji [that is, Portuguese] came here [to China], they brought pepper, sappanwood, ivory, sappan oil, agarwood, sandalwood, and other aromatics to exchange with the people on the [coastal] frontier at an exceptionally reasonable price.[37] As to foodstuffs and daily necessities they had to get from us, such as rice, flour, pigs, and chickens, they paid the people twice the market price. Therefore, the coastal people were happy to trade with them. [The Folangji] have never invaded our land nor slaughtered our people nor plundered our belongings. Furthermore, when they first came to China, they chased away the [sea] bandits on our behalf because they were afraid that they might be implicated. The bandits became scared and did not dare to cause any trouble. A strongman by the name of Lin Jian had been pillaging in our coastal waters and the government was incapable of controlling him. [The Folangji] pacified him and eradicated the pirates that had been rampaging for about twenty years. Thus we see that the Folangji have not been pirates but have been chasing off pirates on our behalf. They have not done us any harm, but have been benefitting our people. I can by no means see the reason why the government insists on punishing them.

Source: Lin Xiyuan 2018, 146. Translation by the author.

DOC. 13. COMMENTARIES ON THE PORTUGUESE AMBASSADORIAL MISSION OF GIL DE GÓIS BY JOÃO DE ESCOBAR, 1564

João de Escobar was a clerk for Gil de Góis's ambassadorial mission sent to China by King Sebastian in 1563 to attempt formalizing Luso-Chinese relations and to obtain permission for the Fathers of the Society of Jesus (Jesuits) to enter China. That year João traveled from Goa to Macau on board the ambassador's ship and likely visited Canton on several occasions. He also took part in the military campaign against mutinous Chinese troops-turned-pirates in 1564, jointly organized by the Chinese and Portuguese authorities. Although the account is somewhat exaggerated about the pirates plundering Canton, nonetheless it is one of the few firsthand descriptions in Portuguese concerning early Luso-Chinese relations that reiterates the Portuguese justification for its settlement of Macau, namely for aiding the Ming government fight pirates. João prepared two extensive Comentários, but only the second part has survived as a copy kept in the Jesuit Archives in Rome. This

---

37. Sappanwood, agarwood, and sandalwood are aromatic woods from India and Southeast Asia used for incense and medicines.

important document had remained unknown until 1996. The following passages from this document present the Portuguese version of events.

The Governor of [the Portuguese State of India] . . . had discharged the Captain-Major [of Macau] Diogo Pereira[38] . . . to the grandees [that is, provincial officials] of Canton. . . . [During the embassy] the grandees, who dared an unheard of thing never before occurring in China, requested the assistance of the Portuguese in the fight against a number of wild thieves [that is, pirates]. . . . And the events happened in the following way:

There was a certain war commander and great mandarin [official] who was in charge of a mighty fleet belonging to the king [of China].[39] That fleet consisted of eighteen junks, which were as imposing and portentous vessels as our own, besides a number of other smaller and lighter vessels. Coming from the coast of Chincheo,[40] [this great mandarin] arrived with his armada in Canton, crowned with the glory and fortune of having defeated his enemies. And upon arriving there he requested from the grandees of Canton payment for his men, as they had not been paid for a long time. . . . The grandees delayed the matter for a few days engrossing him in verbal exchanges and afterward implicating him in a number of misdeeds, all with the intent of canceling the requested silver payment. [Finally], as they were much in fear of him, they ordered him to return to Chincheo, leaving his brother behind, [and promising that he] would soon join him with all the requested silver. Trusting their words he did as was told, but after his departure [the grandees] had the brother flogged, which was a common practice among the Chinese.

Having found out about the insult to his brother, the mandarin sailed back with his fleet and, to redress the nonpayment of the silver that was due, he rampaged all his men through the town, killing and ravaging all and everyone, stealing as much as they could get their hands on. It is said that all this happened so suddenly and unexpectedly that in an attempt to escape the robbers, the grandees, their families and staff, and the people [of Canton] rushed through the gates of the walled city [in such panic that] more than two

---

38. Diogo Pereira, who was one of the wealthiest Portuguese merchants trading in Asia at this time, was the brother-in-law of Gil de Góis; Diogo assumed leadership of the embassy after Góis returned to Goa, but nothing ever came of this mission.

39. In the summer of 1564, rioting troops led by Xu Yongtai, who had been stationed in Chaozhou in western Guangdong on the border with Fujian province, suddenly arrived at the entrance to the Pearl River at Humen (Bogue) demanding pay and provisions from the provincial authorities. Their unexpected appearance just outside the provincial capital posed a serious threat to Canton, which at the time was defended with only a few troops. Diogo Pereira offered to help the Ming government suppress the mutiny. Afterward, under the command of Diogo and Luís de Melo, three hundred Portuguese soldiers joined several Chinese warships to attack and rout the insurgent troops. The king of China refers to the Jiajing emperor.

40. In early Portuguese documents, Chincheo referred to the southern coastal region of Fujian province, and more specifically in this context the area around Chaozhou bordering Fujian and Guangdong.

thousand souls died either by drowning [in the river] or being trampled over. And this is not exaggeration because the city center has more people than [the whole of] Lisbon, and all those who visit it agree that it is indeed much larger, most of its population living in the suburbs. [The Chinese, however,] are an effeminate and weak people and the fact that they are not allowed to carry or own weapons makes them even more cowardly. So being, the robbers, used to war and having plenty of arms and artillery on their ships, were able to plunder the whole of Canton without confrontation. . . .

And after such deeds, they openly declared themselves as robbers and corsairs. . . . Such victories made these robbers even more audacious, thinking that they could disembark at night to our settlement [in Macau], burn the houses, steal and kill the Portuguese so that after they could be able to prey on and rout our vessels and junks which arrive at [Macau] with the monsoon from India and all other regions. . . .

By the middle of June [1564], at the arrival time of the vessels belonging to the Portuguese at the aforesaid harbor, . . . the robbers came too. It was in the afternoon, [when they] entered the anchorage close to the shore, nearing the western side of the settlement. And when they appeared all the people rushed to the beach to see them; they did not carry their weapons because, being daylight, they knew that [the robbers] would not come ashore. The robbers remained quiet and tranquil as if in their own land, harbor, and city, not displaying in the slightest their purposes or sending any message stating their intentions. Faced with such nonchalance the Captain-[Major] ordered a *falcão pedreiro*[41] to be set on a hillock right before them and to ask them about their intentions. But not even the many shots [from] . . . the *falcão* . . . intimidated them to depart or budge in any way, as if the cannonade had not disturbed them in the slightest. The morning of the following day they raised anchor and left toward the high seas, halting with the greatest of confidence between two of our vessels berthed in the middle of the robbers' waterway, which were about to depart for Japan. And despite the heavy gunfire of the vessels nevertheless the [robbers'] junks meandered between them and continued toward the high seas.

It was immediately understood that the robbers' intention was to stay put at the bar awaiting the arrival of unsuspecting junks and vessels. Their designs were made clear when they attacked Luís de Melo's[42] ship moored in Langbai Bay,[43] its heavy artillery safeguarding it from their assault. And giving up

---

41. *Falcão pedreiro* is a type of small cannon able to shoot stone balls.
42. Luís de Melo, who had been granted the royal concession of a "Japan voyage," had just arrived on the coast of China from Java loaded with a precious cargo of pepper. He soon joined Diogo and the Chinese to fight the pirates.
43. Langbai Bay, also known as Lampacau, was situated on the coast west of Macau and during the 1550s it served as an important offshore trading area for the Portuguese.

such prey, [the robbers] returned to the bar of our harbor, confident that the vessels coming into the Portuguese harbor would be easier prey. Thus, while maintaining their position at the mouth of the sea, approached a junk belonging to Pêro Veloso, a Portuguese from Malacca married to a native, which arrived from Timor, loaded with sandal[wood].[44] And within everyone's sight who were helpless to be of any assistance, the [robbers] attacked it and would have captured it had not Dom João Pereira's vessel lagged behind and remained at the bay awaiting high tide.[45]

Becoming despondent with such a reinforcement and the strong defenses they had previously encountered, the robbers [finally] decided to give up capturing Portuguese ships. And thus disappointed they sailed to Canton to get compensation for the losses we had inflicted on them, but the division of these spoils gave rise to such dispute and contention that they split into two groups. And so divided, nine [of their] junks returned to Fujian while the other nine remained on the side of the mandarin. . . . From there [that is, Bogue] they repeatedly tormented Canton, helpless to oppose them, thus inflicting great losses to the merchants unable to ship their merchandise [downriver] to the Portuguese [in Macau]. . . .

The restless boldness of Diogo Pereira saw in this an opportunity to turn this adversity to our advantage and [conceived that, in capturing the robbers, the Portuguese would gain the good graces of] the grandees of Canton. Thus he approached [them] in the name of the King of Portugal and his ambassador [Gil de Góis], offering them all possible assistance and any support they might deem necessary from the Portuguese in order to crush the robbers. And he dealt with such diligence and secrecy that no one became aware of this offer nor of the speculations that were brooding in Canton about the aforesaid assistance; first because he knew that the Chinese would never openly acknowledge their weakness to the Portuguese, and [second] because [he knew that the Chinese] would never entirely trust [the Portuguese]—such was Diogo Pereira's instincts derived from the experience of his [past] dealings with them. . . .

However, thanks be to God, [the Chinese] soon decided it would be beneficial to accept such assistance, and the one to acquiesce was the *chong-bing*, captain-general of the armies of all provinces in China, second in command only after His Majesty,[46] who, holding such a high rank, was not to be con-

---

44. The Portuguese first set foot on the Island of Timor around 1515, with the intention to purchase sandalwood to trade in China. This aromatic wood was in great demand in China for the making of furniture and as an ingredient of incense, burned in large quantities during daily religious practices.

45. Dom João Pereira also had arrived from Malacca; he succeeded Diogo as Captain-Major. In 1565 he arrived in Japan, near Nagasaki, where his small flotilla repulsed an attack by the Japanese lord of Hirado.

46. Here the author has made a mistake; the *chong-bing* (*zongbing*) was commander of provincial armed forces (likely Yu Dayou), not commander-in-chief of the empire's army.

tradicted by the grandees. The *chong-bing* promptly sent a message to both the ambassador and Diogo Pereira stating that he accepted their offer of assistance and that in doing so the ambassador was rendering a great service to the King of China, adding that he promised he would remain in charge of the expenses of the embassy and would convey them to the king [that is, Chinese emperor]. . . . And together with these words were many others of thanks and friendly salutations.[47]

Source: Escobar 1997, 68–74. Translation adapted by the author from Fiona Clark in *Review of Culture* (English edition), vol. 32 (undated and unpaginated online edition).

DOC. 14. THE PEARL THIEVES SU GUANSHENG AND ZHOU CAIXIONG IN THE GULF OF TONKIN, 1573–1581

During the Ming period in the Gulf of Tonkin the most typical pirates were Chinese and Vietnamese "pearl thieves" (zhuzei). Although they mostly operated in small gangs, they nonetheless were well organized and, as the cases of Su Guansheng and Zhou Caixiong demonstrate, sometimes even expanded into formidable forces that posed a significant challenge to the authorities. In the Ming period the government monopolized the pearl industry and strictly regulated collection and distribution of pearls, much to the disadvantage of the pearl divers who found it increasingly difficult to earn a living. There were therefore frequent reports of pearl thieves operating in the gulf. These thieves were mostly poor Dan fisherfolk from China and Vietnam who clandestinely gathered and sold pearls to merchants in China and Vietnam. By the early sixteenth century residents of Weizhou Island and the Dan villages of Wutu and Duolang on the coast had notorious reputations for pearl thievery and resisting officials. In the 1570s, as this document reveals, the pirates Su Guansheng and Zhou Caixiong recruited thousands of followers to foment the largest Dan disturbance in the Ming period. From bases in the gulf their forces sallied forth in violent protest against corrupt and malicious officials (in this case particularly imperial eunuchs) who oversaw the government-monopolized pearl trade. Although Su was captured with more than four hundred followers in 1581, Zhou's plight remains unknown.

Su Guansheng and Zhou Caixiong belonged to Dan households in Shicheng.[48] Their ancestors were all foreigners from Annan who often came

---

47. In the end, the joint Luso-Chinese forces did defeat the pirate-insurgents, but as for the Portuguese embassy, after many delays, it was finally abandoned.
48. Shicheng is a county on the northwest corner of the Leizhou peninsula bordering Lianzhou Prefecture.

to the [Chinese] outposts in Shicheng. Wailing in tears they pleaded: "We are people from the frontier and desire to become your servants" [that is, willingly submit to Ming authority]. Thus they became [registered as] Dan households,[49] occupying the strategic areas of Wutu and Duolang.[50] Two chieftains [Su and Zhou], who realized that profits could be made from the pearl beds, borrowed money from the big traders to hire desperadoes from far and near. Day and night they trained to use weapons and prepared armor. Then they plundered our emperor's pearl beds [in the Gulf of Tonkin]. . . . [Later] they gathered thousands of people to attack the areas around Leizhou and Lianzhou prefectures. . . .

Previously the chieftain Luo Hanqing defended Zhonglu harbor, but the [Dan pirates] deviously attacked and killed him. At the time Zeng Guobin, with some thirty boats, entered Haikang [in Leizhou] and [later] plundered Beihai. That was in the 1st year of the Wanli reign [between 1573 and 1574]. Then in the 2nd year, they plundered Shang Village, and in the 4th year they plundered Hepu and Guantouling. In the 5th year they pillaged Yongan, and afterward returned to Dalianjiao. Zeng Guobin, who deeply regretted his actions, stripped off his upper garments as a token of submission and asked for permission to surrender. But in the 7th year, on the pretext of being cheated by the pearl merchants, he again went out to sea [as a pirate]. After he attacked Nanban Village and killed Zhou Ying and abducted Lin Yi, soldiers once again pacified him.[51]

That year [1579] Su Guansheng and Zhou Caixiong, with eighteen boats, entered Hepu and plundered Qianti Village, beheading the Dan villager Lin San and burning to death six other men and women, as well as destroying their livestock and property. Afterward they pillaged Yongan (Vinh Yen in Vietnamese) Prefecture in Vietnam.[52] Our soldiers closely followed after them. Su Guansheng and the others escaped to Wutu, which to the north has high mountains and to the south a vast sea. Because of its strategic location this was an area often fought over. [Su Guansheng] then ordered woodsmen to gather huge trees, each one with a circumference of ten people, to construct [a fortress and] living quarters and ordered his troops to protect his strong-

---

49. In the early Ming dynasty Dan boat people were registered in the so-called *lijia* system, originally designed to help in the collection of land, labor, and other taxes, such as the fish tax levied on Dan fishers.

50. The exact locations of Wutu and Duolang are unclear, but according to extant documents both were located on a deep bay between Yongan and Shicheng. Duolang was also known as Minglang.

51. Other sources give slightly different dates for these events, but they all occurred between 1573 and 1579.

52. Here the author may be mistaken about the location of Yongan as being in Vietnam (Annan). Although there is a Vinh Yen in Vietnam, it is located deep in the Red River valley, quite far from the coast. There is, however, a Yongan located near Hepu, which is along the Lianzhou coast in China.

hold. . . . [He] then gathered more than a thousand brigands and more than thirty large warships, and once again set out to sea.

In the 9th year [1581], his forces attacked Duanzhou, an area near Yongan. [What follows is a detailed description of a series of battles between the Dan pirates and the Ming navy]. . . . On the 18th day of the 9th lunar month [October 15], guardsmen under Commanders Fu Daming and Zhu Dazhen captured Su Guansheng and another 72 pirates. . . . At the time countless other Dan [pirates] and their boats perished in an enormous storm that arose from the southwest. Most survivors surrendered to the authorities.[53]

Source: Qu Jiusi 2002, 436:238–40. Translation by Lanshin Chang and the author.

---

53. During this campaign, according to other sources, soldiers captured more than four hundred pirates in total.

2. Piracy in the Ming-Qing Transition (1620–1684)

DOC. 15. THE PIRATE CUI ZHI, C. 1620

During the turbulent Ming-Qing transition there was a great confusion of merchants, adventurers, renegades, smugglers, and pirates, including among them a person named Cui Zhi. Among his cohorts were Zheng Zhilong and Liu Xiang, who would both soon become famous pirates in their own right. What we know about these colorful figures comes from writers who either despised them as wicked criminals or admired them as local heroes. The following sketch of Cui Zhi comes from a virtually unknown late Ming literatus named Zhang Linbai, whose short tract depicts the chaotic situation along the Zhejiang and Fujian coast at the outset of the dynastic transition in the 1620s. In this vivid portrayal of Cui Zhi the author reveals a man who was cunning yet esteemed as a "benevolent thief" among his contemporaries.

His original surname was Zhou, but because he became a pirate he changed his name to Cui Zhi and took the nickname "Nine Clouds" (Jiu Yun) [a name indicative of an imposing personality]. He came from a large lineage from Rongtan in Fuqing [a coastal county in Fujian province]. His great grandfather, who attained the rank of Assistant Censor, was honored in the family temple. Cui Zhi was intelligent, courageous, and skillful with all sorts of domestic and foreign weapons. He befriended both scholars and soldiers and was known for his generosity. He especially liked to help the poor and needy. . . . In his youth he was studious . . . but was unable to advance, so he dabbled in farming, hunting, and fishing. He became a jack of all trades, even learning medicine and fortune telling. When he was twenty he slipped away into the underworld of rivers and lakes (*jianghu*), traveling everywhere. He associated with foreign sea merchants and [through them] acquired business skills. He traveled back and forth to Japan. His peers all admired and listened to him because he was cunning and skillful.

Cui Zhi envied the merchants who became wealthy from maritime trade. So instead of filling his ships with merchandise, he had his crews carry many weapons, including cannons and bows and arrows. Cui Zhi henceforth became remarkably successful, so much so that plundering ships became routine. Among his associates were [the pirates] Liu Xiang and Zheng Zhilong. Because Cui Zhi asked his sailors not to kill their victims, and to only take half of the goods of boat owners who could afford the loss of merchandise, but not to rob those who could not afford the loss, therefore all across the seas he became known as the "benevolent thief" (*rendao*). Later, after he secretly returned home, he was arrested and spent two years in jail. His colleagues collected money that he used [to purchase his] release from the jailers and to share with other prisoners. Everyone regarded him as a virtuous person. Later, after his escape, he again fled to sea [as a pirate] and changed his surname to Cui to avoid having his family implicated for his actions.

Source: Zhang Linbai 1978, 9–10. Translation by Lanshin Chang and the author.

DOC. 16. THE PIRATE-ADVENTURER ZHENG ZHILONG, 1625–1628

Zheng Zhilong was one of the most famous and powerful pirates during the Ming-Qing transition. In his late teens he left home to seek his fortune in the Portuguese enclave of Macau, where he converted to Christianity, taking the baptismal name of Nicholas Gaspard. At first as a small-time trader he traveled to Manila and Hirado, and later to Taiwan where in the early 1620s he joined the pirates under Yan Zhenquan (Yan Siqi) and Li Dan. After Yan Zhenquan's death in 1625, Zheng Zhilong pursued piracy full-time and within a few years controlled most of the shipping in the South China Sea. According to local legends, as retold here, Zheng Zhilong became the pirate leader in Taiwan through divine intervention, but in truth he only obtained leadership after a bitter and bloody power struggle. After repeatedly defeating the Ming navy in battles between 1626 and 1628, he surrendered to the Ming government in exchange for a naval commission (figure 7.1). Then in 1646, just two years after the Manchus captured Beijing, Zheng surrendered to the new Qing court, but instead of being rewarded he was arrested and finally executed in 1661.

2. Piracy in the Ming-Qing Transition (1620–1684)

Zheng Zhilong was a native of Stone Well Village in Nan'an County in Quanzhou Prefecture [Fujian province]. His father, Zheng Shaozu, was a granary clerk in the prefectural seat.[1] The prefect was Cai Shanji. The rear of his yamen[2] faced the granary on the same street. Once when Zhilong was ten years old, he was fooling around throwing rocks and carelessly hit Prefect Cai in the head. The prefect grabbed Zhilong intending to punish him, but noticing the boy's handsome and charming appearance, instead let him go, lightheartedly saying: "[One day] you will become a high-ranking official." Not many years afterward, Zhilong and his younger brother, Zhihu, ran off to the island [of Taiwan] to join Yan Zhenquan's band of pirates.[3] After Zhenquan died [in 1625], his followers were leaderless and at odds about how to choose a new leader. So they all prayed to Heaven [to seek a sign] by inserting a sword into a bushel of rice, declaring that "whoever is praying when the sword shakes and leaps out of the rice, then he is the one chosen by Heaven to be our leader." To everyone's amazement, only when Zhilong came to pray did the sword leap from the rice onto the ground. He did this three times, each with the same result. In this way he became their leader.

Now unrestrained, the pirates caused havoc on the seas, and soldiers and officials were unable to repulse them. Hence [the government] began to discuss how to pacify [Zheng Zhilong and the pirates].[4] Because Cai Shanji, who had been promoted to circuit intendent of Quanzhou, had earlier treated Zhilong kindly, [Grand Coordinator Zhu Qinxiang] requested him to summon the pirate to surrender. Zhilong agreed to surrender . . . but his younger brother, Zhihu, refused to capitulate and slipped back to sea where he continued to rebel. . . . [Because the negotiations failed Zhilong also returned to pirating.]

In the spring [of 1626], Zhilong occupied the island of [Nan'ao] from which he sent forth his gangs to plunder rice from merchant ships.[5] [At that time] Fujian suffered a succession of famines, but no rice had arrived by sea. Many starving refugees seeking food joined the pirates. By the 7th lunar month, his plundering of merchant and civilian ships had greatly enhanced

---

1. Other sources identify Zhilong's father with the name Xiangyu or Shibiao. Whatever his correct name, Zhilong's father was a member of the lower class and had a low-level job as a Ming functionary with only a rudimentary education.
2. Yamens were the administrative offices and residences of local civil and military officials in imperial China. Normally officials lived in the rear section of their yamen.
3. Actually, before going to Taiwan, Zheng Zhilong, while in his late teens, first went to Macau around 1610, and only sometime later went to Taiwan.
4. The Chinese term "to pacify" is *zhaofu*, literally "to summon and appease." Although distasteful to many officials, nonetheless pacification was a time-honored policy, dating back to the ancient Han dynasty, for dealing with pirates, bandits, and rebels who could not be suppressed by military means. Accordingly, officials would coax and appease dissident leaders to surrender by promising them pardons, monetary rewards, and official positions or titles. Rank-and-file followers would be offered pardons and then resettled back into mainstream society under bond.
5. At about that time Zhilong defeated the Ming navy off the Fujian coast at Tongshan.

his power. His gangs also attacked the Haifeng coast in Guangdong taking the village of Kantou and using it as a base. Later in the 12th lunar month [January 1627], Zhilong returned to Fujian where he anchored his fleet at Baizhen in Zhangpu [County]. The [new] grand coordinator [of Fujian], Zhu Yifeng, deployed naval forces under Commander Hong Xianchun to attack him. Squadron leaders Xu Xinsu and Chen Wenlian also joined [in the attack]. After fierce fighting for a day no one could declare victory. . . . Afterward from Jiuzhen, Zhilong's fleet advanced on Amoy,[6] defeating the provincial commander Yu Zigao, who fled in a hurry. Zhilong allowed him to flee.[7] When the residents of Amoy opened the city gates and begged the pirates not to kill them, Zhilong benevolently spared the city.

Knowing the situation in detail, the prefect of Quanzhou, Wang You, commented: "Zhilong's situation is such that since he did not pursue [our navy], or kill [civilians], or loot and burn down [homes], it is time for [the government] to exonerate his crimes. Because it is now too difficult to exterminate him, we should instead seek to appease him, to ask him to sail his ships out to sea and allow him to gain merit to atone for his crimes [by annihilating other pirates]. Once he has obtained [sufficient] merit we can then offer him an official rank." Deng Liangzhi, the circuit intendent of Xinghua and Quanzhou, agreed and dispatched someone to negotiate [with Zhilong]. . . . Yan Jizu[8] added: "The pirate Zheng Zhilong, who was born and raised in Quanzhou, has several tens of thousands of followers. He robs the rich and helps the poor. The people are not in awe of officials but are in awe of the pirates." . . .

In the 3rd lunar month [of 1628, the emperor issued another] ban prohibiting ships in Zhangzhou and Quanzhou from setting out to sea. Zhilong continued to plunder the seas off Fujian and Zhejiang. In the 6th lunar month [July 1628] the Board of War deliberated about the pacification of the pirate Zheng Zhilong, and in the 9th lunar month he surrendered to the [new] grand coordinator, Xiong Wencan.

Source: "Zheng Zhilong shoufu" 1658, 76:1a–2b. Translation by Lanshin Chang and the author.

---

6. Amoy maintained a naval base, while at the same time was also an important trading and smuggling port.

7. The squadron leader, Xu Xinsu, however, was not so fortunate. The pirates not only looted and torched his home but also captured and killed him as he tried to flee the city. After this Zhilong had de facto control over Amoy, which he now made his primary base of operations.

8. Yan Jizu was a palace steward at the Office of Scrutiny in the Board of Works in the Ming capital. He accused Yu Zigao of malfeasance and incompetence and the imperial court stripped him of his command, put him under arrest, and finally executed him in 1628.

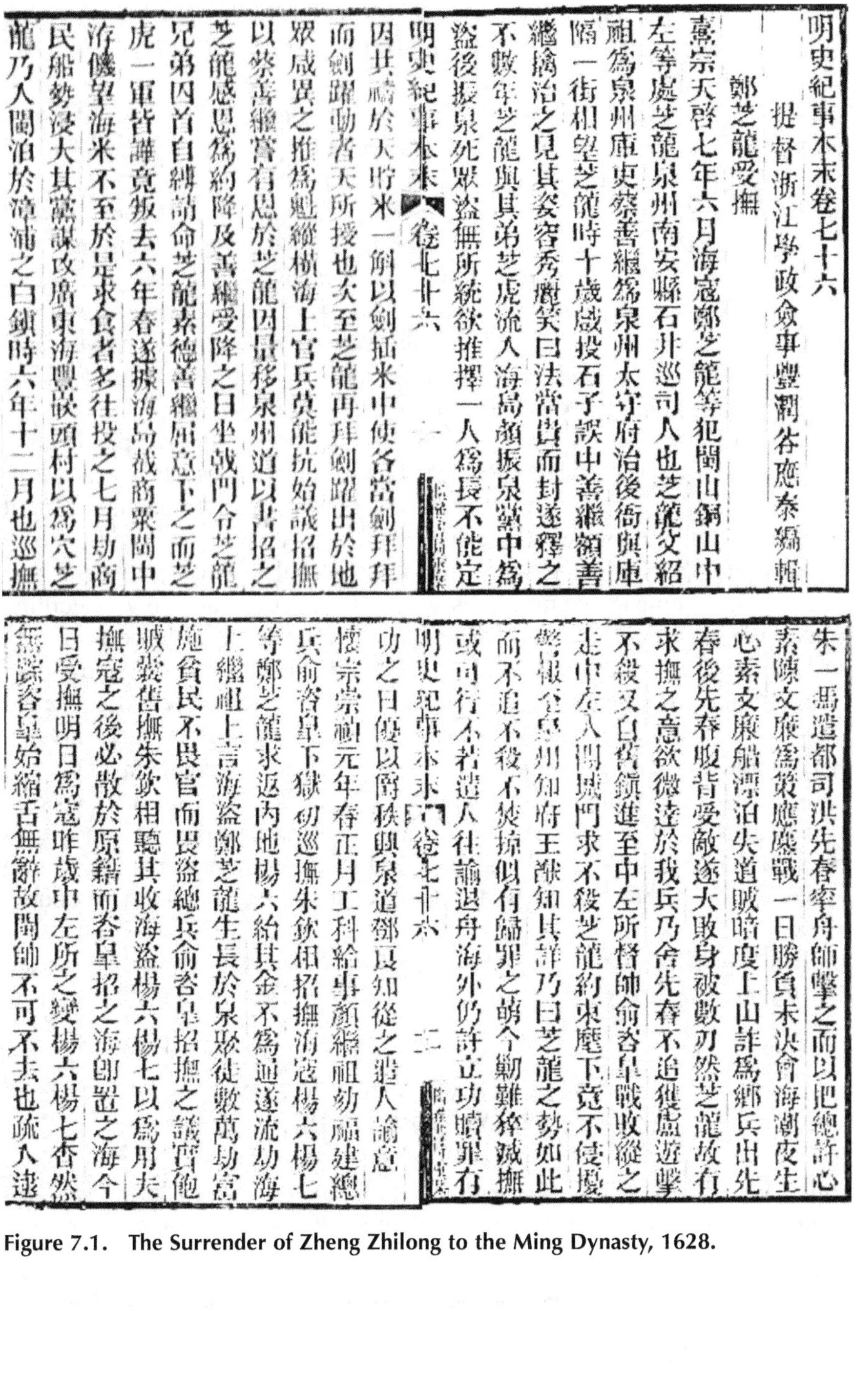
明史紀事本末卷七十六
提督浙江學政僉事豐潤谷應泰編輯
鄭芝龍受撫
熹宗天啓七年六月海寇鄭芝龍等犯閩山銅山中
左等處芝龍泉州南安縣石井巡司人也芝龍父紹
祖爲泉州庫吏蔡善繼爲泉州太守府治後衙與庫
隔一街相望芝龍時十歲戲投石子誤中善繼額善
繼擒治之見其姿容秀麗笑曰法當貴而封遂釋之
不數年芝龍與其弟芝虎流入海島顏振泉黨中爲
盜後振泉死衆盜無所統欲推擇一人爲長不能定
明史紀事本末 卷七十六 一
因共禱於天貯米一斛以劍插米中使各當劍拜拜
而劍躍動者天所授也次至芝龍再拜劍躍出於地
衆咸異之推爲魁縱橫海上官兵莫能抗始議招撫
以蔡善繼嘗有恩於芝龍因量移泉州道以書招之
芝龍感恩爲約降及善繼受降之日坐戟門令芝龍
兄弟囚首自縛請命芝龍素德善繼屈意下之而芝
虎一軍皆譁竟叛去六年春遂據海島截商粟閩中
洊饑望海米不至於是求食者多往投之七月劫商
民船勢浸大其黨謀攻廣東海豐嵌頭村以爲穴芝
龍乃入閩泊於漳浦之白鎮時六年十二月也巡撫
朱一馮遣都司洪先春率舟師擊之而以把總許心
素陳文廉爲策應鏖戰一日勝負未決會海潮夜生
心素文廉船漂泊失道賊暗度上山詐爲鄉兵出先
春後先春腹背受敵遂大敗身被數刃然芝龍故有
求撫之意欲徼達於我兵乃舍先春不追獲盧遊擊
不殺又自舊鎮進至中左所督帥俞咨皐戰敗縱之
走中左人開城門求不殺芝龍約束麾下竟不侵擾
警報至泉州知府王猷知其詳乃曰芝龍之勢如此
而不追不殺不焚掠似有歸罪之萌今剿難猝滅撫
或可行不若遣人往諭退舟海外仍許立功贖罪有
明史紀事本末 卷七十六 二
功之日優以爵秩與泉道鄧良知從之遣人諭意
懷宗崇禎元年春正月工科給事顏繼祖劾福建總
兵俞咨皐下獄切巡撫朱欽相招撫海寇楊六楊七
等鄭芝龍求返內地楊六紿其金不爲通遂流劫海
上繼祖上言海盜鄭芝龍生長於泉聚徒數萬劫富
施貧民不畏官而畏盜總兵俞咨皐招撫之議實他
賊裝售撫朱欽相聽其收海盜楊六楊七以爲用夫
撫寇之後必散於原籍而咨皐招之海卽置之海今
日受撫明日爲寇昨歲中左所之變楊六楊七杳然
無蹤咨皐始縮舌無辭故閩帥不可不去也疏入逮

Figure 7.1. The Surrender of Zheng Zhilong to the Ming Dynasty, 1628.

DOC. 17. ZHENG ZHILONG'S PRIVATEER VENTURES UNDER THE DUTCH, 1625

About the same time that Zheng Zhilong had joined up with Cui Zhi, Yan Zhenquan, and other pirates, he also began collaborating with the Dutch in Taiwan, who on several occasions dispatched Chinese privateers to intercept Chinese, Spanish, and Portuguese ships sailing to and from Manila. Zheng Zhilong actually commanded a freelance privateering navy, which the Dutch had commissioned and supplied with provisions and weapons. In February and March of 1625, Zheng's ships plundered several Chinese and Portuguese ships off the western coast of the Philippine Islands and took their prizes and booty back to Taiwan to share with their Dutch backers. The following passage is from the official report of the Dutch Governor of Taiwan, Martinus Sonck.

The two Chinese junks brought 2,400 rials in silver, and three piculs [and] forty catties of raw silk, which were plundered from various Chinese and Portuguese vessels in waters near Pangasinan,[9] according to the commanders of the above-mentioned junks. These junks and their crews were hired to serve the Company[10] and should have been supplied with the same victuals and beverages as the Company's employees were. These junks have now (according to them) left the fleet with the consent of Commander Muijser because they were afraid that, once the Spanish galleons sailed out, their mission would be over. . . . As for their voyage home, they had received no provisions at all, including their wages and other expenses incurred by the junks, weaponry and ammunition. In view of their performance we decided to grant them 1,500 rials instantly, without waiting for ratification by Commander Muijser, and to permit them to distribute it among their officers and seamen. If we pay the salaries and the fitting out and some other costs incurred by the commanders of the above mentioned junks, they will not be able to make any further claim [on the booty].

Source: Hayashi Fukusai 1912–1913, 5:557. Translation adapted by the author from Cheng 2013, 40.

DOC. 18. PIRATE PROTECTION FEES LEVIED ON FISHERS, C. 1630

With the advent of several large fleets in the 1620s and 1630s, piracy once again became an increasingly powerful force all along the southern coast of

---

9. Pangasinan is a province of the Philippines located on the western side of the island of Luzon; the Spanish began colonizing the area in 1571.
10. This refers to the powerful Dutch East India Company.

China. During those years all ships operating in Chinese waters were liable to pirate attacks unless they bought safe conduct passes. This form of extortion was actually a major source of pirate income. In the following report the grand coordinator of Zhejiang, Zhang Yandeng, clearly reveals his concern that large numbers of Fujian fishers were under the protection, if not the control, of pirates who collected protection money from them. As the report explains, most fishers viewed paying protection fees to pirates as an acceptable custom or simply as another type of taxation.

The massive number of fishing boats causes problems. The fishing grounds in Zhejiang province, off the Taizhou, Changguo, and Ningbo [coasts], yield ribbonfish. Only the Fujian fishers in Putian and Fuqing counties are skilled [at catching this species]. Several hundreds of their fishing boats arrive every July and August. This really huge gathering only disbands in December. The coastal defense force is mortified by the [uncontrollable] situation. . . . Pirates live on the nearby islands. They choose their leader themselves and issue passes [to the fishing junks], which they sell according to the size of the junks, at a price ranging from 20 to 50 taels of silver. Before anyone can begin to gather in their catch, they must show them [that is, pirates] the pass which they have purchased. To issue a license before the merchandise is sold is called a "water fee" (*baoshui*), and to levy silver after the merchandise has been sold is called a "delivery ticket" (*jiaopiao*). This payment has always been collected efficiently in certain periods and has become a kind of custom. No one has ever suggested that such a practice is illegal.

Source: Zhang Yendeng, "Bingke chaochu Zhejiang xunfu Zhang Yandeng tiben" [Report from the grand coordinator of Zhejiang, Zhang Yandeng], dated May 16, 1629. Translation adapted by the author from Cheng 2013, 64–65.

DOC. 19. THE QING SCHOLAR YU YONGHE DESCRIBES ZHENG CHENGGONG

Zheng Chenggong, who is better known in the West as Koxinga, is one of the most colorful and controversial figures in Chinese history. Born in the Japanese port town of Hirado in 1624, his father was Zheng Zhilong and his mother a Japanese woman named Tagawa Matsu. Chenggong was raised by his mother in Japan until the age of seven, when his father recalled him to the ancestral home in southern Fujian. Chenggong received a conventional Confucian education during the waning years of the Ming dynasty. After the fall of the dynasty, he remained a loyal subject, for which the Ming court in exile conferred upon him the imperial surname, Zhu, whereupon he became known as Lord of the Imperial Surname (Guoxingye), corrupted by the Dutch into Koxinga. For more than two decades he battled Qing forces on land and sea, fought the Dutch in Taiwan, and plundered countless towns, villages, and ships, while at the same time building one of the wealthiest maritime empires in the world. Historians have depicted him as a warrior, Ming loyalist, pirate, and national hero. He is even venerated as a deity today in Taiwan. The Qing scholar Yu Yonghe, writing from his personal experiences in Taiwan in the mid-1690s, gives us a candid description of Chenggong during the several years before his death in June 1662.

Zheng Chenggong, while still a young man, collected followers and occupied Quemoy and Amoy. Although he was on the sea, he kept close ties to the land. [Because] the Fujian coast has numerous harbors and bays where [his] troops could land, it was difficult to avoid his surprise attacks. To guard the harbors and bays Chenggong often landed troops and established many stockades in those places. What is more, he had spies everywhere. Everything, whether great or small, that happened in the yamens of the governor-general, governor, and the provincial military commander [in Fujian] were reported to him, thereby allowing him to prepare beforehand. Because he held areas close to [Qing territory], he could resist large armies without being defeated for a period of thirty years. His plans were indeed farsighted. . . .

Chenggong, on the small island [of Taiwan], successfully maintained a fully equipped army of more than one hundred thousand soldiers . . . and [a fleet of] several thousand warships.[11] What is more, he spent a great deal [of time and effort] cultivating relations with people on the mainland and winning their support. . . . The reason for his boundless wealth was maritime trade. To the contrary, because our [Qing] dynasty strictly prohibited any ships going out to sea—not a single plank was allowed to go out to sea—merchants had to bribe guards [stationed on the coast] in order to secretly deal with the Zheng family at Amoy to conduct overseas trade. Foreigners who wanted the goods of China all needed to go to the Zheng family to obtain them. Thus the profit of the sea trade was entirely monopolized by the Zhengs, whose resources only increased.

Source: Yu Yonghe 1959, 47–51. Translation by the author.

---

11. Zheng Chenggong's troops landed in Taiwan in April 1661, finally driving the Dutch from the island by February 1662.

DOC. 20. EARLY QING SEA BAN AGAINST ZHENG CHENGGONG, 1656

Once the Manchus came to power in 1644 as the Qing dynasty, the new government reissued many of the same strict maritime policies as in the previous dynasty. As an alien dynasty from the far northeast corner of Asia, with military forces based on swift-moving cavalry, the Manchus were apprehensive about any challenges emanating from the sea, and in particular the formidable naval forces of the pirate-rebel Zheng Chenggong. The following document is one of the early imperial rescripts by the Shunzhi emperor, issued August 6, 1656, calling on coastal officials to strictly enforce new sea bans.

I [that is, the emperor] instruct the governors-general, governors, and garrison commanders of Zhejiang, Fujian, Guangdong, Jiangnan,[12] Shandong, and Tianjin as follows: The sea rebel (*haini*) Zheng Chenggong has found refuge in inaccessible areas on the coast and so far he has not been exterminated. Certainly there are traitors who secretly contact him and who, in seeking great profits, trade with him and provide him with supplies. If I do not firmly prohibit this by law, how can these noxious sea vapors [that is, pirates] ever be cleared away? From now on . . . it is strictly forbidden for merchant junks and civilian boats to set out to sea on their own and anyone who is found trading foodstuffs or goods with the sea rebels will be brought to our attention and sentenced to death by decapitation. Their goods will be confiscated and their private fortunes will go to those who denounce them. . . . As for those coastal areas where large and small pirate ships can moor and the pirates can go ashore, local mutual responsibility units (*baojia*) and officials should devise plans to establish blockades and construct earthen ramparts or wooden palisades to thwart [pirates]. Everywhere we must have stern defensive [measures] so as to not allow any [pirate] ships to enter the harbors or allow even one pirate to set foot on shore.

Source: *Qing Shizu Shilu* 1985, 102:789–90. Translation by the author.

DOC. 21. THE GREAT CLEARANCE PROCLAMATION IN GUANGDONG, 1662

Unable to militarily eradicate Zheng Chenggong and other pirates along the coast, in 1661 and 1662 the Qing government announced a new harsh

---

12. Jiangnan, literally "south of the [Yangtze] river," refers to a large geographic area that included parts of Zhejiang, Jiangsu, and Anhui provinces, as well as such major cities as Hangzhou, Ningbo, Shaoxing, Wenzhou, and Suzhou. Jiangnan has long been one of China's most prosperous regions due largely to domestic and overseas trade.

policy that forced the entire coastal population from Shandong to Guangdong to abandon their homes and livelihoods and to relocate inland some ten to twenty miles. While there was some relaxation of the policy in some areas after 1669, it remained in force in much of Fujian and parts of Guangdong until 1683, when the Qing conquered Taiwan and destroyed the Zheng regime on the island. Originally the goal of this policy was to combat piracy and the anti-Qing movement based in Taiwan under Zheng Chenggong and his heirs. The following text, dated 1662, is taken from an original placard, today housed in the Chenghai County Museum, publicizing the imperial command to evacuate the Guangdong coast. Although such public notices of the new policy must have been widespread at the time, this is one of the few known to have survived.

In the name of the Southern Pacification King of Guangdong [Shang Kexi],[13] Imperial Inspector Ke [Erkun], Vice Military Director Jie [Shan], Admiral Wang, General Shen, and Governor-General Li—On Receipt of the Imperial Decree:

Based on the seashore inspections of the Feudatory, officials, imperial commissioners, and commanders, the area starting from Chenghai to [a long list of place names along the Guangdong coast follows] . . . is now designated as the boundary line. All [people living in] villages outside the boundary [and] all places on the seacoast must obey and move inland. Let this serve as notice of our imperial will. All villagers and residents outside the boundary, hearing this, must spread this order and move immediately inside the border; no hesitation or resistance will be tolerated. Once you have removed behind the borderline, you shall not cross it to farm the land. You shall not cross it to build houses in which to live. Violators will be executed for treason. Our imperial order is severe. If you commoners linger, delay, or wait and see, you will be exterminated as rebels. Those who have removed to the interior will wait for the governor-general and governor to investigate and provide land and housing. Obey this.

[Posted on the] 1st month, 19th day of the 1st year of the Kangxi reign [March 8, 1662].

---

13. Shang Kexi was born into a military family in northeastern China's Liaoning province in 1604. Originally he served as a Ming general defending the northeastern frontier, but in 1634, before the Manchus invaded China, he switched his loyalty to the rising new state in Manchuria. By the time that the Manchus had entered Beijing in 1644, Shang was a prominent general in the new Qing dynasty. In 1649 the Shunzhi emperor bestowed on him the title Southern Pacification King (*Ping Nan Wang*) and sent him to conquer the southern province of Guangdong. Afterward he became the feudatory governor of the province with full civil and military authority. At the time of his retirement in 1673, another southern general, Wu Sangui, rebelled, thus setting off the Revolt of the Three Feudatories, which was not crushed until 1681. Shang, however, remained loyal to the Qing until his death in 1676.

Source: *Zhanglin xiangtu shiliao* [Local historical sources on Zhanglin], Chenghai County Museum, Guangdong. Translation adapted by the author from Ho 2011, 204–5.

DOC. 22. REPORTS ON REPERCUSSIONS FROM THE GREAT CLEARANCE

The forced coastal evacuation policy never worked as well as officials had planned. As the following reports from Fujian and Guangdong show, the policy actually had the opposite impact—in fact, it produced an escalation of piracy and other social disturbances along the coast. The first report is an excerpt from a memorial by Li Zhifang, a circuit intendent, in which he described the sufferings of the people along the coast of Fujian.

There has not been a period when there were no mountain and sea bandits. The aim [of our policies] should be to control them so as to enable the people to enjoy peace. One never hears of an imperial government removing the people in order to avoid bandits. . . . Now in removing the coastal population, as soon as the soldiers arrive on the spot at the designated time fixed by decree for removal, the people leave their homes and property, separate from their ancestral tombs, and depart in tears. This is simply driving away the people to die in ditches. How can the compassion of the parents of the people [that is, officials] permit such a thing to happen? . . . [Additionally] because the land in the south is not fertile . . . families must supplement farming with fishing to buy food. But this is unsatisfactory. Although the imperial decree promises allotments of land and houses to placate those removed, the people being sent in all directions are at a loss as to what to do. What is more, the authorities make no preparations but are only eager to drive the people away [from their homes]. The poor may carry food for a few days and the rich for a few months. When they gather in some interior locality, they become homeless without food. Afflicted by hunger and cold, they cannot help resorting to evil ways and becoming either pirates on the seas or bandits in the mountains. When one man raises the standard of revolt will not others flock to him?

The following documents come from the Qing Veritable Records and are dated between 1663 and 1665.

October 9, 1663. The [forced coastal] removal policy aimed to stop piracy, but it hasn't helped. If anything, piracy has now gotten worse, as people on the coast are revolting. [This year] more than 2,300 people led by Zhao Pishi revolted. Also many of these people have fled to offshore islands on the Xiangshan coast [of Guangdong], and these places have now become pirate nests.

January 13, 1664. The Southern Pacification King Shang Kexi reports several military engagements against pirates, in which 276 were captured, including bogus general Zhou Yu and bogus military advisor Lin Fubang; we [also summarily] beheaded 2,637 pirates and burned 131 pirate ships.

September 22, 1665. The Southern Pacification King Shang Kexi reports that Dan pirate-rebels occupied the island of Dongyong [off the Guangdong coast], and that we deployed soldiers [to the island], capturing the pirate chief Tan Lin'gao and killing 153 people. We have also pacified 85 men and women [living on the island]. In addition, a Dan boatman named Huang Mingchu jointly cooperated with other ships to supply [the pirates] with rice and other provisions in the vicinity of Maliumen. . . . Our soldiers captured and [summarily] beheaded more than 430 of these pirates and supporters.

The passage that follows comes from a long memorial by Fan Chengmo, Governor-General of Fujian and Zhejiang, submitted to the throne in 1673.

The livelihood of the people of Fujian depends on either farming or fishing. After shifting the boundary to the interior more than two million hectares (*mu*) of land have been left uncultivated, causing a loss in normal resources valued at more than two hundred thousand taels of silver. The result has been a shortage in revenue and the fields have become wastelands. The old and weak, women and children have struggled [to survive] in ditches and burrows. Those who had wandered about in all directions are uncountable, and the few remaining [in place] are without work. Recently the suffering is extreme and people's minds are troubled. The cost of rice is rising daily and unless the people are provided for, they will, oppressed by hunger and cold, turn to robbery. No one can guarantee that they will remain law-abiding subjects.

Sources: Jiang Risheng 1692, 202–3; *Qing Shizu Shilu* 1985, 4:84; *Qing Shengzu Shilu* 1985, 10:164, 16:239; Hsieh 1932, 572. Translation by the author.

DOC. 23. THE DAN PIRATE-REBELS ZHOU YU AND LI RONG, 1662–1664

One of the major disturbances resulting from the Kangxi emperor's Great Clearance policy was that of Zhou Yu and Li Rong, two leaders of large Dan fishing fleets operating in the Pearl River estuary, not far from the metropolis of Canton. Although at first both men had cooperated with local officials to help police the region, once Shang Kexi imposed the oppressive forced coastal removal policy Zhou Yu and Li Rong gathered their forces and revolted under the banner of "Great Army to Restore Guangdong." Labeled as pirates by officials, for more than a year they continually attacked government installations and plundered shipping in the coastal areas around the core Pearl River Delta. They even threatened to seize Canton on more than one occasion. What follows is an excerpt from an anthology of stories collected by the early Qing literatus Luo Tianchi.

As recorded in the collection "The Leftover Calabash" (*Piaosheng*): Zhou Yu and Li Rong, who were Dan fishermen from Panyu [County in Guangdong province], operated a fleet of several hundred large three-masted galleys, which had raised forecastles and were heavily armed.[14] Their ships were so fast they flew across the waves. Because they were skilled in naval combat, the Southern Pacification King Shang Kexi gave them the ranks of commanders. Whenever an alarm sounded at sea, they would swiftly deploy their ships in defense, so that the waters along the coast remained secure and calm. [However,] after the Kangxi emperor decreed the sea bans in 1662, their ships were impounded and moored along different branches of the [Pearl] River, and their family members were relocated inside cities.

Zhou Yu, who displayed the characteristics of hawks and otters,[15] could not be caged. So he deceived Shang Kexi by saying he had to return home for a funeral, a request that Shang Kexi granted. That very day Zhou Yu took his entire family and escaped to sea where he gathered many other desperadoes fleeing the law. In December 1663 he assembled a mighty fleet of warships that he led to the outskirts of Canton. Along the way they burned and plundered military installations so that the whole sky was ablaze. Only the homes of the common people were not harmed. Then they broke into the county seat of Shunde taking Magistrate Wang Yin as prisoner. When Shang Kexi got wind of this he immediately sent warships to attack and arrest the pirate leader Zhou Yu, [causing] his gang to disperse. Magistrate Wang Yin, who had not been killed, was rescued from a pirate boat. At the time Shang Kexi concealed this incident [from the emperor] and only relieved Wang of his duties.

Source: Luo Tianchi 1985, 153. Translation by Lanshin Chang and the author.

---

14. These ships were a type of *zengchuan*, literally "silk ships," which were commonly used as fishing junks and warships in the Ming and Qing dynasties.

15. The characterization of Zhou Yu's personality as resembling hawks and otters indicated that he acted as swift as a hawk and swam like an otter in water. In fact, the word *otter* was a common name given to Dan boat people.

DOC. 24. RECORD OF EVENTS IN THE GULF OF TONKIN, 1650–1681

During the Ming-Qing transition the Gulf of Tonkin was a hotbed of piracy and insurgency. The innumerable islands and fuzzy jurisdictions between China and Vietnam assured widespread and persistent piracy, as well as the continuance of clandestine trade. The gulf was a wild maritime frontier where fisherfolks and traders indiscriminately mingled and colluded with refugees, fugitives, dissidents, smugglers, bandits, and pirates. In this period of warfare and anarchy it became impossible to differentiate pirates, rebels, and merchants. Like their wokou *predecessors a century earlier, they combined commerce raiding with trade, but with the addition of political entanglements often associated with affiliations to the Zheng camp in Taiwan. As reported in the* Fangcheng County Draft Gazetteer, *pirates, such as Deng Yao, Xian Biao, Yang Yandi, and Yang San, formed a second maritime front of resistance against the Manchus in the gulf. It is also noteworthy that the gazetteer compilers mentioned incessant natural disasters and cosmic revelations accompanying piracy during those tumultuous times. Because the draft gazetteer was written in the early twentieth century soon after the founding of the republic that overthrew the Qing dynasty, its authors promoted strong anti-Manchu and nationalist interpretations about piracy. On the one hand, we can view this interpretation as a bias, yet on the other hand, it illustrates the mythologizing process by which Chinese pirates became patriotic heroes, a view still held by many Chinese.*

February 1650. Remnants of the [defeated] Ming dynasty under Deng Yao occupied Longmen Island and opened up communications with Zheng Chenggong to make plans to restore the Ming.

June 1653. Floods.

1655. Deng Yao plundered the Confucian Temple [in Qinzhou], stealing a bronze incense burner weighing 300 catties, two bronze urns weighing 100 catties, and a bronze bell weighing a thousand catties. He melted these down to make weapons.

February 1658. Deng Yao led his troops from Longmen to attack Qinzhou, but failed to take the city.

June 25, 1659. A comet was seen over Longmen, [an omen officials believed] to presage the collapse of the pirates.[16] [Yang Yandi and other pirates plundered the west coast of Hainan Island.]

---

16. Chinese people from emperors to peasants considered comets, apparitions of dragons, vapors in the shapes of knives and weapons, etc., as cosmic revelations or omens foretelling impending disasters. The trust in omens was predicated on the universal acceptance that man, nature, and the cosmos were so interdependent and intertwined that they operated as a single complex or harmonious whole. Any disharmonies or irregularities in the cosmic order were interpreted as supernatural warnings of approaching natural catastrophes, social disorders, defeats of pirates and rebels, or even the fall of dynasties.

August 1659 to May 1660. No rain. Rice cost three silver [taels] per peck. The Qinzhou magistrate opened granaries and had rice transported to the city by sea. The drought lasted more than a year and many people starved to death. The cost of rice became exorbitant.

July 1660. Mountain bandit Lu Guoxiang saw a monstrous apparition [in the sky] and afterward went to implore the Qinzhou magistrate to allow him to surrender.

October 1, 1660. At noontime people saw dragons [flying across the sky]. In the following month, Qing troops pacified Longmen Island. Deng Yao fled to a Buddhist temple on Qianlong Mountain in Guangxi [province].

February 1661. Yang Yandi and Yang San reoccupied Longmen Island and began to communicate with Zheng Chenggong in Taiwan, planning to restore the Ming dynasty.

1662. Emperor Kangxi ordered the coastal removal of the population in Lianzhou prefecture from Qinzhou to Fangcheng. Coastal residents were ordered to move 50 *li* [about 15 miles] inland. Qing soldiers constructed a line of watchtowers and palisades in order to [keep people out of the evacuation zone and thereby] stop people from aiding the Zheng [camp] in Taiwan.

March 1663. Qing forces attacked rebel-pirates [in the Gulf of Tonkin]; Yang Yandi and Yang San were defeated and fled to Fujian and later to Taiwan [to join forces with Zheng Jing].

June 1663. Plague [devastated Lianzhou prefecture].

November 1664. A comet was seen in the southeast. [The following year there was an earthquake and devastating fire in Lianzhou city.]

1666. The Vietnamese king received investiture as King of Annan from the Qing emperor. Vietnam [once again] began sending tributary missions to Beijing.

February 1667. A comet was seen in the night sky.

March 7, 1668. A strange white vapor in shape of a lance and two nights later three lines of black vapor in the shape of a knife were seen crossing the sky and then disappeared.

March 26, 1668. The moon turned the color of the sun. [That summer there was a large number of severe storms and floods in the gulf region, and in the next year man-eating tigers appeared in Lianzhou city.]

July 1668. The Qing court began to relax the forced coastal removal policy from Hepu to the Vietnam border.

March 1669. People began to return home along the coast.

December 1673. Wu Sangui started the Revolt of the Three Feudatories in Yunnan and Guizhou; next year the revolt spread to Lianzhou Prefecture.[17]

---

17. The Revolt of the Three Feudatories was led by the three hereditary lords of the fiefdoms in Yunnan, Guangdong, and Fujian provinces against the Qing government. These three lords had been prominent Han Chinese defectors who had been rewarded with fiefdoms or feudatories from

1677. Flooding began on July 23 and lasted a month; floodwaters reached the city walls of Qinzhou.

1677. Yang Yandi and Xian Biao received orders from Zheng Jing to return to the Gulf of Tonkin to retake Longmen Island; they set out from Taiwan in eighty ships with more than a thousand men.

September 1678. Yang Yandi attacked Qinzhou but failed to take the city.

1679. Confucian schools were restored in Lianzhou Prefecture.

April or May 1681. A comet was seen in the sky moving from southeast to northwest, accompanied by a loud crashing sound on the earth. Officials believed this was an omen predicting the defeat of the pirates. [In fact] not long afterward Yang Yandi was defeated and fled to Vietnam. [The Revolt of the Three Feudatories was crushed, but also that year famines and epidemics devastated the entire region.]

Source: *Fangcheng xianzhi chugao*, unpaginated. Translation by the author.

DOC. 25. TWO TALES ABOUT THE PIRATE CHIEF YANG YANDI

Although little-known in Chinese history, Yang Yandi or Yang Er became the most influential and formidable pirate in the Gulf of Tonkin between the 1650s and 1680s. He began his outlaw career as a local, petty pirate in the 1640s, and within ten years came to command nearly a thousand pirates. In the 1670s, he collaborated with the Zheng regime in Taiwan, and after the latter's demise Yang led several thousand followers back to the gulf where they established a fortified stronghold on Longmen Island. In 1682, when the Qing military drove the pirates from their lairs, Yang led more than a thousand followers to settle in southern Vietnam. The first tale comes from the scholar-official Wu Qi (1619–1694), who published a short book on the customs of Guangdong based on stories he had collected while prefect of Chaozhou in the late seventeenth century, including the following about Yang Yandi's outrageous attacks on two women on Hainan Island (figure 7.2).

I was told this story by Zheng Shangzhi from Danzhou: When the pirate Yang Er pillaged Hainan Island, on the wedding day of a certain local gentry,[18] as his bride crossed the threshold at the start of the ceremony, pirates

---

the first Qing emperor for helping the Manchus conquer China in the 1640s. After the revolt erupted Zheng Jing in Taiwan supported the revolt and sent forces to invade mainland China. In Guangdong, although Shang Kexi did not join the revolt, his son and successor did. Qing forces finally crushed the revolt in 1681.

18. The unnamed man had the lowest civil service degree called *xiangsheng* or *shengyuan*, usually translated into English as licentiate.

鄭儋州尚智為予言海寇楊二寇瓊州時一庠生方娶婦入門交拜賊突至遂掠入舟婦見賊怒曰我雖猶女子然已為士人妻矣狂賊何敢污我遂躍入海而死一家埋金於室一婢守之賊入詰其資婢始猶乞哀備受榜掠知不得免乃大聲極罵賊剮其齒斷其舌終不告以金之所在遂至於死二事皆節義之尤者惜其姓氏不傳也

Figure 7.2. Yang Yandi's Atrocities Against Two Women on Hainan Island.

suddenly seized her and then forced her aboard their ship. Seeing that they were pirates, she angrily said: "Although I am but a female, nonetheless I am the wife of a gentry man. How dare you wild thieves defile me!" Thereupon, she jumped into the sea and drowned. [In another episode] there was a family who had buried gold inside their home and had a female servant watch over it. [When] the pirates entered the home they flogged and interrogated her about the valuables. She begged for mercy, but realizing that there was no way to avoid being tortured, refused to tell them and harshly cussed at them. The pirates knocked out her teeth and cut off her tongue, but she still would not reveal where the gold was hidden, and so she was [slowly] tortured to death. In these two rare cases of chastity,[19] unfortunately we do not know the women's names.

The next tale, also from Hainan, is taken from the 1820 edition of the Chengmai County Gazetteer. *Although the story focuses on the filial son Li Chaoqin, nevertheless it also provides a somewhat kinder depiction of the pirate chief, which hints to why he became known locally as "Righteous Yang."*

Li Chaoqin, who styled himself Yuanzhe [a somewhat ostentatious name meaning primal sage], was a native of Tangyi. In the 20th year of the Kangxi reign [1681], the pirate chief Yang Er attacked Chengmai. The pirates seized Chaoqin's father, Shuirong. At the time although Chaoqin was sixteen, he was willing to risk his own life to save his father. When the pirates demanded 300 silver [taels], however, he was unable to pay them. The pirates then forced his father aboard their ship. Chaoqin steadfastly begged to go with them [to care for] his father who suffered from dysentery and was foul smelling and dirty. The pirates intended to throw him into the sea, but Chaoqin beat his head to the ground and wept. [Once aboard the pirate ship] he [continuously] cleaned up [his father's] mess and scrubbed the ship. The pirate chief [Yang Er] was deeply moved. When they arrived at Yangjiang, he said [to Chaoqin]: "You have disregarded your own life to serve your father. Because I pity you I will spare your lives. You and your father can go." Chaoqin thereupon helped his father ashore and they left.

Sources: Wu Qi 1780, 11:48–49; *Chengmai xianzhi* 1820, 7:33b. Translation by the author.

---

19. Since the Song dynasty (960–1279) chastity (rendered here as *jieyi*) had been held in China as the foremost honor for women, so much so that (at least in theory) for a woman to lose her virtue was worse than death.

DOC. 26. JAPANESE DOCUMENTS ON YANG YANDI IN VIETNAM AND CAMBODIA, 1682–1687

After being driven from his stronghold on Longmen Island in 1682, Yang Yandi continued to roam about the Gulf of Tonkin, plundering ships and coastal towns and villages. He eventually settled in My Tho in the Mekong Delta (about 45 miles from present-day Saigon), where he and his followers received protection and support from the Nguyen rulers. Once resettled Yang and his compatriots engaged in trade, farming, and fishing, as well as the occasional plundering of passing ships. To repay his new lords for granting him asylum, Yang helped the Nguyen rulers consolidate control over southern Vietnam by fighting their Cambodian rivals. The following documents are reports by Chinese junk captains that were prepared for Japanese authorities in Nagasaki, who were gathering intelligence on conditions in China and Southeast Asia. These reports are key sources for information on Yang's affiliation with the Zheng regime in Taiwan and his piratical activities in the Gulf of Tonkin between 1682 and 1687, when he was assassinated.

Ship No. 5, June 25, 1683. A ship came from Cambodia last year [1682] with Zhang Xiaoguan as captain. It left Cambodia on the 1st day of the 6th lunar month [June 25] last year. At dawn of the same day the ship wrecked in the shallow waters called Linlangqian off the coast of Champa.[20] . . . The captain of the wrecked ship is now in Siam. The purser Lin Xiangguan, who had [also] been in Siam, is aboard our ship. When he was ashore at the site of the shipwreck he heard about a recent development in Cambodia. Regional Commander Yang Er, a retainer of Qinshe in Dongning,[21] had been cruising around the islands off the coast of Guangdong for several years on Qinshe's orders, so as to establish control over the Guangdong coast. From time to time the [Qing] imperial navy ventured out from Guangdong to expel [Yang Er's forces] and it became difficult for them to stay in the sea bordering Guangdong [and Vietnam]. They roamed about, appearing sometimes in Quang Nam [central Vietnam] and Cambodia.

Ship No. 9, September 4, 1683. You might have heard about Regional Commander Yang Er, one of the followers of Qinshe on Dongning, from the ships which entered earlier [e.g., Ship No. 5 above]. On the pretext of escorting trading ships from Dongning,[22] [last year in the 11th lunar month]

---

20. Champa refers to the area of today's south-central Vietnam. Before 1832 Champa consisted of a collection of semi-independent polities with close ties to both Vietnam and Cambodia. In 1653 Vietnam annexed most of Champa.

21. Dongning or Eastern Peace refers to Taiwan. Qinshe or Zheng Kezang was the eldest son of Zheng Jing, the crown prince and regent of Taiwan. In 1681 his uncle killed him during the power struggle following the death of Zheng Jing. Taiwan fell to the Qing two years later.

22. These trading ships would have belonged to the Zheng family conglomerate based in Taiwan, which monopolized maritime trade in the South China Sea at this time.

seventy-odd military ships with 3,000 soldiers on board [under the command of Yang Er] had been patrolling the coastlines of Guangdong, Quang Nam, Tonkin [northern Vietnam], and Cambodia. . . . In Cambodia, a remote country with a small population, the King[23] and his people were surprised by the unexpected arrival of Yang Er's forces, which they thought had come to attack them. They fled to the mountains. Ever since then, and up until the time of our departure [from Siam], Yang Er and his forces have been in Cambodia.

Ship No. 107, August 30, 1687. When we were about to leave Siam, we heard the following news about Cambodia. Rather than return to Dongning, the navy of Qinshe under Commander Yang's authority in Cambodia has been roaming around the neighboring seas for several years with several thousand men aboard large and small military vessels. Since they had nothing to do and nowhere to stay, they went to Cambodia to expel the King . . . and place the Cambodian coast under their control. While the King of Cambodia had retreated to the mountains, General Yang's adjunct commander Huang [Jin] revolted against his master and killed him.[24]

Source: *Tôsen Fusetsu-gaki* [Reports and tales from Chinese junks]. Translation adapted by the author from Ishii 1998, 29–32, 42.

---

23. At the time the Cambodian king was Chey Chettha IV (1656–1725).
24. Other sources reported that Yang Er died in 1688.

3. Piracy in the Mid-Qing Dynasty (1775–1810)

DOC. 27. DEPOSITION OF A KIDNAPPED BOY NAMED XIAN YASHENG, 1777

This piracy case took place in the Gulf of Tonkin in 1777 and involved a petty gang of amateur pirates. Pang Shunyu, the leader, came from Wuchuan County, in southwestern Guangdong, but in 1775 he moved his family to Jiangping (Giang Binh in Vietnamese), a notorious black market on the Sino-Vietnamese border, where he tried to find work as a day laborer. At the time of his arrest Pang was thirty-nine years old (sui). As was so often the case, poverty and the hardships of making an honest living were driving forces behind Pang's decision to turn pirate. It was not difficult for him to convince other men, who, like him, had ended up in Jiangping and were unable to find steady work, to join his gang. In a short time Pang recruited sixteen men, who after procuring a boat and purchasing two muskets, a peck of gunpowder, several knives, and lances from markets in Jiangping, set out on their adventure at dawn on the 1st day of the 6th lunar month (July 5). Over the next three months they plundered one Vietnamese and five Chinese boats, which carried cargoes of rice, clothing, fresh and salted fish, tobacco, and areca or betel nut, as well as small amounts of copper cash. After each heist they returned to Jiangping to sell their booty, buy supplies and weapons, and recruit new gang members. The following deposition was that of a fourteen-year-old boy named Xian Yasheng, whose family fishing boat fell first victim to Pang's gang on the evening of July 5. Because the victims knew Pang and other members of his gang, the pirates brutally murdered the entire family, except the boy, to ensure their silence. At the trial in Canton, Xian Yasheng made this statement to the court.

I am from Xinhui County [near Canton] and this year I am 14 years old (*sui*). My father is Xian Shengxiang and my mother's maiden name is Fan. Together with a hired sailor, Wu Sige, we operated a fishing boat that went everywhere to catch fish. This year [1777] in the 5th lunar month our boat got blown off course in a storm and we ended up in the waters near White Dragon Tail (Bailongwei) off the coast of Lianzhou prefecture [in the Gulf of Tonkin]. My father decided to fish there. On the 1st day of the 6th lunar month, we ran into an old acquaintance named Pang Shunyu, whose boat happened to pass by. He approached my father to buy fish, but didn't pay us any money. He asked my father to join his gang, but my father refused. Pang then ordered Li Dezi and the others to jump aboard our boat. They grabbed and tied up my father and threw him down on the deck. Pang next grabbed a knife and killed my father and flung him into the sea. Our sailor, Wu Sige, also tried to resist but was overpowered and tied up; [one of the pirates] Lu Baisheng took his knife and killed Wu and then threw him overboard as well. They next took all our rice and money [which amounted to three pecks of rice and two silver dollars], and grabbed me and my mother and forced us to go over to their boat. Pang then locked me inside the hold [of his boat], not allowing me to see my mother. Later I learned that Pang and Li Dezi [fought over who would] rape my mother. Li Dezi lost. Afterward he told Lu Yushen and the others to kill my mother and throw her into the sea. At that time I was locked in the hold and didn't see anything. Later I found out what happened and wept. Pang wanted to also kill me, but I knelt down before him and begged him to spare my life and that I would obediently serve all of them. Because I was so young the others asked that I not be killed. My job aboard their boat was to help cook food; I was not allowed to come out of the hold. They continued to rob boats but I don't know how many times or how many people they killed. On the 3rd day of the 9th lunar month [October 3], while our boat was stranded in the waters off Dazhou [a small island near Hainan], Fang Shifa and other fishermen captured Pang and his men. They also rescued me.

Source: *Xingke tiben*, dated 9th day, 6th lunar intercalary month, 43rd year of the Qianlong reign (August 1, 1778). Translation by the author.

DOC. 28. THE EARLY CAREER OF MO GUANFU AND HIS GANG, 1794–1796

Mo Guanfu grew up in a poor fisher family in Suixi County on the western coast of the Leizhou peninsula in a village facing the Gulf of Tonkin. He began his outlaw career in 1787 after being abducted by pirates and deciding

3. Piracy in the Mid-Qing Dynasty (1775–1810)

to join them. Over the next few years he seems to have worked on and off as a pirate and fisherman. At some point he joined up with Zheng Qi, a notorious pirate whose family had been pirates in the Pearl River Delta for several generations. At the same time, both men became acquainted with the Cantonese pirate Chen Tianbao, who became affiliated with the Tay Son rebels in Vietnam as a brigade general in 1784. Mo and Zheng were soon afterward also commissioned as brigade generals in the Tay Son cause. In 1796 Mo was promoted and given an additional title as the "King of the Eastern Sea" in recognition of his bravery and skills as a military commander. In 1801, however, he was captured by Tay Son rivals and extradited to China where he was beheaded. At that time he commanded a large fleet with more than a thousand pirates. This document is taken from a lengthy memorial written to the Jiaqing emperor by Governor-General Zhu Gui on July 29, 1796. In it he relates the capture and trial of several members of Mo Guanfu's gang, at a time when he was still a local pirate boss. Like many other pirates at this time, they operated from lairs near the black market town of Jiangping. In this case, most of the action took place in the Gulf of Tonkin, either in China's or Vietnam's territorial waters. Two gang members, He Yuli and Ye Long, gave the following testimony at their trial in Canton, as transcribed by the court scribe.

He Yuli and Ye Long, natives of Suixi County [on the Leizhou peninsula], were fishermen in Jiangping, where they fished together with several acquaintances including Mo Guanfu. On January 19, 1794, He Yuli and Ye Long met with friends on Mo Guanfu's boat, where they complained about their poverty and hardships. Mo Guanfu suggested that they form a gang to plunder boats at sea and then split up the booty. He Yuli and the others agreed. . . . [Next, they recruited more gang members.] Mo Guanfu recruited Mai Ya'er, Hainan Yang, and six other men; He Yuli recruited Mai Yayin, Liang Yashun, and five other men; and Ye Long recruited two men. Afterward Mo bought cannons, guns, and other weapons [at a market in Jiangping]. Two days later, after all twenty men gathered on Mo's boat, they set off. On the 22nd, in Vietnamese waters they plundered a cargo junk, which they kept as a prize. [Now with two boats] they set off again, robbing and killing so many times that He Yuli and Ye Long could not remember clearly. . . . Then on February 4, 1795, they robbed a large junk carrying a cargo of green oil[1] and other items. On the 28th of that month they plundered a boat carrying areca or betel nuts; on April 26 they robbed a boat carrying pottery bowls; and on May 7 they robbed a boat carrying white radishes. For the rest of the year [1795]

---

1. Green oil (*qingyou*) refers to Chinese tallow seed oil, which was used mainly in paints and varnishes.

they continued to plunder trading and fishing boats in Vietnamese waters [in the Gulf of Tonkin], but He Yuli and Ye Long could not remember how many.

[In January 1796] they returned to Jiangping to sell their loot, refit their boats, and recruit more men. . . . Now with a total of forty men and two ships, they again set sail on April 6, and plundered a fishing boat in the gulf off the Shicheng coast, abducting Wen Yada, who they tried to coerce into joining the gang. When he refused Wen was ordered to serve as a cook. On April 15 they kidnapped two more fishermen in Vietnamese waters, but when they refused to join the gang, they were forced to haul water and clean the boats. Three days later, in Huanglong harbor in Lin'gao county [Hainan], they kidnapped a fisherman, Chen Yachen, who was sodomized by the pirate Mai Ya'er. On April 20, they came across three salt junks in Vietnamese waters; when the pirates fired their cannons and guns, the sailors [on the salt junks] abandoned ship and fled in three small sampans.[2] Because his boats were in disrepair Mo Guanfu decided to scuttle them and take the three captured salt junks in their place. . . . On the 25th they plundered another fishing boat and killed the captain, and two days later off the Xuwen coast they robbed a passage boat with a cargo of white radishes and abducted Wan Kaichao, who after refusing to join the gang was forced to clean the ships.

On May 2, off the coast of Haikang, they plundered a fishing boat and abducted a young boy named Zhou Yapei, who the pirates ordered to maintain fires for cooking and smoking. Later they locked him below deck because he cried. The next day the pirates kidnapped a fisherman, Wang Wenhuai, who Hainan Er sodomized. On the 5th, off the Vietnam coast, they kidnapped Deng Laosan, a sailor on Chen Lixing's boat, and after refusing to join the gang, Deng was locked below deck. On May 18, off Xuwen, they abducted a fisherman named Lin Jiazhai, who after refusing to join them also was locked below deck. On the 21st, they plundered two boats carrying lumber, and six days later they raided the home of a wealthy man named Wang Jizhuan on the Suixi coast, . . . stealing cloth and clothing and kidnapping for ransom Wang, his mother, wife, and Wang Jiguo [his younger brother], who the pirates ordered to return home to collect the ransom money. That same day three of the other captives took the occasion to escape. They were soon afterward arrested by soldiers in Suixi, where local officials interrogated them. On May 28, the pirates abducted three sailors on board a small boat used for cutting grasses along the eastern coast of Leizhou;[3] they too were locked below deck when

---

2. Sampans are the most common type of small boat in Chinese waters; they generally have sharp bows and large sterns, with the after portion of the gunwale and deck usually raised. While some are rigged for sailing, sometimes with two masts, most are rowed with large sweep-type oars. They are mostly used for transportation and fishing in coastal waters and on rivers.

3. Chinese made fans, mats, and baskets from grasses and reeds growing in the brackish waters along the coast.

they refused to join the gang. The next day, the pirates were spotted by a naval patrol who gave them chase. After a short skirmish off the Wuchuan coast, in which about thirty pirates were reported killed or drowned, He Yuli, Ye Long, and eight others were apprehended and brought to justice. [Mo Guanfu, although reported to have been killed, escaped.]

Source: *Gongzhongdang*, dated 25th day, 6th lunar month, 1st year of the Jiaqing reign (July 29, 1796). Translation by the author.

DOC. 29. BIOGRAPHICAL SKETCH OF THE PIRATE CHIEF CAI QIAN

Cai Qian was the most feared pirate in Fujian in the early nineteenth century. According to one account, he was born in the small coastal village of Xiapu in Tong'an County in Quanzhou Prefecture. We know little about his early life, except that as a child he was orphaned and as an adolescent he wandered about Fujian's fishing villages and port towns eking out a subsistence living at various menial jobs. About 1794 he became a pirate. Making his way up the ranks by defeating his rivals, in a short time he became the most powerful pirate chief on the Fujian coast. The following story was recorded by Wang Songchen, who had heard it when he was a child from his father, who in turn had heard it from a low-ranking official in Quanzhou named Wu Zhipu (figure 8.1). This anecdotal story, although based largely on hearsay, nonetheless presents a telling depiction of how Cai Qian was remembered in his home area soon after his death in 1809, and how his legend was born. These stories are still being told today along Fujian's coast.

From early in life Cai Qian was poor. Previously [when still a boy] he purchased sugar cane on credit at a store and cut the cane into sections to sell. However, he accumulated a debt of a thousand-odd cash [copper coins] that he was unable to repay. One day, while selling sugar cane at a temple, Cai Qian suddenly encountered the store owner, who seized and flogged him. An opera was being performed at the temple and the spectators had formed a barrier. None of them uttered a word on his behalf. Among the people watching the play, there was a man surnamed Chen, who was a native of the provincial capital [Fuzhou] and served in Tong'an County as the director of studies. Commiserating with Cai Qian's tender age and poverty, Chen took out a Spanish silver dollar and cleared off the boy's debts. To express his gratitude, Cai Qian knelt in front of Chen and knocked his forehead upon the ground [as a sign of respect]. Then he requested his benefactor's name and left the scene. Later, when Cai Qian became a great pirate chieftain, whenever he mentioned

Director Chen, he always emotionally burst into tears, covered his heart with his hands, and cried aloud that he owed a lot to Chen's kindness. . . .

Afterward, Cai Qian suffered repeated defeats at the hands of official forces. Government posters were also hung in marketplaces and streets offering an official position of the second rank and ten thousand in gold [coins?] to anyone who could capture Cai Qian alive and hand him over to the authorities. This excited Cai Qian, who pounded [his fists on] the surface of a table and declared in a determined tone: "Now I have a way to repay Mr. Chen." Dressing in ordinary clothes and taking two robust retainers along with him, Cai Qian sneaked into Director Chen's yamen at night. Prostrating himself and knocking his forehead on the ground, he said: "Allow me to repay your favor with great wealth and high position." Having been the director of studies in Tong'an County for several tens of years, Chen was very senile and had long forgotten the incident when he had redeemed Cai Qian's debt. He also did not know that the boy who had suffered humiliation on that day was Cai Qian. He lifted Cai Qian up and enquired about the matter. Cai Qian told him the whole story in detail, saying: "There is no way for me to repay the great favor I received; and having learned that an official position of the second rank and ten thousand in gold are to be afforded to anyone who captures Cai Qian, I am willing to be tied up and sent to the authorities by you to repay your great virtue." Upon learning that the man [before him] was Cai Qian, Director Chen became furious, recounted his crimes, and ordered him to leave his house. Cai Qian persisted in his request, but Director Chen cursed him without stopping. Cai Qian thereupon stationed himself outside the door and entrusted his two able retainers to continue the persuasion. The two men repeated Cai's offer, but Director Chen cursed Cai even more vigorously and the sound of his swearing carried outside the yamen. Fearing the denunciation might be heard by patrolmen, Cai Qian quickly left.

By nature Cai Qian liked the color of aqua blue. On board ship his canopy and bedding were all pure aqua blue. He frequently wore an aqua blue crepe jacket as well as a pair of aqua blue trousers. He carried two knives at his waist and was as nimble [as a bird] in flight. [Cai Qian] and his wife, surnamed so and so, smoked opium together. When he became a bit tired and bored, he opened the hold of his ship and brought out male captives. He then slit open their chests and took out their livers, which were fried and eaten. He did this several times a day. His junks all had abundant amounts of [looted] goods. When there was a shortage of firewood, they burned more than ten bolts of silk and satin instead. When they ran out of lead shot [for their cannons], they used Spanish silver dollars. . . .

Just a few years after Cai Qian was vanquished, Honorable Wu Zhipu served as director of studies in Quanzhou and was my late father's mentor.

Wu, who was familiar with tales about Cai Qian, once told my father this story.

Source: *Maxiang tingzhi* 1893, addendum 1:55a–57a. Translation by the author.

DOC. 30. ANECDOTAL SKETCHES OF MADAM CAI QIAN

We know little about the wife of Cai Qian, and what we do know is mostly anecdotal. We do not even know her true name, although some sources say that she was surnamed Lü. She was likely born into a Dan boat family in Pingyang County in Zhejiang province sometime between 1770 and 1780. According to stories that circulated along the waterfronts, she was well known for her uninhibited love affairs, even after marrying Cai Qian. Nonetheless, she was said to be a forceful and capable woman, as well as someone who determined her own fate. The following composite of Cai Qian's wife is taken from two sources, first from the Gazetteer of Pingyang County.

In the port of Yanting [in Zhejiang province to the south of Wenzhou] there was a local beauty, who, although married, enjoyed sleeping about [with men] at night. Because her husband could not stop her, he sold her to a barber, but she continued her old ways. One day when the pirate Cai Qian went ashore to have his head shaven,[4] he was delighted to see [the barber's lovely wife], so he bought her for several tens of gold [coins]. She assisted Cai Qian in organizing and disciplining his fleet. She was a fierce warrior unsurpassed in battle. People along the coast called her Cai Qian Ma or Madam Cai Qian.

The next passage comes from the Gazetteer of Maxiang Subprefecture *in Fujian (figure 8.1).*

[Cai Qian's] wife fought bravely and was skillful in battle. She regularly led a separate [squadron of] several junks of female warriors. Those who encountered her frequently stood off. When she had nothing to do she would take the handsome male captives out of the hold to satisfy her carnal desires. If captives begged for their lives she would set them free. Even Cai Qian dared not interfere or try to stop her.

Sources: *Pingyang xianzhi* 1925, 59:22b–23a; *Maxiang tingzhi* 1893, addendum 1:56b–57a. Translation by the author.

---

4. During the Qing period the government imposed on the male population a hairstyle, referred to as a queue, to signify submission to the alien dynasty; originally Manchu men wore this hairstyle in which the hair on the front of the head was shaved off above the temples every ten days or so and the remainder of the hair was braided into a single long pigtail. Noncompliance to wearing the queue was considered treason and punishable by death.

初牽爲童子貧甚嘗賣蔗竿於某肆斷而賣之瘢欠千餘錢不能償一日賣蔗某猝遇肆主執而笞之廟方演劇觀者如堵皆無言同安學官陳某省視人亦在戲場憐其幼而窮也取泮番一併代價所負牽即頓謝訶姓名而去爲巨盜言及陳教官則感激流涕撫心呼負狽屢爲官軍所敗官又懸激昻曰吾今有以報陳君矣徵服攜兩船乍夜闖入榜衙市鬮生禽牽以歸者二品職賞萬金乃拊儿陳教官學箓伏地搏顙曰謝以一塲大富貴報君陳教官任同安學數十年龍鍾甚久總代牽償債事亦不知當日受辱童子郎蔡牽扶起問之牽具道前事且言受大恩無以報今聞購某者予二品職賞萬金願就縛送官以酬大德陳教官聞其爲牽也大怒愍數其罪麾使出牽請不已陳教官罵亦不已牽乃屬兩健卒婉勤之而自立門外以待兩健卒復申前說牽教官屬益烈聲徹戶外恐爲邏者所間俠快去牽性喜青船中帷幄被褥悉純青色常以靑巾帕首衣青綢短褂下着縹絝腰斃刃趫捷如飛與妻某氏相對吸鴉片烟倦則開戾艙取所掠男子十餘卷以代鉛子竭則代以番錢幼亦勇悍善戰別率數船縮爲嬭子軍當輒擇易收泊無事則亦開底艙取所掠男子捍美好者與淫哀詞乞有則竟縊之逸齡不敢問亦不能禁也吳芝圃太先生徵君業師此嘉慶間任泉州教授距牽滅僅數年知其遺事甚悉嘗爲先君言之如此

Figure 8.1. A Sketch of Cai Qian and His Wife.

DOC. 31. THE GUANGDONG PIRATE PACT OF 1805

*In 1805 seven of the most powerful pirate leaders in Guangdong, all of them pirate bosses who previously had been commissioned by the Tay Son rulers in Vietnam, came together and signed a pact (*yue*), which formally established a loose confederation that numbered more than 50,000 pirates and several thousand large and small ships (figure 8.2). They made this agreement, not to guarantee equality and democracy aboard their ships (as was the case among some eighteenth-century Western pirates) but rather to bring stability and regularity to the unruly gangs. For several years previous to signing this pact chaos and fighting prevailed among the numerous bands of pirates. Specifically, the pact established rules to normalize operating procedures among the different fleets and gangs and to create a code of conduct to regulate their rowdy behavior. Harsh punishments were prescribed for violations of the agreement. However, it is unclear how or if these rules were carried out. During the next two years the confederation stabilized at six self-sustaining fleets or branches, each one designated by a separate colored banner, and this remained the situation until its collapse in 1810.*

We the signatories to this pact—Zheng Wenxian [Zheng Yi], Mai Youjin [Wushi Er], Wu Zhiqing [Donghai Ba], Li Xiangqing [Jin Guyang], Zheng Liutang [Zheng Laotong], Guo Xuexian [Guo Podai], and Liang Bao [Zongbing Bao]—have discussed it among ourselves and have willingly agreed to its terms. If regulations are not harsh they will not be obeyed and therefore trade will be harmed. Today we have achieved a great accomplishment by agreeing to join forces and making this pact. . . . No matter if the commands are big or small, or if the ships are far or near, everyone must obey these rules. . . .

The regulations are as follows:

1. We have agreed that our large and small seagoing ships will be arranged in seven branches designated as Heaven (*Tian*), Earth (*Di*), Black (*Xuan*), Yellow (*Huang*), Universe (*Yu*), Cosmos (*Zhou*), and Vast (*Hong*). Each branch must record the sobriquet of their commanders in a register. Every fast boat[5] must have its branch name and registration number written on the bow and must fly the branch's banner on its foremast.[6] If the bow does not display the branch name and registration number or the foremast displays a banner with the wrong color, then that vessel and its weapons will be confiscated and the commander executed.

2. Each branch shall have its own name and number. If any [vessel] falsely displays another branch's name and banner, then as soon as it is discovered the vessel and its weapons will become the property of the whole group. [Because] the commander has intentionally cheated the whole group then the whole group will decide his fate.

3. If a fast boat disregards the regulations to stop and damage a vessel [with one of our safe conduct passes], and then sells its cargo or steals its money and clothes, the value of the booty must be estimated and [the victim] compensated. The offending vessel's weapons will be confiscated and the commander will be punished according to the circumstances of the case. If the offending vessel cannot pay the compensation then the amount will be deducted from its share [of the common fund].

4. Whenever attacking merchant junks [without passes], all of the captured cargo will become the property of the vessel that attacks it first. If others forcefully take it from the initial captors, the value of the prize must be estimated and the initial captor must be compensated with a sum double the original value. Anyone who disobeys this rule will be subject to attack from the entire group.

5. No matter which branch's fast boats stop a junk with a pass, those who witness the action and apprehend the culprits will be rewarded with 100 silver dollars. If any of our brothers is wounded in the action the entire group consents to their medical care. Moreover, the amount of compensation that the offenders must pay will be decided by the whole group. Those witnesses who do not come forward to act [against the offenders] will be punished as accomplices.

---

5. Fast boats were two-masted vessels commonly used for fishing and coasting; they were also a favorite among pirates because they handled well both at sea and in coastal waters.

6. In fact this system mimicked the Qing government's boat surveillance system (called *aojia* in Chinese) that required every boat to register with port authorities and to display the boat's name and registration number on the ships.

6. If there are ships that sail without permission to oceans and harbors to rob small trading boats and the money of merchants who have [safe conduct] passes, once they are captured by any of the branch's patrol boats, then the [offenders'] boat will be burned, their weapons confiscated, and their bosses executed.

7. If there are merchants on either land or sea who had been the enemies of one of us, but who [now] openly continue to do business [with us], we must restrain our personal anger for the good of the whole group. We cannot use our power as a pretext to harm them on the grounds that they are our enemies or implicate their kith and kin as an excuse to kidnap them. Once such violations are discovered they will be punished for false implication.

8. If [the commander of a] flagship has something to discuss concerning the whole group then he should hoist a flag on his mainmast and the big bosses of each branch should come to confer. If a branch leader has an order to transmit to his fast boats, he should hoist a flag on the third mast, and all junks [in that branch] must assemble to listen to the orders. Those who do not assemble will be held in contempt and punished accordingly.

By order of our highest commanders, [this pact] shall be copied and sent to each ship so as to be obeyed.

Heavenly Circle Reign, Yiqiu year, 6th lunar month [1805]
[The pirate's vermillion seal was affixed over the above reign date][7]
Prepared by Wu Shangde[8]

Source: *Zhupi zouzhe*, dated 22nd day, 11th lunar month, 10th year of the Jiaqing reign (January 11, 1806). Translation by Lanshin Chang and the author.

DOC. 32. DEPOSITIONS OF LI CHONGYU, 1806

It was not uncommon for pirates to collaborate with local bandits and secret society members, who fenced their stolen goods; sold them food, weapons, and other provisions; acted as spies and local guides for village raids; and helped them recruit gang members. One of the most famous cases during this period involved a notorious Lufeng gangster and secret society boss named Li Chongyu. Official records described him as "a man of moderate wealth who liked to loaf about and spend money freely." Around 1804 he helped a bandit named Shi Chenglian organize a Triad society in nearby Haifeng County. In his hometown, the port of Jiazi, he opened a rice shop, which in fact was a

---

7. The use of a reign date and affixing a vermillion seal indicated imperial pretentions of the pirates.

8. Wu Shangde was one of several literate men who joined the pirates and functioned as scribes to write ransom letters and safe conduct passes, keep accounts, and, as in this case, compose pacts.

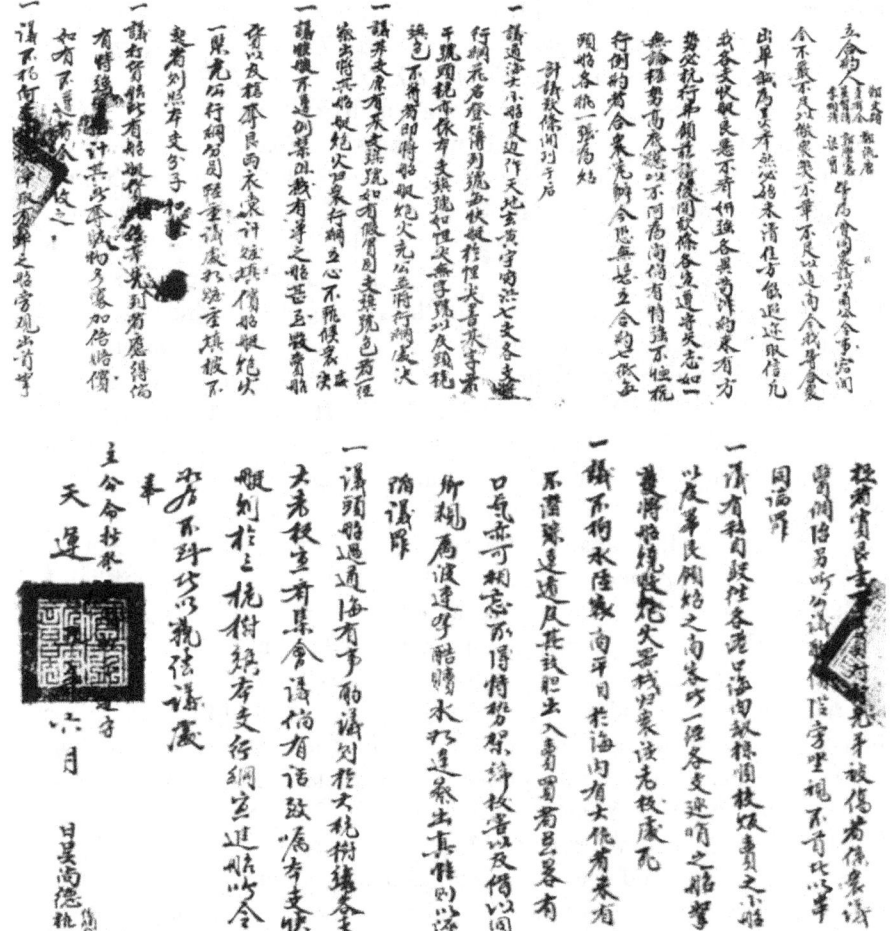

Figure 8.2. The Guangdong Pirate Pact of 1805.

front for buying and selling the booty of pirates and bandits. He also operated a gambling den and brothel in Jiazi and was involved in other criminal activities, including robbery, kidnapping, extortion, and murder. After several run-ins with the law, Li fled to sea and joined the pirates, becoming close friends with Zhu Fen among others pirate bosses. According to his own testimony, after hearing about Governor-General Nayancheng's offer of pardon, Li turned himself in to the authorities in 1806. He was not only pardoned, but Nayancheng also commissioned him as a naval captain and gave him a silver placard. However, because the governor-general had overstepped his authority, the Jiaqing emperor dismissed Nayancheng and sentenced him to military exile in Ili in the far northwestern frontier. The following are two excerpts from Li Chongyu's deposition, taken on different occasions and under torture. The first deposition was recorded on March 16, 1806.

I am from Lufeng County [Guangdong] and live at a place called Jiazi. I am now forty-five years old (*sui*). Both my father, Li Yuanjun, and my mother, who is surnamed Tian, died of illnesses last year [1805]. My elder brother is Li Chongyun and my younger brothers are Li Chongyin and Li Chongfang. I am married to a woman surnamed Cai and have three sons. The oldest is Yazhao, the second is Yahong, and the youngest is Yajin.[9] I used to earn my living as the owner of a rice shop. In the third year of the Jiaqing reign [1798], I organized a Society of Filial Sons[10] to help take care of funeral arrangements for all those society members in the village whose parents died of illness.

Afterward, Circuit Intendent Wu Huichao arrested me for no apparent reason. I was harshly interrogated and then sentenced to exile [penal servitude] in Lienzhou[11] for five years. [At that time, however,] the emperor issued a general amnesty and my father offered a guarantee so I could return home. Nonetheless, Circuit Intendent Wu not only refused to set me free but also had my father imprisoned in order to compel him to say I was unfilial. My father had to comply and presented a petition, signed jointly with Du Lao, Chen Fengjia, and others, charging me with insubordination. While on route to serve my sentence, one night after my guards fell asleep, I jumped into the river and made good my escape in Qujiang County.[12] I then slipped back home and hid myself in the house without going out. I asked someone to run the rice business for me. I also changed my name to Li Qingxing and purchased a brevet title as Student of the Imperial Academy.[13]

Last year [1805], on February 13, local officials learned I was living at home and suddenly led several constables to Jiazi to arrest me. At that time, I was at my rice shop. Upon hearing the noise of the crowd and gunshots, I climbed to the roof of my shop and saw many people searching for me at my house. I then ran to the seashore, boarded a small boat, and escaped to sea. When I reached Hudong harbor, about 30 *li* [roughly 9 miles] from Jiazi, I

---

9. The names of Li Chongyu's immediate relatives were recorded because according to Chinese law family members were also held culpable and could be punished with floggings or even death, depending on the severity of the crime.

10. In the eyes of the Qing state, such societies were regarded as illegal associations or secret societies and whenever uncovered severely suppressed. Often, too, these associations were fronts for criminal racketeering activities, which is likely the case here.

11. Lienzhou is a remote mountainous independent department in the far northwestern corner of Guangdong bordering Hunan and Guangxi provinces.

12. Qujiang is on the North River and at that time about a day's journey to Lienzhou.

13. In the Qing dynasty the purchase of civil service degrees was common, and in fact by the early nineteenth century had become an important means for the central government to obtain extra revenue. Li had purchased a collegian or *jiansheng* degree, which gave him some status as a lower gentry in his home community.

came across Li Yafa's junk and boarded it. Later I transferred to Zhu Fen's junk on the ocean off Zhaoan in Fujian.[14] Zhu Fen gave me a small boat and also assigned to me about thirty men to assist him in committing acts of piracy. Then, I do not remember what day it was, Zhu Fen was surrounded and attacked by General Li. Only my vessel escaped to the high seas, where I encountered a large trading junk that I seized and plundered.

In October, I returned to the area near Jiazi. There, Wang Tengkuei a former pirate who had switched to the government side under a previous imperial amnesty, came aboard my ship and informed me that Lord Na[yencheng] had posted notices offering pardons to pirates. But because I was afraid, I dared not go ashore to surrender. Later a collegian from Jiazi and some of my kinsmen came aboard my ship and said that if I would give myself up as soon as possible then my crimes would be pardoned. Thus, I felt at ease and went ashore. The officials [at first] did not offer me any monetary reward. I also returned the ship I had seized to the merchant [owners]. I led Tian Qiannan and another hundred or so men to Lord Na's encampment where we turned ourselves in. Lord Na first granted me a shiny white button for my hat decoration. After learning that I had returned the trading junk to its owners, Lord Na said that I was a man of conscience and further granted me a blue button,[15] 1,500 [Spanish silver] dollars for my personal use, and 1,000 [Spanish silver] dollars for the renovation of my house. I only personally knew Lin Yafa and Zhu Fen; I did not make the acquaintances of Zheng Yi, Wushi Er, Zongbing Bao, Liu Tangbo, and other [pirate chiefs]. Furthermore, while I was on Zhu Fen's ship, I only heard him say that Cai Qian had written him a letter asking him to join him. I really did not meet Cai Qian. This is true.

The second deposition was recorded a week later on March 22, 1806.

I called Zhu Fen Honorable Eldest Brother and he addressed me as Elder Brother Chongyu. Among ourselves, the most respectful title is Master of the Seas, the next in order is Honorable Eldest Brother, and for the lesser chiefs, we addressed them as Elder Brother So-and-So. Actually, I was a subordinate of Zhu Fen and not the head of the pirates. Moreover, when I seized the trading junk on the high seas, the sailors and passengers all remained on board and were not molested. When I came ashore to turn myself in, I returned the vessel and its cargo to the merchants in front of the authorities. Now, having undergone three or four harsh interrogations, I dare not quibble, but admit in the face of irrefutable evidence that I have unforgivably killed people in two

---

14. Lin Yafa was a local pirate chief who operated in the coastal areas of Huizhou and Chaozhou prefectures, Guangdong, in the early nineteenth century. Zhu Fen was the most powerful pirate boss operating on the Guangdong and Fujian border.

15. Colored hat buttons signalized official ranks in the Qing dynasty; the white and blue buttons were of low rank.

armed affrays, am on friendly terms with Zhu Fen, and seized a trading junk by force. This is true.

Sources: *Shangyudang*, dated 27th day, 1st lunar month, 11th year of Jiaqing reign (March 16, 1806), and 3rd day, 2nd lunar month, 11th year of Jiaqing reign (March 22, 1806). Translation by the author.

DOC. 33. JOHN TURNER'S FIRSTHAND DESCRIPTIONS OF THE LADRONES, 1806–1807

On December 7, 1806, near Macau, pirates kidnapped John Turner, the chief mate of the merchant ship John Jay, *and five Lascars. Pirates held him prisoner for five and a half months, only releasing him after a ransom of $6,000 was paid. He has left us a compelling account of his captivity and vivid descriptions of the size, armaments, and organization of the pirate gangs when they were at the height of power. His captors belonged to the Red Banner Fleet, the most powerful pirate fleet in Guangdong, which was led by Zheng Yi Sao and Zhang Bao. The term "Ladrones," which was derived from Spanish or Portuguese, was commonly used for pirates and thieves.*

The total number of vessels engaged in acts of piracy on the south coast of China . . . is as nearly as I can conjecture between five and six hundred sail; these are of different sizes; the largest maybe about two hundred tons burthen, the smallest does not exceed fifteen, but the majority are from 70 to 150 tons. Like other Chinese vessels, their draught of water is much less than the generality of Europeans of the same burthen, as they have not been built by the pirates themselves, but are vessels which from time to time have fallen into their hands. There is nothing in their construction, or their appearance, to distinguish them from the common Chinese trading vessels.

The largest mount twelve guns, from 6 to 12 pounders, and some of them have even a few 18 pounders; the rest carry metal according to their size, with long wall pounders, match locks, pikes with bamboo shafts from 14 to 18 feet in length, which they throw at a distance like javelins, also, shorter ones with shafts of solid wood; the pike part being similar to the blade of a dirk,[16] and made sharp on both edges, those they use when at close quarters, for which they also use short swords, about eighteen inches in length (figure 8.3). Like the guns of the Chinese forts and junks, those of the Ladrones are mounted on carriages without trucks, having neither breechings nor tackles, . . . and never pointed fore and aft, they are obliged (when making an attack)

---

16. A dirk was a long-bladed thrusting dagger that European naval officers used as a boarding weapon and in hand-to-hand combat.

3. Piracy in the Mid-Qing Dynasty (1775–1810)

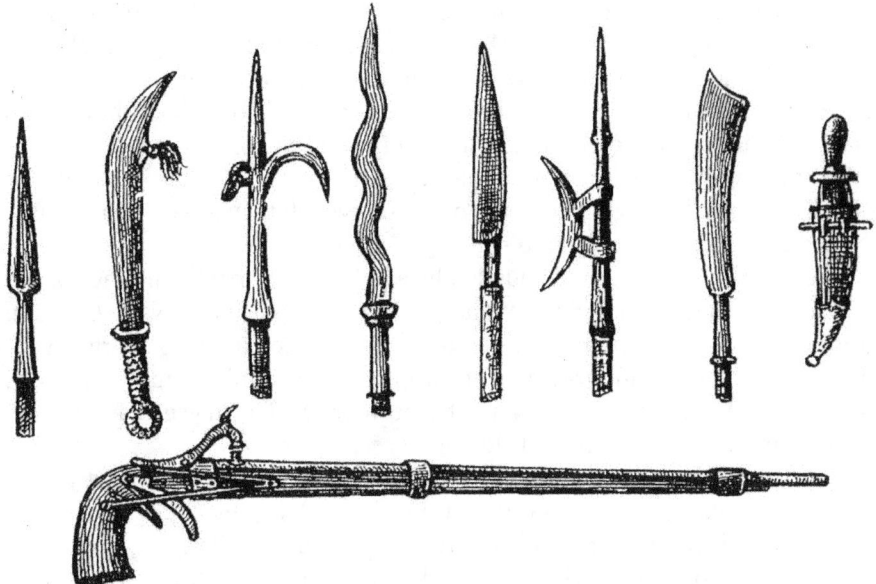

Figure 8.3. Weapons of Chinese Pirates, Late Nineteenth Century.

to bear off in order to bring the guns to bear on the object, a man standing by to fire when having good aim. The guns are previously elevated or depressed according to the distance, having in this manner discharged their broadside they haul off to reload.

The number of men in each junk is generally considerable for its size, the largest have upward of one hundred men, and the smallest seldom ever less than thirty, I have averaged the whole at fifty men, and the number of junks at five hundred, neither of which suppositions, exceeds the truth. The total number of those pirates [in the Red Banner Fleet] amount to twenty-five thousand men.

Independent of the fore above-mentioned, several vessels have belonging to them, a row boat, mounting from six to ten wall pieces and swivels,[17] also well armed with boarding pikes and swords, and according to their size, carry from eighteen to thirty-six men; these are rigged with one or two masts, and sail like the Chinese boats, and pull from fourteen to twenty oars, they are more particularly employed in going close along shore at nights, plundering and desolating villages, that do not pay them tribute, and carrying off such of

---

17. Wall pieces were a type of smoothbore firearm or large matchlock referred to as gingals in China. Swivels or swivel guns were types of small cannons, mounted on a swiveling stand that allowed a wide arc of movement. Both weapons were used extensively in Asia mainly in naval combat as short-range antipersonnel ordnance.

the inhabitants as fall into their hands; they chiefly infest the mouths of the rivers, Maccoa [Macau], and such places as have small trading vessels; . . . though they [that is, pirates] are sometimes absent two or three days, lying at anchor during the day, so as not to be seen by those on whom they intend making their depredations. At dusk they sally forth and plunder whatever may fall in their way. Sometimes when unsuccessful they go on the sides and tops of hills, and on perceiving any boat or vessel, which they are able to capture, immediately give chace [sic] to it.

The Chinese Ladrones are abundantly supplied with shot from Maccoa and Whampoo [that is, Huangpu or Whampoa]; stolen I presume, by the Chinese, from the forts and shipping at those places. . . . When at close quarters they frequently use nails, the fragments of iron pots, etc., which supply the place of grape and cannister [sic] shot. The powder is of Chinese manufacture, which they readily procure at different places.

Their numbers are kept up and even considerably augmented, partly such of their captives as are unable to ransom themselves; and by Chinese who volunteer their services daily from different parts of the coast. . . . I have frequently seen from five to ten come at one time, and on one occasion upward of thirty, some of these were, doubtless, vagabonds, induced by poverty and idleness, to embrace this criminal mode of life, but many were men of decent appearance, and some of whom brought money with them. The only reason I heard them assign for their conduct was that the Mandarins [officials] of their district were unjust and they came to avoid their oppression. These men are at liberty to leave the Ladrones when they think proper; as several went away after being only a month with them. At one time they used to come and go, in such quick succession, that the chief I was with refused to allow any to join them, unless they agreed to remain eight or nine months, at the expiration of which time they were at liberty to go or remain. But greater numbers of them remain four years, and it is on them that the command of their junks chiefly devolve. . . .

With respect to the women who fall into their hands, the handsomest are reserved by them for wives and concubines; the chiefs frequently have three or more, the others seldom more than one. And having once made choice of a wife, they are obliged to be constant to her. No promiscuous intercourse being allowed among them, but the greater part of the crew are satisfied without them.[18] A few are ransomed and those that possess no beauty are turned on shore. Children taken, are generally brought up among them as servants etc.[19]

. . .

---

18. Turner here implies homosexual relationships, which, in the absence of females, were apparently common aboard pirate ships.

19. In fact, among kidnapped boys, those not ransomed were usually raised among the pirates and later joined their ranks, as was the case of the pirate chieftain Zhang Bao.

When a vessel is taken and the owners do not ransom her (which is sometimes done) both vessel and cargo are destroyed, if not wanted by the captors, but in general the best vessels are made use of and armed as Ladrones, the cargo when of use to them is distributed to the ships of the squadron, and it is in this way they are partly supplied with necessaries. Whatever monies is found in their prizes is brought to the commander of the squadron, as also the sums received for ransom of prisoners and goods. Of this a trifle is given to the immediate captors, part of which is reserved to purchase provisions and other necessaries, for the use of the squadron. And a certain proportion, I know not what, is paid to the chief of the division.[20] From this source and that of the tributes formerly mentioned, there is generally a large quantity of specie [that is, coined money] on board of their vessels, I have been told from fifty to one hundred thousand dollars [kept in their common fund]. Out of this they supply such squadrons as have been unsuccessful in their cruizes [sic]. The Ladrones find not the least difficulty in procuring provisions and all other necessaries on the coast, for which they pay honorably. The fishermen are generally the bearer of those supplies.

Source: Turner 1814, 28–42.

DOC. 34. MEMORIAL ON THE DESTRUCTION OF THE PIRATE BASE ON WEIZHOU ISLAND, 1808

For centuries Weizhou Island in the Gulf of Tonkin served as a major pirate base, home for illegal squatters, and anchorage for fishing fleets. The following excerpt comes from a lengthy memorial written on July 18, 1808, by Wu Xiongguang, the governor-general of Guangdong and Guangxi provinces. The Jiaqing emperor had specifically tasked Wu to conduct an aggressive military campaign against the pirates in Guangdong. This memorial reported to the emperor the results of that action in the Gulf of Tonkin, where naval forces captured more than five hundred pirates and killed as many in battle. Significantly, during this campaign soldiers destroyed the pirate base on Weizhou Island and took 423 prisoners, including pirates, their family members, and illegal squatters and traders. Most of these pirates were members of Wushi Er's Blue Banner fleet. While some of the prisoners in this case testified that they had voluntarily become pirates, others claimed that they had been kidnapped before joining gangs. This document is also important for what it tells us about how the Qing government differentiated the criminal culpability of pirates based on the degree of involvement in acts of piracy.

---

20. In general, pirate bosses received two shares and ordinary pirates one share of the loot.

On the 1st day of the 3rd lunar month [March 27, 1808] Chen Menghu again personally led soldiers and runners from the Lianzhou, Hepu, and Suixi battalions to Weizhou Island, where they apprehended the deserter Chen Wuzhao, the [sea] bandit Lu Shanghuan, and others, a total of 423 men, women, and children. They also torched the straw huts on the island and [during their search for pirates] they discovered the coffin of Wushi Er's father, which they reduced to ashes.[21] All of the prisoners were forwarded to Lianzhou Prefecture for interrogation.

The total number of prisoners [from the campaigns at sea and on Weizhou Island] came to 510. Because of so many prisoners I [that is, Wu Xiongguang] thought it impractical to forward them all to the provincial capital [Canton] for trial. Among them there are those who acted as bandits and therefore should be treated harshly according to the [full extent of] the law, but there are others who are foolish people who were coerced into helping the pirates and should be treated accordingly. . . . [Based on the preliminary investigation in Lianzhou officials designated 97 prisoners as dangerous criminals and had them forwarded to Canton for trial, while 406 less serious offenders remained in Lianzhou for investigation. Of the remaining prisoners six died in jail and one escaped.]

[At trial in Canton] after being harshly questioned [under torture], the criminal Chen Wuzhao, who is a native of Dongguan [a county near Canton], confessed that he originally served as a sergeant in the Leizhou battalion. [Later] fearing punishment for negligence in his investigation of secret society bandits Lin Tianshen and others, he deserted and joined Wushi Er's band, sharing in the pirate's booty.

Lu Derong . . . and ten other criminals, natives of Danzhou, Shunde, Guishan, Xinhui, and Panyu [all in Guangdong], confessed that they had been abducted at sea by pirates and had afterward either voluntarily joined or had been coerced to join [Wushi Er's band]. They have committed numerous robberies and kidnappings at sea and were apprehended aboard their [pirate] vessels. Lu Shanghuan . . . and sixteen other criminals, who were seized on Weizhou Island, confessed that they had joined the pirates after being abducted. Some have committed one or two robberies and kidnappings, others have committed three or four robberies and kidnappings, while others have committed six or seven robberies and kidnappings. The two criminals Fang Meimu and Hu Linshou confessed that they had been kidnapped by pirates and [afterward] had twice helped them receive and handle booty. The criminal Chen Sheng confessed that he had once clandestinely transported and

---

21. It was common practice for officials to order the desecration of graves of parents and grandparents of rebel and bandit chieftains in order to destroy the geomantic forces (*fengshui*) believed to protect family members.

sold rice, vegetables, melons, and raw opium to pirates. The criminal Zong Guangsheng confessed that he once sold masts, wood, iron, nails, and other items to pirates.

Li Pangui . . . and sixty-three other criminals confessed that they had been kidnapped and forced to help pirates receive and handle booty once, or had once acted on the pirate boss's behalf as go-betweens to collect ransom money, or had one or more times covertly transported and sold vegetables and other provisions to pirates aboard their vessels. [For their help they all received a share of the spoils.]

[The other 406 prisoners remained in Lianzhou for questioning.] According to Circuit Attendant Yang Wei's investigation, Li Chengtai and another 127 criminals had been abducted by pirates and forced to work for them [at various menial chores, such as cooking and washing clothes]; according to evidence, Chen Bingyi and another 149 individuals had illegally planted crops on Weizhou Island; Long Yalai and another 71 individuals, including women and children, had gone to Weizhou Island where they eked out a living as hired laborers and beggars. None of them were bandits or had colluded with pirates.

According to the evidence, Huang Yasan and another forty-one individuals had been abducted and held prisoners [by the pirates on the island. These also included] Mrs. Chen, whose maiden name is Ye, and thirteen other women who are the wives and relatives of pirates [who had settled on Weizhou Island]. . . .

After completing the investigation I [that is, Wu Xiongguang] immediately requested the summary execution by royal mandate . . . of said criminal Chen Wuzhao, whose sentence of death by slicing was thereupon carried out at the [execution grounds in the] market.[22] Afterward his severed head was publicly displayed on the coast [where he had committed his crimes] to serve as a warning to others. As for Wen Weixing, Chen Xing, and Zhu Ruichao, who had died of illnesses in custody, their corpses were likewise desecrated in accordance with the law. [Lu Shanghuan, Lu Derong, and another twenty-seven pirates were also summarily beheaded at this time.]

[The following prisoners all received provisional sentences from Wu Xiongguang.][23] Chen Sheng, who clandestinely sold rice and other items to pirates at sea, should be sentenced to immediate strangulation according to

---

22. Normally executions were the prerogative of the emperor and could take months before they were actually carried out. To expedite punishment the emperor allowed certain high-ranking civil and military officials to summarily execute convicted rebels and pirates. Death by slicing, also called lingering death, was the most severe form of capital punishment in imperial China. These executions were carried out in Canton.

23. All cases involving sentences of exile and capital punishment (excepting summary executions) had to be reviewed by the high courts in Beijing and approved by the emperor before being carried out. Provincial officials could only decide in cases having penalties of penal servitude and floggings.

the substatute on wicked scoundrels who aid and supply pirates with rice and other staples. Zong Guangsheng, who was greedy to make profits by selling masts, wood, iron, nails, etc. to pirates, should be sentenced to strangulation after the assizes according to the substatute on coastal merchants who sell iron and other such provisions to pirates; and although he testified that he is [his family's] sole representative and was needed to care for his elderly kinfolk,[24] because his crimes of aiding pirates are too serious his punishment should not be reduced on this account.

Li Pangui and another forty-two criminals, who were adjudged to have been kidnapped and coerced into helping the pirates receive and handle booty once, should be sentenced to exile in Heilongjiang [Manchuria] . . . as [military] slaves. [Among these criminals] Hou Huanying . . . and four others testified to be sole representatives or the only sons of widows, but because their crimes of helping pirates handle their booty are too serious their punishments should not be reduced. Yang Xiongyu and nineteen other criminals only had carried melons and vegetables [one or more times] to sell to pirates aboard their ships. Because there are no laws to punish such specific crimes, Yang Xiongyu and the others should be adjudged by analogy according to the aforementioned substatute on selling rice to pirates, but with the punishment reduced by one degree [because the crime of selling vegetables was considered less serious than selling rice to pirates]. . . . Nonetheless, because at this time in Guangdong [officials] are making every effort to prosecute criminals who aided pirates and because the said criminals had the audacity to sell vegetables and other items to pirates, their crimes are especially horrendous; therefore, their punishment should be increased to exile to Heilongjiang as [military] slaves. [Although] Li Kezheng testified that he is the sole representative, his sentence should not be reduced; and even though Huang Chaoju is over seventy years old (*sui*), he should not be allowed to redeem his sentence with a monetary payment. The criminal Zhu Yuxi, who was adjudged to have collected ransom payments for pirates for which he received payment for his services, should be sentenced with one hundred blows of the heavy bamboo and exile of 3,000 *li*, according to the substatute on gangsters who extort ransoms for others; but because his crime is more serious [than ordinary extortion], his sentence should be changed to exile to Heilongjiang as a [military] slave. In each case the prisoners also were tattooed [with the names of their crimes] in accordance with the law.

[In the following cases sentences were carried out in Lianzhou prefecture.] Li Chengtai and another 127 criminals, who were adjudged to have been abducted and coerced to serve the pirates, were all sentenced to floggings

---

24. According to law, in ordinary cases involving only sons of elderly parents their sentences were commuted so that they could care for their parents. A similar law applied to the only sons of widows.

of one hundred blows of the heavy bamboo and three years' penal servitude. However, because Li Chengtai . . . [and six others] were underage, they are to be allowed to redeem their penalties with monetary payments. Luo Wancai . . . [and five others], who testified that they were either sole representatives or the sons of widows, were sent back to their respective home districts for further investigation.

Chen Bingyi and another 149 individuals, who were adjudged to not be bandits or to have aided the pirates, but to have [only] illegally gone to [Weizhou] Island to open up lands and plant crops. [Because their case is] analogous to those poor Cantonese who [clandestinely] go into the mountains to put up huts and plant hemp and indigo, but do not report this to the authorities, . . . they have been adjudicated in accordance with the statue on illegally cultivating land of others . . . and have been sentenced variously with floggings of thirty to fifty blows of the light bamboo, reduced to twenty blows, . . . and returned to their home counties where they have been placed under the strict supervision of the local constabulary to assure that they will not cause any further trouble.

As for Long Yalai and the [other] seventy-one men, women, and children who were on Weizhou Island as laborers and beggars, but who had not put up any huts, they are not guilty of any crimes. They were all sent back home and released. As for Huang Yasan and the other forty-one people who Circuit Intendent Yang Wei adjudged to have been kidnapped and held prisoners by pirates, together with Mrs. Chen and the other wives of pirates, they were all returned home and released.

There is no need to deliberate any further.

Source: *Gongzhongdang*, dated 25th day, 5th intercalary month, 13th year of the Jiaqing reign (July 18, 1808). Translation by the author.

DOC. 35. ZHANG BAO AND THE SEA GODDESS NAMED THE THIRD OLD LADY

Like other sailors and fishers, pirates also worshipped any number of sea deities, such as the Empress of Heaven (Tianhou) or, as she was known more colloquially, Maternal Ancestor (Mazu). Zhang Bao, in particular, worshipped a little-known deity called the Third Old Lady (Sanpo) at her temple on the Huizhou coast, not too distant from present-day Hong Kong. Although Yuan Yonglun does not mention this in his account, the Sanpo cult was especially vibrant in the Gulf of Tonkin among fishers, smugglers, and pirates since at least the fifteenth century. In fact, it was these same groups of seafarers who later brought Sanpo to the Pearl River Delta and Huizhou coast, probably in the late eighteenth century. Zhang Bao, like other pirate chiefs, always consulted their deities to obtain their oracles before starting any campaigns as well as to ask for their blessings and protection. Although we have little direct information concerning the religious beliefs of pirates, we can assume that they would have been little different from other seafarers. The following two episodes, which were recorded by Yuan Yonglun, provide a rare glimpse into Zhang Bao's religious practices (figure 8.4).

On the Huizhou coast [of Guangdong] there is a temple dedicated to the sea goddess named Sanpo, who is said to be very efficacious. Whenever the pirate ships pass her temple they always disembark to worship Sanpo, for to not do so would mean certain disaster on their piratical ventures. One day [in 1807] when each of the [pirate] commanders gathered to worship [in her temple], they planned to take away her statue to place on one of their boats so they could conveniently beseech her instructions both day and night. [However] her statue could not be budged. Only Zhang Bao was able to lift the statue and bring it back to his ship. . . . Whenever they set off on raids, the pirates first earnestly prayed to their goddess to decide [on their actions and to keep them out of harm's way]. Whatever she predicted always proved to be true. . . .

[During the 10th lunar month of 1809], when the pirates had assembled off Lantau Island [near Hong Kong], our navy planned to use fireboats to attack. On the 20th there was a strong northerly wind and our commander made ready twenty fireboats to attack Dongyong where the pirates had anchored. That place, however, was protected by mountains from the wind and as a consequence, when our warships approached [on the next morning], two were destroyed by our own fireboats. . . . Nonetheless, our commander ordered the attack to continue and when more than three hundred pirates were killed, Zhang Bao became apprehensive and implored Sanpo for an oracle. The oracle predicted "to attack would be inauspicious, but to head to the east would be auspicious." Zhang Bao then asked whether or not to act on the following day, and the oracle replied that it would be auspicious. He repeated the request three times and each time the answer was the same. On the 22nd day Zhang Bao's fleet weighed anchor and with a strong southerly wind broke the blockade and escaped to the outer ocean.

Source: Yuan Yonglun 1830, 1:6b–7a, 2:5b–7a. Translation by the author.

惠州有廟曰三婆神者在海旁數著靈異，賊舟過必虔祀稍不盡誠禍咎立至賊事之甚謹。一日各頭領齋詣羅拜欲捧其像以歸俾朝夕求問皆持之不動張保一扶而起遂奉以歸舟。如有風送到船者屺往來出沒搶却打仗皆取決於神每有祈禱休咎悉驗。

Figure 8.4. An Account of Zhang Bao and the Third Old Lady.

DOC. 36. RICHARD GLASSPOOLE'S REMARKS ON MANNERS AND CUSTOMS OF THE LADRONES, 1809

Richard Glasspoole was returning to his ship, the British East India Company's Marquis of Ely, *when members of the Red Banner Fleet kidnapped him near Macau on September 21, 1809. He remained a prisoner for more than two months, during which time he was able to observe their treatment of women and daily habits. He was finally released after a huge ransom of $4,200, two bales of superfine cloth, two chests of opium, two casks of gunpowder, and a telescope was paid to his captors.*

At the period of my captivity [in 1809] they [that is, the pirates in Guangdong] were supposed to amount to near seventy thousand men, eight hundred large vessels, and nearly a thousand small ones, including row-boats. They were divided into five squadrons,[25] distinguished by different coloured flags; each squadron commanded by an admiral or chief. . . .

The Ladrones have no settled residence on shore, but live constantly in their vessels. The after-part is appropriated to the captain and his wives; he generally has five or six. With respect to conjugal rights they are religiously strict; no person is allowed to have a woman on board, unless married to her according to their laws. Every man is allowed a small berth, about four feet square, where he stows with his wife and family.[26]

From the number of souls crowded in so small a space, it must naturally be supposed they are horridly dirty, which is evidently the case, and their vessels swarm with all kinds of vermin. Rats in particular, which they encourage to breed, and eat them as great delicacies;[27] in fact, there are very few creatures they will not eat. During our captivity we lived three weeks on caterpillars boiled with rice. They are much addicted to gambling, and spend all their leisure hours at cards and smoking opium.

Source: Glasspoole 1831, 127–28.

---

25. Actually there were at this time six pirate squadrons or fleets organized into a loose confederation in Guangdong.

26. While this space appears quite small, it was not unusual. On British sailing vessels in the early nineteenth century, typically passengers were berthed in two-by-six-foot compartments, and sailors slept in cramped quarters below deck in the forecastle in hammocks and stowed their personal belongs and any trade goods they had acquired during the voyage in one or several sea chests.

27. Among the Cantonese rats were a common food. Whereas the wealthy ate a particular sort of rat, which was large and of a whitish color, the poor ate wild rats whenever they could be caught.

DOC. 37. OFFICIAL REPORTS ON THE PIRATE RAID INTO THE PEARL RIVER DELTA IN 1809

Following a severe famine in Guangdong, in the summer and fall of 1809 Zheng Yi Sao, Zhang Bao, and Guo Podai led their fleets of pirates deep into the Pearl River Delta, even reaching as far as the suburbs of Canton. The sudden appearance of large gangs of pirates just outside the provincial capital caused panic among the populace and officials, who hurriedly prepared the city's defenses. Throughout that summer and autumn Zhang Bao and his cohorts continued their raids, gathering food and other provisions, and collecting "tribute" from trading and salt junks, villages, and market towns along the coast and in the delta. At the same time other pirate leaders conducted raids along the coasts in southwestern Guangdong and Gulf of Tonkin, in search for booty, food, and supplies. Here are excerpts from two documents written in 1809 by high-ranking provincial officials in Guangdong. The first document, dated September 13, 1809, is a proclamation written by Prefect Ying of Guangzhou.

Prefect Ying of Guangzhou proclaims: The linguists[28] Yang Chao and others have been informed on the [following] matter: Let it be known that the ocean bandit, Ya Bao Zai [that is, Zhang Bao], etc., and his hideous band of outlaws have been increasing daily. Recently, because of difficulties in getting supplies of food, they began to enter the inner rivers at Weijia and Yaimen [at the entrance to the West River] in Xiangshan and Xinhui counties. . . . At Humen [that is, Bogue] they continue to rove about to pillage [towns and villages]. I have gathered several boats and soldiers nearby to await the chance to catch them. . . . According to reports from the Hong merchants, currently at the foot of Whampoa anchorage there is a foreign ship equipped with cannons and prepared to assist [us]. . . . I hereupon report to [Governor-General Bailing] that the Hong merchants leased the foreign ship, as well as a contingent of able-bodied sailors to set out to sea to engage and capture the pirates.[29] . . . However, because I am afraid that these foreigners are unfamiliar with the surroundings of our water channels . . . I order the linguists to immediately and personally take two compradors[30] and two river guides, and

---

28. Linguists were more than translators. They were licensed professionals who were essential in helping foreign merchants negotiate daily transactions, while at the same time working with Chinese officials to monitor foreigners in Canton.

29. The Hong merchants formed a guild of Chinese merchants who were sanctioned by the Qing government to monopolize foreign trade at Canton. The ship was undoubtedly the 250-ton British country ship *Mercury*, which we know was leased by the Hong merchants at the request of the Guangzhou prefect in August 1809. It was equipped with twenty cannons and fifty American volunteers, who joined the imperial fleet in battles with pirates between Lintin and Lantau islands in late summer.

30. Compradors were officially licensed Chinese provision purveyors for the foreign ships and factories in Canton.

together with the foreign ship to set out to blockade [the entrance to the river] and to apprehend pirates. . . .

The following document is taken from a memorial written by Governor-General Bailing to the Jiaqing emperor, dated October 11, 1809.

Ocean bandits come and go everywhere on the high seas and now they even dare to plunder inland villages [in the Pearl River Delta]. To do so they must have local bandits acting as their guides and supplying them with rice and provisions. . . . According to a report from the magistrate of Shunde County, soldiers of the Huizhou Brigade captured a bandit guide named He Zongpei and nine receivers, who were forwarded to the prefect of Huizhou for initial questioning. . . . According to He Zongpei's confession he is from Shunde and is a close friend of the [sea] bandit Chen Bosheng, who is a member of Guo Podai's band. Twice at Chen's request, He bought liquor, rice, and weapons for the pirates, which he transported to their ships. He also became well acquainted with the pirate chief Guo Podai. . . . On the 4th and 5th days of the 7th lunar month in the 14th year of the Jiaqing reign [August 14–15, 1809], Guo and his band entered the inland river in Shunde County to raid and pillage. Because He cherished resentment for one of his clansmen, He Yishao, who had not loaned him money, He Zongpei decided to guide the pirates to [his clansman's] village to plunder and to extort money. However [seeing the pirates coming] He Yishao ran off and hid. The pirates then attempted to extort his father and son, but just at that time a military patrol came along and captured He Zongpei. . . . [At his trial in Canton, although] He Zongpei was sentenced to beheading, according to a law on wicked coastal people who collude with pirates to allow them to pillage villages, [because his crimes were so serious] instead he was summarily executed right after trial and his head was publicly displayed in the area where he committed his crimes. . . .

Sources: *Foreign Office Records* (FO 1048.9.9), proclamation dated 4th day, 8th lunar month, 14th year of the Jiaqing reign (September 13, 1809); *Gongzhongdang*, dated 3rd day, 9th lunar month, 14th year of Jiaqing reign (October 11, 1809). Translation by the author.

DOC. 38. RICHARD GLASSPOOLE'S EYEWITNESS ACCOUNT OF THE PIRATE RAID INTO THE PEARL RIVER DELTA, 1809

The following excerpt is Richard Glasspoole's exceptionally detailed and valuable firsthand account of the pirate raid into the Pearl River Delta in the autumn of 1809, at a time when he was being held prisoner by Zhang Bao's gang. Most of his account is corroborated by other Chinese documents.

About nine o'clock [at night, September 21, 1809,] a boat came and hailed the chief's vessel; he immediately hoisted his mainsail, and the fleet weighed apparently in great confusion. They worked to windward all night and part of the next day, and anchored about one o'clock in a bay under the island of Lantow,[31] where the head admiral of Ladrones [that is, Zhang Bao] was lying at anchor, with about two hundred vessels and a Portuguese brig they had captured a few days before, and murdered the captain and part of the crew. . . .

Tuesday the 25th, at day-light in the morning, the fleet, amounting to about five hundred sail of different sizes, weighed, to proceed on their intended cruize up the rivers, to levy contributions on the towns and villages. . . .

Wednesday the 26th, . . . [a]bout noon we entered a river to the westward of the Bogue, three or four miles from the entrance [of the Pearl River]. We passed a large town situated on the side of a beautiful hill, which is tributary to the Ladrones; the inhabitants saluted them with songs as they passed. The fleet now divided into two squadrons [the red and the black][32] and sailed up different branches of the river. At midnight the division we were in anchored close to an immense hill, on the top of which a number of fires were burning, which at day-light I perceived proceeded from a Chinese [military] camp. At the back of the hill was a most beautiful town, surrounded by water, and embellished with groves of orange-trees. The chop-house [that is, customhouse][33] and a few cottages were immediately plundered, and burnt down; most of the inhabitants, however, escaped to the camp. The Ladrones now prepared to attack the town with a formidable force, collected in row-boats from the different vessels. They sent a messenger to the town, demanding a tribute of ten thousand dollars annually, saying, if these terms were not complied with, they would land, destroy the town, and murder all the inhabitants. . . . The inhabitants agreed to pay six thousand dollars, which they were to collect by the time of our return down the river. . . .

October the 1st, the fleet weighed in the night, . . . and anchored very quietly before a town surrounded by a thick wood. Early in the morning the Ladrones assembled in row-boats, and landed; then gave a shout, and rushed into the town, sword in hand. The inhabitants fled to the adjacent hills, in

---

31. Lantow or Lantau, located near the mouth of the Pearl River, is the largest island belonging to Hong Kong. In the past, this and several nearby islands were referred to by Western sailors as the Ladrones or Pirate Islands because they had served as lairs where pirates settled their families, conducted trade, and launched raids.

32. The red and black banner fleets were the two most powerful fleets in the Guangdong pirate confederation, the former commanded by Zheng Yi Sao and Zhang Bao and the latter by Guo Podai.

33. In pidgin English, the trade language spoken at Canton to facilitate communication between Chinese and Western merchants, there was an indiscriminate use of the word *chop*, in this case meaning a stamp or seal placed on documents, such as a custom's declaration. Thus a chop-house referred to a customs station. The plundered chop-house was likely the Zini customhouse, only sixteen miles from Canton, which pirates held for several months using it as a headquarters for collecting tribute and ransom payments, as well as a staging area for further raids.

numbers apparently superior to the Ladrones. . . . The old and the sick, who were unable to fly, or to make resistance, were either made prisoners or most inhumanly butchered! The boats continued passing and repassing from the junks to the shore, in quick succession, laden with booty, and the men besmeared with blood! Two hundred and fifty women, and several children, were made prisoners, and sent on board different vessels. . . . Twenty of these poor women were sent on board the vessel I was in; they were hauled on board by the hair, and treated in a most savage manner. When the chief came on board, he questioned them respecting the circumstances of their friends, and demanded ransoms accordingly, from six thousand to six hundred dollars each. . . . The fleet remained here three days, negotiating for the ransom of the prisoners, and plundering the fish-tanks and gardens.[34] . . .

October the 5th, the fleet proceeded up another branch of the river, stopping at several small villages to receive tribute, which was generally paid in [silver] dollars, sugar and rice, with a few large pigs roasted whole, as presents for their joss [that is, the idol or deity they worship].[35] Every person on being ransomed is obliged to present him with a pig, or some fowls, which the priest[36] offers him with prayers; it remains before him a few hours, and is then divided amongst the crew. Nothing particular occurred 'till the 10th, except frequent skirmishes on shore between small parties of Ladrones and Chinese soldiers. They frequently obliged my men to go on shore, and fight with the muskets we had when taken, which did great execution, the Chinese principally using bows and arrows. They have matchlocks, but use them very unskillfully. . . .

On the 17th, the fleet anchored abreast four mud batteries, which defended a town. . . . The Ladrones remained perfectly quiet for two days. On the third day the forts commenced a brisk fire for several hours: the Ladrones did not return a single shot, but weighed in the night and dropped down the river. The reasons they gave for not attacking the town, or returning the fire, were, that Joss [likely Sanpo or some other deity] had not promised them success. They are very superstitious, and consult their idol on all occasions. If his omens are good, they will undertake the most daring enterprizes.

The fleet now anchored opposite the ruins of the town where the women had been made prisoners. Here we remained five or six days, during which time about an hundred of the women were ransomed; the remainder were

---

34. The Pearl River Delta had a long-established and famous aquaculture industry; the gardens referred to the many fruit orchids, which were also well established in the delta. Both enterprises played substantial roles in making the delta one of the richest areas in China.

35. Joss was a corruption of the Portuguese word *Dias* or God.

36. Aboard nearly every Chinese ship, including pirate ships, was a religious specialist who was a member of the crew and who had the daily job of burning incense and making offerings to the deities while at sea. Glasspoole refers to this person as the priest.

offered for sale amongst the Ladrones, for forty dollars each. The woman is considered the lawful wife of the purchaser, who would be put to death if he discarded her. Several of them leaped over-board and drowned themselves, rather than submit to such infamous degradation.

The fleet then weighed and made sail down the river, to receive the ransom from the town before-mentioned. As we passed the hill, they fired several shots at us, but without effect. The Ladrones were much exasperated, and determined to revenge themselves; they dropped out of reach of their shot, and anchored. Every junk sent about a hundred men each on shore, to cut paddy,[37] and destroy their orange-groves, which was most effectually performed for several miles down the river. During our stay here, they received information of nine boats lying up a creek, laden with paddy; boats were immediately dispatched after them.

Next morning these boats were brought to the fleet; ten or twelve men were taken in them. As these had made no resistance, the chief said he would allow them to become Ladrones, if they agreed to take the usual oaths before the Joss. Three or four of them refused to comply, for which they were punished in the following cruel manner; their hands were tied behind their back, a rope from the mast-head rove through their arms, and hoisted three or four feet from the deck, and five or six men flogged them with three rattans twisted together 'till they were apparently dead; then hoisted them up to the mast-head, and left them hanging nearly an hour, then lowered them down, and repeated the punishment, 'till they died or complied with the oath.

October the 20th, in the night, an express-boat came with the information that a large mandarin [that is, government] fleet was proceeding up the river to attack us. The chief immediately weighed, with fifty of the largest vessels, and sailed down the river to meet them. About one in the morning they commenced a heavy fire 'till day-light. . . . Two or three hours afterwards the chief returned with three captured vessels in tow, having sunk two, and eighty-three sail made their escape. The admiral of the mandarins[38] blew his vessel up, by throwing a lighted match into the magazine as the Ladrones were boarding her; she ran on shore, and they succeeded in getting twenty of her guns. . . .

On the first of November, the fleet sailed up a narrow river, and anchored at night within two miles of a town called Little Whampoa. In front of it was a small fort, and several mandarin vessels lying in the harbour. The chief sent the interpreter to me, saying, I must order my men to make cartridges and clean their muskets, ready to go on shore in the morning. . . . A few hours afterwards he sent to me again, saying, that if myself and the quarter-master

---

37. Paddy refers to unhusked rice either growing in the field or already harvested.
38. The admiral refers to Provincial Commander Sun Quanmou. In fact, it was one of his subordinates who blew up his own warship, while Sun escaped to safety.

would assist them at the great guns, that if also the rest of the men went on shore and succeeded in taking the place, he would then take the money offered for our ransom, and give them twenty dollars for every Chinaman's head they cut off. To these proposals we cheerfully acceded, in hopes of facilitating our deliverance.

Early in the morning the forces intended for landing were assembled in row-boats, amounting in the whole to three or four thousand men. The largest vessels weighed, and hauled in shore, to cover the landing of the forces, and attack the fort and mandarin-vessels. About nine o'clock the action commenced, and continued with great spirit for nearly an hour, when the walls of the fort gave way, and the men retreated in the greatest confusion. . . . The mandarin vessels still continued firing, having blocked up the entrance of the harbour to prevent the Ladrone boats entering. At this the Ladrones were much exasperated, and about three hundred of them swam on shore, with a short sword lashed close under each arm; they then ran along the banks of the river 'till they came abreast of the vessels, and then swam off again and boarded them. The Chinese thus attacked, leaped over-board, and endeavoured to reach the opposite shore; the Ladrones followed, and cut the greater number of them to pieces in the water. They next towed the vessels out of the harbour, and attacked the town with increased fury. The inhabitants fought about a quarter of an hour, and then retreated to an adjacent hill, from which they were soon driven with great slaughter. . . .

I must not omit to mention a most horrid (though ludicrous) circumstance which happened at this place. The Ladrones were paid by their chief ten dollars for every Chinaman's head they produced. One of my men turning the corner of a street was met by a Ladrone running furiously after a Chinese; he had a drawn sword in his hand, and two Chinaman's heads which he had cut off, tied by their tails,[39] and slung round his neck. I was witness myself to some of them producing five or six to obtain payment!!! . . .

Source: Glasspoole 1831, 107–19.

DOC. 39. ZHANG BAO'S PETITION TO SURRENDER, 1810

There is some debate about whether or not Zhang Bao, or rather one of his scribes, actually composed this petition to surrender. Some scholars have suggested that Governor-General Bailing wrote it on behalf of the pirates in order to justify his pacification policy. Nonetheless, it does fairly represent

---

39. Here tails refer to pigtails or queues, a hairstyle required to be worn by male subjects of Qing China as a sign of submission.

the sentiments of many pirates at that time—that they were victims of circumstances beyond their control and that they acted in the same manner as the brave heroes of the past. Written during the height of the pirate disturbances in the Pearl River Delta and at the time of a severe famine in Guangdong, the petitioner explains that the pirates were poor and hungry and had no choice but to rob if they were to survive. Zheng Yi Sao and Zhang Bao, in fact, surrendered in April 1810 with more than seventeen thousand followers, including men, women, and children.

It is my humble opinion that the enterprises of heroes have different origins. So do the hearts of officials, for there are differences of benevolence and tolerance. Therefore, the bandits of Mount Liang,[40] who thrice plundered cities, were graciously pardoned and eventually made pillars of the state. The bandits of Wagang,[41] who repeatedly resisted the imperial soldiers, not only received no death penalties but also became cornerstones of the empire. Other examples are Kong Ming, captured by Meng Huo seven times; Guan Gong thrice set Cao Cao free;[42] Ma Yuan[43] never pursued a desperate enemy; and Yue Fei[44] never killed those who willingly submitted. Therefore chivalrous heroes from the four seas[45] pledged their allegiances and services, and among the heroes of the world, those from afar came forward and those nearby rejoiced. Although no single track runs through all these events, in essence each of these stories share the same vision.

Today we, your humble petitioners, live in a prosperous age. Originally we were meek and obedient subjects, but we became [sea] bandits [for many reasons]. Because some of us were not careful in choosing friends we thus fell into [the marshes of] Huanfu.[46] Others were unable to make a living or were kidnapped and forced into [the realm of] rivers and lakes [that is, join the pirates]. Still others, because of having been accused of a crime, joined this watery world to escape punishment or to seek revenge. At first there

---

40. The mountain lair of the 108 bandit-heroes in the novel *Suihu Zhuan* (*Water Margin*).
41. A bandit-infested marshland in Henan province in the Sui dynasty (581–618) and the subject of many popular legends.
42. These men were all heroes during the turbulent Three Kingdoms period (220–280). Kong Ming, which was another name of Zhuge Liang, and Guan Gong, or Guan Yu, served Liu Bei, one of the three most powerful rulers. Cao Cao was another powerful ruler. Meng Huo was one of the foreign leaders who threatened China at this time. Their legends were made famous in the novel *Sanguo yanyi* (*Romance of the Three Kingdoms*).
43. The heroic general of the Later Han dynasty (25–220) who reconquered southern China and northern Vietnam.
44. Another famous general in the early Southern Song dynasty (1127–1279), who became a tragic hero who fell victim to court intrigues that ultimately cost him his life in 1141. Ever since he has been regarded as one of China's greatest patriots.
45. The "four seas" was used metaphorically for the boundaries of ancient China, each representing one of the four cardinal directions.
46. Another bandit-infested marshland in Henan in northern China; thus the implied meaning is to join the bandits.

were only a few of us in a band, but later we increased to thousands and tens of thousands. Moreover, because of the successive famines [in recent years], people had nothing with which to maintain their livelihoods, and as days and months passed more and more of us had to take extraordinary measures to endure. Had we not resorted to robbery we could not have survived. Had we not resisted our ill fate, we would have perished. Therefore, we violated the imperial laws and wrecked trade. This was unavoidable.

Yet, once we left our native villages, there were none among us who did not yearn for our families. Drifting along with wind and tide, every day we were deeply troubled by our rootless lives. If we ran into government patrols, their cannons and arrows struck terror in our hearts. If we met a display of power by the god He Bo,[47] the great tempests and towering waves [that he made also] caused us great fear and alarm. We fled to the east and to the west in hopes of avoiding the constant pursuit of navy warships. Having to sleep without shelter and take our meals in the winds, we suffered all the bitterness of the boundless sea. At those times, we wanted to break away and return to our villages, but our fellow countrymen refused to accept us. We considered surrendering ourselves as a group but did not know what dedicated officials would do with us. Therefore, we could not but remain on the islands and pace back and forth in hesitation.

Alas! According to the law our crimes most certainly deserve the death penalty [and] we cannot evade the emperor's justice. However, our situation is extremely pitiful and our survival must depend on benevolent men. We are happy that Your Honor [that is, Governor-General Bailing] has returned to Guangdong to rule, . . . for you regard others as yourself and love the people as your own sons.[48]

We have respectfully read your proclamation several times. You advise us to surrender and you will take pity on our reasons for having become [sea] bandits. Your principle is to use both severity and leniency, and you understand that to spare lives is a heavenly virtue. In your justice you righteously employ both extermination and appeasement.[49] Even birds flying in the dust seek clean air, so how can a fish be content in boiling water? For these reasons, we have gathered our followers to present to you this petition with our signatures. We humbly submit the remaining years of our lives to your mercy, hoping you will save us from flood and fire, pardon our former misconduct,

---

47. God of the Yellow River, worshipped as a sea deity.
48. Bailing, a Chinese bannerman, had served earlier as governor of Guangdong province in 1805, when he was recognized for his capable and fair administration. The emperor later appointed him governor-general in 1809, with the specific task of putting an end to the rampant piracy in the region.
49. Once he arrived in Canton in April 1809, Bailing initiated an ancient stratagem known as "extermination and appeasement" (*jiaofu*), a carrot-and-stick approach in which military campaigns were coupled with liberal offers of amnesties and rewards to pirates who surrendered.

and permit us a new way of life from this day forward. We solemnly promise to sell our swords to buy oxen to plow the fields. In appreciation of your greatness we burn incense and praise you all the days for your benevolence. If we dare to act with duplicity you may instantly have us executed.

Source: Yuan Yonglun 1830, 2:10b–12b. Translation by Lanshin Chang and the author.

DOC. 40. A BRIEF ACCOUNT OF THE FEMALE PIRATE ZHENG YI SAO

One of the most remarkable women in Chinese history was a pirate. In 1807 Zheng Yi Sao became the leader of Guangdong's largest and most powerful pirate fleet, the Red Banner Fleet, with roughly twenty thousand pirates, including men and women, and several hundred ships. Through an extensive protection racket she controlled the seas and coastal areas around the Pearl River Delta, one of China's most densely populated and prosperous regions. When the pirates surrendered in 1810, Zheng Yi Sao had played a crucial role in negotiations with local officials and Governor-General Bailing. Few accounts of Zheng Yi Sao provide as much detail as the following firsthand record by Yuan Yonglun. The first episode describes Zheng Yi Sao's rise to power over the Red Banner Fleet after her husband, Zheng Yi, suddenly died at sea, as well as her organizational skills as a formidable chieftain who promulgated a strict code of behavior for her followers.

In the 12th year of the Jiaqing reign on the 17th day of the 10th lunar month [November 16, 1807], Zheng Yi drowned at sea in a typhoon. His wife, surnamed Shi [Stone], assumed command of his fleet, making Zhang Bao her lieutenant, while she retained overall command. She was called Zheng Yi Sao, meaning the Wife of Zheng Yi. . . . Day by day their fleet grew in numbers and they made three regulations binding on everyone under their command. First, if anyone sneaks ashore . . . that person shall lose an ear as punishment . . . and if the act is repeated, that person shall be immediately sentenced to death in the presence of everyone. Second, nothing can be taken privately from the plundered goods. [After] being registered, crew members who stole the goods shall be allotted two shares while the remaining eight shares shall be put into a common treasury. Taking anything out of this common treasury without permission shall result in the punishment of death. Third, no person shall debauch captive women who were abducted from villages and brought aboard ship. After their [names] are put into the ship's register, they will be placed in the ship's hold. If anyone rapes them or privately has an affair with them, they shall be immediately punished with death. . . . It was further ordered that villagers shall be paid double the price for liquor, rice, and other provisions, and if anyone does not pay for such items or takes them by force, they shall be immediately punished with death. As a result [of such policies], the pirates were never in want for gunpowder, food, or any other provisions. . . .

The following episode describes Zheng Yi Sao's crucial role at every stage in negotiating the surrender in April 1810.

After taking notice that Guo Podai [pirate leader of the Black Banner Fleet] had been rewarded with an official position after he surrendered [in December 1809], Zheng Yi Sao also considered submitting to the government. She thought to herself, "I am ten times stronger than Guo Podai and so if I surrender, the government will act towards me in the same manner as Guo Podai." But recalling the grave crimes and many offenses against officials committed by the pirates, she became concerned, so [she] began to spread rumors that the Red Banner Fleet was willing to surrender. Once the local official at the Zini station [near Canton] got wind of this, he ordered Zhou Feixiong, who was an apothecary in Macau and someone well acquainted with the pirates, to make inquiries. . . . [Zhou then contacted the pirates and helped arrange for Zheng Yi Sao to meet with Governor-General Bailing.] Zheng Yi Sao and Zhang Bao expressed their sincere desires to surrender with no trickery. . . . The Governor-General then embarked in his ship to meet with the pirates where they assembled near Humen. In anticipation the pirates hoisted flags, beat drums, and set off their cannons. . . . Zhang Bao and Zheng Yi Sao . . . boarded [Bailing's] ship where they both fell upon their knees to *koutou* and beg submission to the throne. . . . Suddenly several large Portuguese ships appeared, and the pirates alarmed that this was some sort of trap, immediately weighed anchor and fled. . . . The governor-general, believing that the negotiations had failed, returned to Canton. . . . [Soon afterward, however, the pirates ascertained that there was no trick and decided to resume the negotiations with Bailing in Canton.] Zheng Yi Sao reasoned with her pirates: "His excellency has been very candid with us and we should treat him in the same manner. . . . I shall go to Canton myself with a few other [pirate] wives to negotiate directly with his excellency, to clear up all doubts, and to agree on the day and place for our submission." . . . [In an audience with Bailing, the governor-general accepted their submission and granted them pardons.] As agreed, Zheng Yi Sao, Zhang Bao, the other wives and children went to Furongsha in Xiangshan [County] to accept the surrender. [In celebration] officials provided each ship with pork and liquor and each pirate received a silver tally for submitting. Those who so desired were allowed to join the military to pursue the remaining pirates, and those who did not desire to become soldiers were ordered to be resettled. In this way the Red Banner Fleet was pacified.

Source: Yuan Yonglun 1830, 1:5a–6b and 2:15a–18a. Translation by the author.

Chronology

1223–1263	Early Japanese pirate (*wokou*) raids on Korea
1368–1644	Ming dynasty
1405–1433	Maritime voyages of Zheng He to Southeast Asia and the Indian Ocean
1513	Portuguese traders first arrive in southern China
1522–1566	Reign of Jiajing emperor; start of the golden age of piracy in China
1523	Disputed Japanese tribute mission and resulting riots in Ningbo
1527	New Ming prohibitions on private maritime trade
c. 1540s	Xu Dong and his brothers establish pirate syndicate on Shuangyu Island
1541	New prohibitions on private maritime trade; Altan Khan raids north China
1543	Wang Zhi helps Portuguese introduce guns into Japan; famine hits Zhejiang
1547	Zhu Wan appointed Grand Coordinator of Coastal Defense in Zhejiang and Fujian provinces
1548	Ming fleet under Zhu Wan destroys pirate-smuggler base on Shuangyu Island
1550	Zhu Wan committed suicide after being impeached by the emperor
1550–1558	Repeated *wokou* raids along the Zhejiang coast
1551	Ming prohibitions on fishing boats going out to sea
1554	Pirates establish new bases along the South China coast and threaten attacks on Nanjing, Hangzhou, and Suzhou

1556–1563	Hu Zongxian appointed Supreme Commander to eradicate the *wokou* menace
1557	Wang Zhi surrenders to the Ming; Portuguese establish foothold on Macau, maintained until 1997
1558	Qi Jiguang's forces win decisive naval battle against pirates at Cen Harbor in Zhejiang
1558–1567	Repeated *wokou* raids along Fujian and Guangdong coasts
1559	Hong Dizhen executed as a pirate
1560	Jiajing emperor orders Wang Zhi's execution
1565	Qi Jiguang's forces destroy Wu Ping's pirate stronghold on Nan'ao Island
1567	Jiajing emperor dies; maritime prohibitions are lifted, except for Japan; *wokou* piracy declines
1567–1572	Reign of Longqing emperor
1572–1620	Reign of Wanli emperor
1579–1581	Disturbances led by the pearl thieves Su Guangsheng and Zhou Caixiong in the Gulf of Tonkin
1592–1598	Japanese invasions of Korea
1600–1874	English East India Company operated in Asia
1602–1799	Dutch East India Company (VOC) operated in Asia
1621–1628	Reign of Tianqi emperor
1622	Portuguese repulse Dutch attack on Macau; Dutch start robbing Chinese trading junks
1624	Dutch settle in Taiwan; VOC hire Chinese privateers, such as Zheng Zhilong
1628–1644	Reign of Chongzhen emperor, last Ming ruler
1628	Pirate lord Zheng Zhilong surrenders to the Ming and is appointed patrolling commander in the Ming navy
1630–1644	Numerous peasant revolts erupt in China against the Ming dynasty
1635	Zheng Zhilong defeats the pirate Liu Xiang off the Leizhou peninsula
1640	Zheng Zhilong appointed regional commander of the military forces in Fujian
1644–1911	Qing (Manchu) dynasty
1644–1661	Reign of Shunzhi emperor, Qing dynasty
1644	Manchu armies enter north China and defeat rebel leader Li Zicheng; the Ming Chongzhen emperor commits suicide in Beijing
1644–1662	Various Southern Ming loyalists resist the Manchu conquest of China

c. 1644–1682	Several thousand pirates, under such leaders as Deng Yao and Yang Yandi, who often professed loyalty to the fallen Ming dynasty, are active in the Gulf of Tonkin
1645	Southern Ming's Longwu emperor granted Zheng Chenggong the title Guoxingye (corrupted as Koxinga), meaning "Lord of the Imperial Surname" for his loyalty
1646	Zheng Zhilong surrenders to the Qing and is put under house arrest in Beijing
1655	Zheng Chenggong establishes stronghold at Xiamen (Amoy)
1657	Zheng Chenggong's forces raid Putian on the Fujian coast, looting towns and villages, raping women, and kidnapping people for ransom and forced labor
1659	Zheng Chenggong attempts to seize Nanjing, but failing retreats to Xiamen
1661–1722	Reign of Kangxi emperor
1661	Zheng Zhilong is executed in Beijing; Zheng Chenggong attacks Dutch on Taiwan
1661–1683	Kangxi emperor promulgates the so-called Great Clearance or the forced coastal evacuation policy
1662	Zheng Chenggong's forces drive Dutch from Taiwan; his forces raid the Philippines; he dies in June and is succeeded by his son Zheng Jing
1662–1664	Zhou Yu and Li Rong lead Dan fishers in a revolt in the Pearl River Delta
1664	Qing dynasty retakes Fujian and Zheng Jing retreats to Taiwan
1673–1681	Revolt of the Three Feudatories against the Qing
1683	Qing general Shi Lang defeats the Zheng regime in Taiwan
1684	Kangxi emperor rescinds most of the maritime bans
1722–1735	Reign of Yongzheng emperor
1735–1796	Reign of Qianlong emperor; this period is often referred to as the High Qing
c. 1740–1840	The "China Century" when Chinese junks dominated trade in the South China Sea
1771–1802	Tay Son Rebellion in Vietnam (Annan)
1796–1820	Reign of Jiaqing emperor
1805	Zheng Yi, Wushi Er, Donghai Ba, and four other pirate chiefs sign a pact creating the Guangdong pirate confederation, lasting to 1810
1805–1806	Cai Qian makes repeated raids on Taiwan and declares himself the "Majestic Warrior King Who Subdues the Sea"

1806	John Turner kidnapped by Guangdong pirates and held for $6,000 ransom
1807	Zheng Yi dies at sea; his widow, Zheng Yi Sao, and Zhang Bao take charge of the Red Banner Fleet, the largest pirate fleet in Guangdong
1809	Cai Qian and Zhu Fen killed in separate naval battles; during severe famine, Zheng Yi Sao, Zhang Bao, and Guo Podai lead pirate raids deep into the Pearl River Delta; Richard Glasspoole kidnapped for ransom by the Red Banner Fleet
1810	Zheng Yi Sao and Zhang Bao surrender to Qing authorities in Guangdong; Wushi Er killed in battle and Donghai Ba surrenders; end of the golden age of piracy in China

Glossary

Amoy	port city in Fujian province; known in Chinese as Xiamen 廈門
Annan 安南	name used in China for Vietnam before 1802
arquebuses	an early type of portable gun supported on a tripod or a forked rest that appeared in Europe and Asia during the fifteenth and sixteenth centuries; in China these firearms had such names as bird-beaked guns
baojia 保甲	a traditional Chinese system of collective neighborhood watch or mutual responsibility system, by which the government aimed to maintain order and control all levels of society, while employing relatively few officials; a corresponding system for boats was called *aojia* 澳甲; the *lijia* 里甲 system, which often worked in conjunction with the *baojia* system, was mainly concerned with local-level tax collection in the Ming dynasty
booty	prize or cargo of a captured ship
Canton	capital of Guangdong province; known in Chinese as Guangzhou 廣州
Canton System	the trading system that remained in effect from 1757 to 1842, served as a means for China to control trade with the West within its own country by focusing all trade on the southern port of Canton (Guangzhou); it ended with the First Opium War
catty (*jin* 斤)	a Chinese measure roughly equal to 1.3 lbs.

Dan/Danmin 蛋民	derogatory term, literally egg people, referring to South China's boat people and fisherfolk
dirk	a long-bladed dagger that European naval officers used as a boarding weapon and in hand-to-hand combat
Dutch East India Company or VOC (Vereenigde Oostindische Compagnie)	a trading company founded in the Dutch Republic in 1602 to expand and protect that country's trade in Asia; the company prospered through most of the seventeenth century as the instrument of the powerful Dutch commercial empire in the East Indies (today Indonesia); the company was dissolved in 1799
East Indies	as the name suggests, the region east of the Indian subcontinent, especially Southeast Asia and parts of East Asia
Folangji 佛郎機	a Chinese term referring to the Portuguese and their breech-loading guns when they first arrived in China in the sixteenth century
galleon	a European square-rigged sailing ship in use from the fifteenth through seventeenth centuries for war and trade; the Manila galleons were used by Spain in voyages between Mexico and the Philippines bringing cargoes of Asian luxury goods such as spices and porcelain to the Americas in exchange for New World silver
galley	a traditional sailing vessel with oars for rowing
Great Clearance (qianjieling 遷界令)	a series of edicts issued between 1661 and 1679 that required the evacuation of all coastal areas from Shandong to Guangdong in order to fight Zheng Chenggong and other pirates; the policy remained in effect until 1683
hagaibune	sixteenth-century Japanese armored warships sometimes used by wokou pirates
haifei 海匪	common Chinese term for pirate, literally meaning sea bandit
haikou 海寇	common Chinese name for pirate, literally meaning sea rebel
haini 海逆	common Chinese name for pirate, literally meaning sea rebel
Hong merchants	a guild of Chinese merchants sanctioned by the Qing government to monopolize foreign trade at Canton
jianghu 江湖	a traditional Chinese term, literally translated as rivers and lakes, used to describe the underworld society and culture of knights-errant, martial artists, bandits, pirates, beggars, and vagabonds

jiaofu 剿撫	a traditional stratagem, literally extermination and appeasement, in which military campaigns were coupled with liberal offers of amnesties and rewards to pirates, bandits, and rebels who surrendered
Joss	a term used by Westerners to refer to a Chinese idol or cult image; it originated from the Portuguese word *Dias* or God
junk	a traditional Chinese sailing vessel; the name derives from Javanese *djong*, meaning ship
koku 石	a Japanese measurement equivalent to about 4.96 bushels
Ladrones	a Spanish or Portuguese term for pirates; also referred to groups of pirate islands near Hong Kong and Macau
li 里	a measure of distance roughly equal to 0.311 miles
mandarin	based on the Portuguese word *mandarim*, this was the term Europeans used for Chinese officials in the Ming and Qing periods
merchant-pirates	a term sometimes used by historians to describe those pirates in the mid-Ming period who had merchant backgrounds but had been forced into smuggling and piracy due to the sea bans; also called smuggler-pirates
mu 畝	a Chinese hectare in which roughly 6.6 *mu* equals one acre
paddy	unhusked rice either growing in the field or harvested
pearl thieves (*zhuzei* 珠賊)	a type of pirate operating in the Gulf of Tonkin who specialized in stealing state monopolized pearls in the Ming dynasty
peck (*dou* 斗)	a measure for grain roughly equal to 13.3 lbs.
Pescadores	an archipelago of ninety islands and islets in the Taiwan Strait; known in Chinese as Penghu 澎湖
picul (*dan* 石)	a dry measure for grain equivalent to roughly 132.3 lbs.
pidgin	a modified form of English used as a trade language between the British and the Chinese, first in Canton and later in other Chinese trade centers, such as Shanghai
political pirates	a term sometimes used by historians to describe those pirates during the Ming-Qing transition who combined predation with political agendas, namely continued loyalty to the fallen Ming dynasty
privateer	a private person or armed ship commissioned by a Western government to attack enemy ships, usually commercial vessels; the 1856 Declaration of Paris that banned privateering was ratified by fifty-five countries, but the United States was not a signatory

prize	a seized vessel, either by pirates or privateers
Quemoy	group of islands located in the Taiwan Strait between Fujian and Taiwan; known in Chinese as Jinmen 金門
rendao 仁盜	a traditional Chinese term meaning benevolent thief or noble robber
ronin 浪人	Japanese term for masterless samurai
sea bans (*haijin* 海禁)	a series of Ming and early Qing isolationist policies that prohibited all private maritime trading and allowed only state sanctioned commerce within the tributary system
silver dollars (*yuan* 圓)	refers to New World Spanish silver dollars, which after the seventeenth century became common currency in China
sui 歲	in China a person's age is reckoned in *sui*, that is, the number of calendar years in which someone has lived, not the actual number of months that have elapsed since birth; because Chinese are born at age one, they are one or two years older under Chinese reckoning when compared to Western reckoning
swivel gun	a type of small cannon mounted on a forked stand that allowed a wide arc of movement; they were used extensively in Asia mainly in naval combat as short-range antipersonnel ordnance since the fifteenth century
tael (*liang* 兩)	in China a traditional type of silver currency or sycee based on weight; although irregular, most taels were equivalent to 1.3 ounces of silver
Tanka	see Dan/Danmin
Tay Son Rebellion	a massive peasant uprising led by three brothers that started in southern Vietnam in 1771, conquered most of the country, and was crushed in 1802
Three Feudatories (*Sanfan* 三藩)	in 1659 Wu Sangui 吳三桂, a Ming general who helped the Manchus conquer China, was rewarded a semi-independent satrapy or fief in Yunnan and Guizhou provinces; at the same time two other commanders were granted similar satrapies in Guangdong and Fujian; between 1673 and 1681 they led the Revolt of the Three Feudatories against the Qing dynasty
tributary system	the common Western name for a set of highly regulated, ritualized exchanges that occurred between the imperial court in China's capital and leaders of other Asian polities

wall piece, wall pounder, or wall gun	a type of smoothbore rampart gun used extensively in Asia in the nineteenth century; known in China as gingals
wokou 倭寇 (*wakō* in Japanese)	a term referring to Japanese pirates, literally meaning dwarf bandits; they were actually composed of pirates of various nationalities who raided the coasts of China and Korea between the thirteenth and sixteenth centuries
yamen 衙門	the administrative offices and residences of local civil and military officials in imperial China
yangdao 洋盜	common Chinese term for pirate, literally meaning ocean bandit
yangfei 洋匪	common Chinese term for pirate, literally meaning ocean bandit
yifei 夷匪	a Chinese term referring to foreign pirates during Vietnam's Tay Son Rebellion (1771–1802); actually most of the pirates were Chinese
zhaofu 招撫	a Chinese term literally meaning to summon and appease, it was a common method used by officials to pacify pirates, bandits, and rebels

A Note on Chinese Documentary Evidence

Although there are many primary sources in Chinese, nonetheless it is no easy task to recover the history of Chinese piracy. The problem is not in numbers but in the reliability of the sources. Because the pirates themselves left us virtually no records, we must rely on the written accounts of officials and scholar elites. It is therefore no exaggeration to say that the sources are biased. Nonetheless, when read with care official documents are valuable and can be used in ways not intended by their authors. There are innumerable official documents that deal with piracy. Overall, one of the most important sources is the official or standard histories of the successive dynasties called the *Twenty-Four Histories* (*Ershsisi shi* 二十四史), which cover a period from roughly 3000 BCE to the end of the Ming dynasty in the mid-seventeenth century. Official histories were always written after a dynasty ended. The *Ming History* (*Ming Shi* 明史) was the last official history. Because the Qing dynasty was not followed by another dynastic regime it does not have an official history, only a *Draft History of the Qing* (*Qing Shi Gao* 清史稿). Both the *Ming History* and the *Draft History of the Qing* are available online at the Chinese Text Project.

Another important source is the *Veritable Records* (*Shilu* 實錄), which are daily accounts compiled from court diaries and administrative records and, as a more comprehensive source, can be used in conjunction with the official histories. While only sections of the *Veritable Records* are extant from before the fourteenth century, we have complete *Veritable Records* from the Ming and Qing dynasties. Each *Shilu* consists of an account of one emperor's reign compiled after his death. Arranged chronologically, the *Shilu* is a collection of notices of court activities, important events, summaries of memorials, debates, imperial edicts, and so forth. For mid-Ming piracy, see the *Shizong Shilu* 世宗實錄, covering the Jiajing reign (1521–1567); the *Muzong Shilu*

穆宗實錄, covering the Longqing reign (1567–1572); and the *Shenzong Shilu* 神宗實錄, covering the Wanli reign (1572–1620). For piracy during the Ming-Qing transition, see the *Xizong Shilu* 僖宗實錄, covering the Tianqi reign (1621–1628); the *Chongzong Shilu* 崇宗實錄, covering the Chongzhen reign (1628–1644); the *Shizu Shilu* 世祖實錄, covering the Shunzhi reign (1644–1661); and the *Shengzu Shilu* 聖祖實錄, covering the Kangxi reign (1661–1722). For mid-Qing piracy, see the *Gaozong Shilu* 高宗實錄, covering the Qianlong reign (1735–1795); and the *Renzong Shilu* 仁宗實錄, covering the Jiaqing reign (1796–1820). Both the Ming and Qing *Veritable Records* are available online at the China Text Project, though beware of typographical errors in the transcriptions.

Official documents found in the central government archives, especially for the Qing dynasty, are among the most direct and useful sources for the study of piracy and its suppression. The best documentary evidence on piracy is found in the collections of palace memorials (*zouzhe* 奏摺), routine memorials (*tiben* 題本), and imperial edicts (*shangyu* 上諭). Memorials were written by both high-ranking provincial civil and military officials to inform the emperors on important events, social disorders and criminal activities, military campaigns, natural disasters, food costs, and so forth. Edicts were detailed instructions from the emperors, often written in response to memorials. The majority of original archival documents are housed in Beijing at the First Historical Archives and in Taibei at the Palace Museum and at Academia Sinica. Many of these archival collections have been published in recent years. In 2004 the National Central Library in Beijing published a four-volume collection of draft memorials on Cai Qian titled *Jiaoping Cai Qian zougao* 剿平蔡牽奏稿 [Anthology of draft memorials on the suppression of Cai Qian]. The Palace Museum in Taiwan in 2015 published a selection of archival materials on Zhang Bao (or Zhang Baozai) in *Yuanzang jiaofu Zhang Baozai shiliao huibian* 院藏剿撫張保仔史料彙編 [Anthology of historical sources on Zhang Baozai in the Palace Museum], compiled by Zhou Weiqiang 周維強 and Chen Longgui 陳龍貴.

Gazetteers (*fangzhi* 方志) of coastal areas that date mostly from the Ming dynasty and afterward are also particularly useful documentary evidence. They are fundamental local histories usually compiled by members of the local elite—the very people most familiar with their home areas about which they wrote—and were produced under the sponsorship of officials. Gazetteers are usually subdivided into provincial gazetteers (*tongzhi* 通志), prefectural gazetteers (*fuzhi* 府志), county gazetteers (*xianzhi* 縣志), and occasionally township gazetteers (*xiangzhi* 鄉志). Gazetteers provide comprehensive accounts of the geography, administration, economy, history, local customs, religion, and civil and military officials, gentry elites, and occasionally even locally famous pirates. While gazetteers vary in quality and scope, nonetheless they generally contain important local information on pirates and their activities, as well as on both official and community responses to piracy. Many Ming and Qing gazetteers are available online. East View, for example, has digitized roughly seven thousand titles in its China Comprehensive Gazetteers database.

Besides official documents, there are a large number of private volumes dating from the Ming and Qing dynasties that were written by officials and literati stationed or living along the coast. In general, these sources are available in various collectanea (*congshu* 叢書), which are anthologies of individual writings. These include the *Siku chuanshu* 四庫全書 [Complete library of the four treasuries] and *Siku quanshu cunmu congshu* 四庫全書存目叢書 [Collectanea of the complete library of the four treasuries], as well as Gu Yingtai's 谷應泰 collection in *Ming shi jishi benmo* 明史紀事本末 [A record of Ming historical events from beginning to end]. These compilations provide important information on the nature of piracy and local conditions, as well as the applications and effects of local-, provincial-, and national-level policies dealing with piracy. In many cases, private writings offer a different, more personal perspective on piracy from that of the official documents.

More specifically for mid-Ming piracy, one important book is *Chouhai tubian* 籌海圖編 [An illustrated discourse on maritime defense], compiled by Zheng Ruozeng 鄭若曾 (1503–1570), which was first published in 1562 and has been continuously republished ever since. This work discusses in detail many of the *wokou* leaders—Xu Dong, Li Guangtou, Wang Zhi, He Yaba, Xu Hai, Hong Dizhen, and others—as well as their activities and organization, the people and areas that they pillaged, and the actions taken by the Ming government to suppress piracy. A useful modern anthology of sources on *wokou* piracy is *Mingdai wokou shiliao* 明代倭寇史料 [Historical sources on wokou in the Ming period], compiled by Zheng Liangsheng 鄭樑生, published in 1987. Matsuura Akira 松浦章 and Bian Tengkui 卞鳳奎 have published a slim volume of Chinese primary sources that covers the entire Ming period titled *Mingdai Dongya haiyu haidao shiliao huibian* 明代東亞海域海盜史料彙編 [Compilation of historical sources on pirates in East Asian seas in the Ming period], published in 2009.

For piracy in the Ming-Qing transition, there are numerous private writings on Zheng Zhilong, Zheng Chenggong, and Zheng Jing. One such source is Yu Yonghe 郁永河, "Wei Zheng yishi" 偽鄭逸事 [Machinations of the Zheng family, or alternatively titled as "Zheng Shi yishi" 鄭氏逸事], in his *Pihai jiyou* 裨海紀遊 [Small sea travel diaries], based on the author's first-hand experiences in Taiwan in the late seventeenth century. Other sources on this period include *Jinghai jilue* 靖海紀略 [An account of the pacification of the seas] by Cao Lütai 曹履泰; *Dongnan jishi* 東南紀事 [A record of events in the southeast] by Shao Tingcai 邵廷采; *Taiwan waiji* 臺灣外記 [An unofficial record of Taiwan] by Jiang Risheng 江日昇; *Haishang jianwenlu* 海上見聞錄 [Record of things seen and heard on the sea] by Ruan Minxi 阮旻錫; and *Ping Min ji* 平閩紀 [Account of the pacification of Fujian] by Yang Jie 楊捷, among many others.

For southwestern Guangdong and the Gulf of Tonkin area, Chen Shunxi 陳舜系, a local scholar and healer in Wuchuan County, kept a diary from the 1630s to 1679, the year that he passed away. His diary, published posthumously as *Luanli jianwen lu* 亂離見聞錄 [A record of the chaos and abandonment seen and heard], provides an intriguingly detailed eyewitness account of the turmoil that marked the Ming-Qing transition in his home area, with accounts of Deng Yao, Chen Shangchuan, and Yang Yandi, among other pirates.

For the mid-Qing period, we have the account of a low-ranking scholar-official, Yuan Yonglun 袁永綸, who had firsthand experience and access to local records dealing with the provincial government's suppression of Zheng Yi Sao, Zhang Bao, and other pirates in Guangdong. His important book, first published in Canton in 1830 (and reprinted many times thereafter), is titled *Jinghai fenji* 靖海氛記 [A record of the pacification of the sea]; it previously was translated into English in 1831 by Charles Neumann as *History of the Pirates Who Infested the China Sea from 1807 to 1810, by Yuan Yung-lun*. There are several online versions of the original Chinese book, such as one provided by Google Books. Besides Yuan Yonglun's book, another shorter eyewitness account of the Cantonese pirate confederation was written by Wen Chengzhi 溫承志 titled *Pinghai jilue* 平海紀略 [A short record of pacifying the sea], first published in Canton in the early 1830s, and is included in the 1968 anthology titled *Shiliao congbian* 史料叢編 [Collection of historical sources], vol. 13, published in Taiwan.

Many of these and other primary sources are available online at the Chinese Text Project (ctext.org), Project Gutenberg (gutenberg.org), Google Books (books.google.com), and at the National Archives of Japan Digital Archives (digital.archives.go.jp). Full bibliographical information on these sources is in the "Works Cited" section in the references and additional readings.

References and Additional Readings

WORKS CITED

Andrade, Tonio. 2011. *Lost Colony: The Untold Story of China's First Great Victory over the West*. Princeton: Princeton University Press.
———. 2004. "The Company's Chinese Pirates: How the Dutch East India Company Tried to Lead a Coalition of Pirates to War against China, 1621–1662." *Journal of World History* 15 (4): 414–44.
Andrade, Tonio, and Xing Hang, eds. 2016. *Sea Rovers, Silver, and Samurai: Maritime East Asia in Global History, 1500–1700*. Honolulu: University of Hawai'i Press.
Antony, Robert J. 2017. "Integrating Maritime Asia with World, Transregional, and Local History: An Introduction." In *Beyond the Silk Roads: New Discourses on China's Role in East Asian Maritime History*, edited by Robert Antony and Angela Schottenhammer, 1–24. Wiesbaden: Harrassowitz Verlag.
———. 2014a. "Violence and Predation on the Sino-Vietnamese Maritime Frontier, 1450–1850." *Asia Major*, Series 3, 27 (2): 87–114.
———. 2014b. "'Righteous Yang': Pirate, Rebel, and Hero on the Sino-Vietnamese Water Frontier, 1644–1684." *Cross-Currents: East Asian History and Culture Review* 3 (2): 319–48.
———. 2014c. "Maritime Violence and State Formation in Vietnam: Piracy and the Tay Son Rebellion, 1771–1802." In *Persistent Piracy: Maritime Violence and State-Formation in Global Historical Perspective*, edited by Stefan Eklöf Amirell and Leos Müller, 113–30. New York: Palgrave.
———. 2012. "Bloodthirsty Pirates? Violence and Terror on the South China Sea in Early Modern Times." *Journal of Early Modern History* 16: 481–501.
———. 2010a. "Piracy and the Shadow Economy in the South China Sea, 1780–1810." In *Elusive Pirates, Pervasive Smugglers: Violence and Clandestine Trade in the Greater China Seas*, edited by Robert J. Antony, 99–114. Hong Kong: Hong Kong University Press.

———. 2010b. "Giang Binh: Pirate Haven and Black Market on the Sino-Vietnamese Frontier, 1780–1802." In *Pirates, Ports, and Coasts in Asia: Historical and Contemporary Perspectives*, edited by John Kleinen and Manon Osseweijer, 31–50. Leiden: International Institute for Asian Studies.

———. 2006. "State, Community, and Pirate Suppression in Guangdong Province, 1809–1810." *Late Imperial China* 27 (1): 1–30.

———. 2003. *Like Froth Floating on the Sea: The World of Pirates and Seafarers in Late Imperial South China*. Berkeley: University of California, Institute of East Asian Studies, China Research Monograph No. 56.

———. 1994. "Pacification of the Seas: Qing Anti-Piracy Policies in Guangdong, 1794–1810." *Journal of Oriental Studies* 32 (1): 16–35.

Blussé, Leonard. 1999. "Chinese Century: The Eighteenth Century in the China Sea Region." *Archipel* 58: 107–29.

———. 1990. "Minnan-jen or Cosmopolitan? The Rise of Cheng Chih-lung Alias Nicolas Iquan." In *Development and Decline of Fukien Province in the Seventeenth and Eighteenth Centuries*, edited by Eduard B. Vermeer, 245–64. Leiden: Brill.

Brown, Delmar M. 1951. *Money Economy in Medieval Japan: A Study in the Use of Coins*. New Haven: Institute of Far Eastern Languages, Yale University.

Calanca, Paola. 2010. "Piracy and Coastal Security in Southeastern China, 1600–1780." In *Elusive Pirates, Pervasive Smugglers: Violence and Clandestine Trade in the Greater China Seas*, edited by Robert J. Antony, 85–98. Hong Kong: Hong Kong University Press.

Cao Lütai 曹履泰. 1969. *Jinghai jilue* 靖海紀略 [An account of the pacification of the seas]. Taibei: Wenhai chubanshe. Also online at the Chinese Text Project.

Carioti, Patrizia. 1996. "The Zhengs' Maritime Power in the Context of the 17th Century Far Eastern Seas: The Rise of a 'Centralized Piratical Organization' and Its Gradual Development into a 'State.'" *Ming-Qing Yanjiu* 5: 29–67.

Chang, Thomas C. S. 1983. "Ts'ai Ch'ien, The Pirate King Who Dominates the Seas: A Study of Coastal Piracy in China, 1795–1810." PhD diss., University of Arizona.

Chen Chunsheng 陳春聲. 2010. "Shiliu shiji Min Yue jiaojie diyu haishang huodong renquan de tezhi: yi Wu Ping de yanjiu wei zhongxin" 十六世紀閩粵交界地域海上活動人權的特質：以吳平的研究為中心 [Characteristics of groups active in the waters bordering Fujian and Guangdong in the sixteenth century: a case study of Wu Ping]. *Haiyang shi yanjiu* 海洋史研究 [Journal of maritime studies] 1: 129–52.

Chen Shunxi 陳舜系. 2010. *Luanli jianwen lu* 亂離見聞錄 [A record of the chaos and abandonment seen and heard]. In *Ming Qing Guangdong xijian biji qizhong* 明清廣東稀見筆記七種 [Seven types of collected writings from Guangdong in the Ming and Qing], 3–47. Guangzhou: Guangdong renmin chubanshe.

Cheng, Wei-chung. 2013. *War, Trade and Piracy in the China Seas, 1622–1683*. Leiden: Brill.

Chengmai xianzhi 澄邁縣志 [Gazetteer of Chengmai County, Guangdong]. 1820. Harvard-Yenching Library.

Chin, James K. 2010. "Merchants, Smugglers, and Pirates: Multinational Clandestine Trade on the South China Coast, 1520–1550." In *Elusive Pirates, Pervasive Smug-*

glers: Violence and Clandestine Trade in the Greater China Seas, edited by Robert J. Antony, 43–58. Hong Kong: Hong Kong University Press.

Chonlaworn, Piyada. 2017. "Rebel with a Cause: Chinese Merchant-Pirates in Southeast Asia in the 16th Century." In *The Maritime Defence of China: Ming General Qi Jiguang and Beyond*, edited by Y. H. Teddy Sim, 187–200. Singapore: Springer.

Connolly, Patrick, and Robert J. Antony. 2017. "'A Terrible Scourge': Piracy, Coastal Defense, and the Historian." In *The Maritime Defence of China: Ming General Qi Jiguang and Beyond*, edited by Y. H. Teddy Sim, 43–58. Singapore: Springer.

Croizier, Ralph C. 1977. *Koxinga and Chinese Nationalism: History, Myths, and the Hero*. Cambridge, MA: Harvard University Press.

Escobar, João de. 1997. "Comentários Sobre a Embaixada de Gil de Góis." *Revista de Cultura* 31 (2): 67–74.

Fangcheng xianzhi chugao 防城縣志初稿 [Fangcheng County draft gazetteer]. Early twentieth century, author's photographic copy, unpaginated.

Fitzpatrick, Merrilyn. 1979. "Local Interests and the Anti-Pirate Administration in China's South-East, 1555–1565." *Ch'ing-shih wen-t'i* 4 (2): 1–50.

Fok, K. C. 1987. "Early Ming Images of the Portuguese." In *Portuguese Asia: Aspects in History and Economic History Sixteenth and Seventeenth Centuries*, edited by Roderich Ptak, 143–56. Stuttgart: Steiner Verlag Wiesbaden.

Foreign Office Records. British National Archives, Kew, London.

Glasspoole, Richard. 1831. "A Brief Narrative of My Captivity and Treatment Amongst the Ladrones." In *History of the Pirates who Infested the China Sea from 1807 to 1810*, compiled by Charles Neumann, 97–128. London: Oriental Translation Fund.

Gongzhongdang 宮中檔 [Palace memorials]. Qing Dynasty. National Palace Museum, Taibei.

Gu Yanwu 顧炎武. 1901. *Tianxia junguo libing shu* 天下郡國利病書 [Book of benefits and faults of the empire's local administration]. Shanghai. Online at https://new.shuge.org/meet/topic/13786/.

Haikang xianzhi 海康縣志 [Gazetteer of Haikang County, Guangdong]. 1938. Taibei: Chengwen chubanshe, 1974.

Hayashi Fukusai 林復齋, comp. 1912–1913. *Tsūkō ichiran* 通航一覽 [Overview of all foreign communications]. 5 vols. Tokyo: Kokusho Kankōkai.

Hang, Xing. 2017. "Leizhou Pirates and the Making of the Mekong Delta." In *Beyond the Silk Roads: New Discourses on China's Role in East Asian Maritime History*, edited by Robert Antony and Angela Schottenhammer, 115–32. Wiesbaden: Harrassowitz Verlag.

———. 2016. *Conflict and Commerce in Maritime East Asia: The Zheng Family and the Shaping of the Modern World, 1620–1720*. Cambridge: Cambridge University Press.

Higgins, Roland L. 1981. "Piracy and Coastal Defense in the Ming Period: Government Response to Coastal Disturbances, 1523–1549." PhD diss., University of Minnesota.

Ho, Dahpon. 2013. "The Empire's Scorched Shore: Coastal China, 1633–1683." *Journal of Early Modern History* 17: 53–74.

———. 2011. "Sealords Live in Vain: Fujian and the Making of a Maritime Frontier in Seventeenth-Century China." PhD diss., University of California, San Diego.

Hsieh, Kuo Ching. 1932. "Removal of Coastal Population in Early Tsing Period." *Chinese Social and Political Science Review* 15: 559–96.

Hu Zongxian 胡宗憲. 1621. *Haifang tulun* 海防圖論 [Illustrated treatise on coastal defense]. In *Bingyuan sibian* 兵垣四編 [Four chronicles on military affairs], section on coastal defense (*haifang* 海防), compiled by Zang Maoxun 臧懋循. Online at the National Archives of Japan Digital Archives.

Hucker, Charles. 1971. "Hu Tsung-hsien's Campaign against Hsu Hai, 1556." In *Two Studies on Ming History*, edited by Charles Hucker, 1–40. Ann Arbor: Center for Chinese Studies, University of Michigan.

Ishii, Yoneo, ed. 1998. *The Junk Trade from Southeast Asia: Translations from the Tôsen Fusetsu-gaki, 1674–1723*. Singapore: Institute for Southeast Asian Studies.

Jiang Risheng 江日昇. 1692. *Taiwan waiji* 臺灣外紀 [Unofficial record of Taiwan]. Taibei: Datong shuju, 1995. Also online at the Chinese Text Project and Project Gutenberg.

Jiang Zuyuan 蔣祖緣 and Fang Zhiqin 方志欽, eds. 1993. *Jianming Guangdong shi* 簡明廣東史 [A brief history of Guangdong]. Guangzhou: Guangdong renmin chubanshe.

Jiaoping Cai Qian zougao 剿平蔡牽奏稿 [Anthology of draft memorials on the suppression of Cai Qian]. 2004. Beijing: Quanguo tushuguan wenxian suowei fuzhi zhongxin.

Kuhn, Philip. 1990. *Soulstealers: The Chinese Sorcery Scare of 1768*. Cambridge, MA: Harvard University Press.

Laver, Michael. 2016. "Neither Here nor There: Trade, Piracy, and the 'Space Between' in Early Modern East Asia." In *Sea Rovers, Silver, and Samurai: Maritime East Asia in Global History, 1500–1700*, edited by Tonio Andrade and Xing Hang, 28–37. Honolulu: University of Hawai'i Press.

Lin Xiyuan 林希元. 2018. *Lin Ciya xiansheng wenji* 林次厓先生文集 [Collected writings of Lin Xiyuan]. Beijing: Shangwu yinshuguan.

Ljungstedt, Anders. 1836. *An Historical Sketch of the Portuguese Settlements in China and of the Roman Catholic Church and Mission in China*. Boston: James Munroe & Co.

Luo Tianchi 羅天尺. 1985. *Wushan zhilin* 五山志林 [Five mountains anthology]. 2 vols. Beijing: Zhonghua shuju.

MacKay, Joseph. 2013. "Pirate Nations: Maritime Pirates as Escape Societies in Late Imperial China." *Social Science History* 37 (4): 551–73.

Matsuura Akira 松浦章 and Bian Tengkui 卞鳳奎, comps. 2009. *Mingdai Dongya haiyu haidao shiliao huibian* 明代東亞海域海盜史料彙編 [Compilation of historical sources on pirates in East Asian seas in the Ming period]. Taibei: Lexue shuju youxian gongsi.

Maxiang tingzhi 馬巷廳志 [Gazetteer of Maxiang Subprefecture, Fujian]. 1893. Also online at Wikimedia Commons.

Ming Qing shiliao wubian 明清史料戊編 [Historical sources on Ming and Qing history, *wu* series]. 1972. Taibei: Academic Sinica.

Ming Shizong Shilu 明世宗實錄 [Veritable records of the Ming Shizong (Jiajing) reign]. 2005. Beijing: Xianzhuang shuju. Also online at the Chinese Text Project.

Murray, Dian H. 1992. "The Practice of Homosexuality among the Pirates of Late 18th and Early 19th Century China." *International Journal of Maritime History* 4 (1): 121–30.

———. 1987. *Pirates of the South China Coast, 1790–1810*. Stanford: Stanford University Press.

———. 1981. "One Woman's Rise to Power: Cheng I's Wife and the Pirates." *Historical Reflections* 8 (3): 147–61.

———. 1979. "Sea Bandits: A Study of Piracy in Early Nineteenth-Century China." PhD diss., Cornell University.

Nan'ao zhi 南澳志 [Gazetteer of Nan'ao, Guangdong]. 1841. Online at the Chinese Text Project.

Ng, Peter Y. L. 1983. *New Peace County: A Chinese Gazetteer of the Hong Kong Region*. Hong Kong: Hong Kong University Press.

Pelúcia, Alexandra. 2010. *Corsários e Piratas Portugueses: Aventureiros nos Mares da Ásia*. Lisboa: A Esfera dos Livros.

Petrucci, Maria Grazia. 2010. "Pirates, Gunpowder, and Christianity in Late Sixteenth-Century Japan." In *Elusive Pirates, Pervasive Smugglers: Violence and Clandestine Trade in the Greater China Seas*, edited by Robert J. Antony, 59–72. Hong Kong: Hong Kong University Press.

Pingyang xianzhi 平陽縣志 [Gazetteer of Pingyang County, Zhejiang]. 1925. Zhejiang Archives. Online at http://data.zjda.gov.cn/col/col212/index.html.

Ptak, Roderich. 1998. "Piracy along the Coasts of Southern India and Ming-China: Comparative Notes on Two Sixteenth Century Cases." In *China and the Asian Seas: Trade, Travel, and Visions of the Others (1400–1750)*, edited by Roderich Ptak, 255–73. Brookfield: Ashgate.

Qing Shengzu Shilu 清聖祖實錄 [Veritable records of the Qing Shengzu (Kangxi) reign]. 1985. Beijing: Zhonghua shuju. Also online at the Chinese Text Project.

Qing Shizu Shilu 清世祖實錄 [Veritable records of the Qing Shizu (Shunzhi) reign]. 1985. Beijing: Zhonghua shuju. Also online at the Chinese Text Project.

Qu Jiusi 瞿九思. 2002. *Wanli wugong lu* 萬曆武功錄 [Record of the military campaigns of the Wanli emperor]. In *Xuxiu siku quanshu* 續修四庫全書 [Sequel to the complete library of the four treasuries], 436: 238–40. Shanghai: Shanghai guji chubanshe. Also online at the Chinese Text Project.

Reid, Anthony. 1996. "Flows and Seepages in the Long-term Chinese Interaction with Southeast Asia." In *Sojourners and Settlers: Histories of Southeast Asia and the Chinese*, edited by Anthony Reid, 15–49. Honolulu: University of Hawai'i Press.

Ruan Minxi 阮旻錫. 1958. *Haishang jianwenlu* 海上見聞錄 [Record of things seen and heard on the sea]. Taibei: Taiwan yinhang. Also online at the Chinese Text Project.

Shangyudang 上諭檔 [Imperial edict record book]. Qing Dynasty. National Palace Museum, Taibei.

Shao Tingcai 邵廷采. 1961. *Dongnan jishi* 東南紀事 [A record of events in the southeast]. Taibei: Taiwan yinhang. Also online at the Chinese Text Project.

Shapinsky, Peter. 2016. "Envoys and Escorts: Representations and Performance among Koxinga's Japanese Pirate Ancestors." In *Sea Rovers, Silver, and Samurai: Maritime East Asia in Global History, 1500–1700*, edited by Tonio Andrade and Xing Hang, 38–64. Honolulu: University of Hawai'i Press.

Sim, Y. H. Teddy, ed. 2017. *The Maritime Defence of China: Ming General Qi Jiguang and Beyond*. Singapore: Springer.

So, Kwan-Wai. 1975. *Japanese Piracy in Ming China during the 16th Century*. East Lansing: Michigan State University Press.

Turner, John. 1814. *A Narrative of the Captivity and Sufferings of John Turner, First Officer of the Ship John Jay of Bombay, among the Ladrones or Pirates, on the Coast of China, Showing the Manners and Customs of the Natives—Their Mode of Warfare, Treatment of Prisoners, and Discipline, with the Difference between the Pirate and the Chinese, in the Year 1807.* New York: C. & R. Waite Booksellers.

Wang, Yuanfei. 2021. *Writing Pirates: Vernacular Fiction and Oceans in Late Ming China*. Ann Arbor: University of Michigan Press.

Wei, Peh Ti. 2006. *Ruan Yuan, 1764–1849: The Life and Work of a Major Scholar-Official in Nineteenth-Century China before the Opium War*. Hong Kong: Hong Kong University Press.

———. 1979. "Internal Security and Coastal Control: Juan Yuan and Pirate Suppression in Chekiang, 1799–1809." *Ch'ing-shih wen-t'i* 4 (2): 83–112.

Wen Chengzhi 溫承志. 1842. *Pinghai jilue* 平海記略 [Brief account of pacifying the seas]. In *Shiliao congbian* 史料叢編 [Collection of historical materials], vol. 13. Taibei: Guangwen shuju, 1968.

Wu Qi 吳綺. 1780. *Lingnan fengwu ji* 嶺南風物記 [A record of the customs of Guangdong]. In *Qinding siku chuanshu shibu* 欽定四庫全書史部 [Imperially endorsed complete library of the four treasuries, history section], vol. 11. Shanghai: Shuliu shanzhuang, 1888. Also online at the Chinese Text Project.

Xiamen zhi 廈門志 [Gazetteer of Xiamen]. 1961. Taibei: Taiwan yinhang jingji yanjiushe. Also online at the Chinese Text Project.

Xingke tiben 刑科題本 [Routine memorials, Punishment Section of the Censorate]. Qing Dynasty. First Historical Archives, Beijing.

Yang Jie 楊捷. 1961. *Ping Min ji* 平閩紀 [Account of the pacification of Fujian]. Taibei: Taiwan yinhang. Also online at the National Archives of Japan Digital Archives.

Yu Yonghe 郁永河. 1959. "Wei Zheng Yishi" 偽鄭逸事 [Machinations of the Zheng family]. In *Pihai jiyou* 裨海紀遊 [Small sea travel diaries], compiled by Yu Yonghe, 47–51. Taibei: Taiwan yinhang. Also online at the Chinese Text Project. It is also known under the title "Zheng shi yishi" 鄭氏逸事.

Yuan Yonglun 袁永綸. 1830. *Jinghai fenji* 靖海氛記 [A record of the pacification of the sea]. Canton, no publisher. Also online at Google Books.

Zhang Linbai 張麟白. 1978. *Fu hai ji* 浮海記 [Record of floating on the sea]. In *Taiwan guanxi wenxian jiling* 臺灣關係文獻集零 [Compilation of fragmentary historical materials relating to Taiwan], compiled by Sun Chengze 孫承澤 et al., no. 503, pp. 7–24. Taibei: Wenhai chubanshe.

Zhaoan xianzhi 詔安縣志 [Gazetteer of Zhaoan County, Fujian]. 1694. Harvard-Yenching Library.

Zheng Liangsheng 鄭樑生, comp. 1987. *Mingdai wokou shiliao* 明代倭寇史料 [Sources on wokou pirates in the Ming period]. Taibei: Wenshizhe chubanshe.

Zheng Lüchun 鄭履淳. 1569. *Zheng Duanjian gong nianpu* 鄭端簡公年譜 [A chronological record of Zheng Xiao]. In *Siku quanshu cunmu congshu shibu* 四庫全書存目叢書史部 [Collectanea of the complete library of the four treasuries, history section], vol. 83. Jinan: Qi lu shushe chubanshe, 1997.

Zheng Ruozeng 鄭若曾, comp. 1562. *Chouhai tubian* 籌海圖編 [An illustrated discourse on maritime defense]. Beijing: Zhonghua shuju, 2007. Also online at the National Archives of Japan Digital Archives.

"Zheng Zhilong shoufu" 鄭芝龍受撫 [The surrender of Zheng Zhilong]. 1658. In *Ming shi jishi benmo* 明史紀事本末 [A record of Ming historical events from beginning to end], compiled by Gu Yingtai 谷應泰, 76: 1a–3a. Online at the National Archives of Japan Digital Archives.

Zhou Weiqiang 周維強 and Chen Longgui 陳龍貴, comps. 2015. *Yuanzang jiaofu Zhang Baozai shiliao huibian* 院藏剿撫張保仔史料彙編 [Anthology of historical sources on Zhang Baozai in the Palace Museum]. Taibei: National Palace Museum.

Zhu Wan 朱紈. 1587. *Piyu zaji* 甓餘雜集 [Miscellany of extraneous glazed tiles]. Online at the National Archives of Japan Digital Archives.

Zhupi zouzhe 硃批奏摺 [Palace memorials]. Qing Dynasty. First Historical Archives, Beijing.

ADDITIONAL READINGS

Anderson, J. L. 1997. "Piracy in the Eastern Seas, 1750–1830." In *Pirates and Privateers: New Perspectives on the War on Trade in the Eighteenth and Nineteenth Centuries*, edited by David J. Starkey, E. S. van Eyck van Heslinga, and J. A. de Moor, 87–105. Exeter: University of Exeter Press.

Andrade, Tonio. 2005. "Pirates, Pelts, and Promises: The Sino-Dutch Colony of Seventeenth-Century Taiwan and the Aboriginal Village of Favorolang." *Journal of Asian Studies* 64 (2): 295–321.

Antony, Robert J. 2021a. "China's Pirate Wars, 1520–1810." *Research in Maritime History*, China Maritime Museum, Shanghai, 27: 1–28.

———. 2021b. "Defending Canton: Chinese Pirates, British Traders, and Hong Merchants, 1780–1810." *Revista de Cultura* 66: 70–95. Online at http://www.icm.gov.mo/rc/viewer/40066.

———. 2021c. "Piracy, Empire, and Sovereignty in Late Imperial China." In *Piracy in World History*, edited by Stefan Eklöf Amirell, Bruce Buchan, and Hans Hägerdal, 173–97. Amsterdam: Amsterdam University Press.

Antony, Robert J., ed. 2010. *Elusive Pirates, Pervasive Smugglers: Violence and Clandestine Trade in the Greater China Seas*. Hong Kong: Hong Kong University Press.

Boxer, C. R. 1980. "Piracy in the South China Sea." *History Today* 30 (12): 40–44.

Couto, Dejanirah Silva. 2000. "Some Observations on Portuguese Renegades in Asia in the Sixteenth Century." In *Vasco da Gama and the Linking of Europe and Asia*, edited by Anthony Disney and Emily Booth, 178–201. New Delhi: Oxford University Press.

Elleman, Bruce, Andrew Forbes, and David Rosenberg, eds. 2010. *Piracy and Maritime Crime: Historical and Modern Case Studies*. Annapolis: Naval War College Press. Online at digital-commons.usnwc.edu/newport-papers/19.

Feign, Larry. 2021. *The Flower Boat Girl: A Novel Based on a True Story*. Hong Kong: Top Floor Books.

Hang, Xing. 2018. "The Seventeenth-Century Guangdong Pirates and their Transnational Impact." In *Early Modern East Asia: War, Commerce, and Cultural Exchange. Essays in Honor of John E. Wills, Jr.*, edited by Kenneth M. Swope and Tonio Andrade, 151–65. London and New York: Routledge.

Higgins, Roland L. 1980. "Pirates in Gowns and Caps: Gentry Lawbreaking in the Mid-Ming." *Ming Studies* 10: 30–37.

Kleinen, John, and Manon Osseweijer, eds. 2010. *Pirates, Ports, and Coasts in Asia: Historical and Contemporary Perspectives*. Leiden: International Institute for Asian Studies.

Kung, James Kai-Sing, and Chicheng Ma. 2014. "Autarky and the Rise and Fall of Piracy in Ming China." *Journal of Economic History* 74 (2): 509–34.

Lane, Kris, and Robert Antony. 2020. "Piracy in Asia and the West." In *Cambridge World History of Violence, v. 3, 1500–1800 CE*, edited by Robert Antony, Stuart Carroll, and Caroline Dodds Pennock, 449–71. Cambridge and New York: Cambridge University Press.

Leung, Man-kam. 1977. "Piracy in South China in the Nineteenth Century." In *Buddhist Thought and Asian Civilization: Essays in Honor of Herbert V. Guenther on His Sixtieth Birthday*, edited by Leslie Kawamura and Keith Scott, 152–66. Emeryville: Dharma Press.

Murray, Dian H. 1997. "Living and Working Conditions in Chinese Pirate Communities, 1750–1850." In *Pirates and Privateers: New Perspectives on the War on Trade in the Eighteenth and Nineteenth Centuries*, edited by David J. Starkey, E. S. van Eyck van Heslinga, and J. A. de Moor, 47–68. Exeter: University of Exeter Press.

———. 1988. "Commerce, Crisis, Coercion: The Role of Piracy in Late Eighteenth and Early Nineteenth Century Sino-Western Relations." *American Neptune* 48 (1): 237–42.

Niu Junkai and Li Qingxin. 2011. "Chinese 'Political Pirates' in the Seventeenth-Century Gulf of Tongking." In *The Tongking Gulf through History*, edited by Nola Cooke, Li Tana, and James Anderson, 133–42. Philadelphia: University of Pennsylvania Press.

Pérotin-Dumon, Anne. 1991. "The Pirate and the Emperor: Power and the Law on the Seas, 1450–1850." In *The Political Economy of Merchant Empires*, edited by James Tracy, 196–227. Cambridge: Cambridge University Press.

Risso, Patricia. 2001. "Cross-Cultural Perceptions of Piracy: Maritime Violence in the Western Indian Ocean and Persian Gulf Region during a Long Eighteenth Century." *Journal of World History* 12 (2): 293–319.

Scammell, G. V. 1992. "European Exiles, Renegades and Outlaws and the Maritime Economy of Asia, c. 1500–1750." *Modern Asian Studies* 26 (4): 641–61.

Wang, Wensheng. 2014. *White Lotus Rebels and South China Pirates: Crisis and Reform in the Qing Empire*. Cambridge, MA: Harvard University Press.

Wang, Yong. 2002. "Realistic and Fantastic Images of Dwarf Pirates: The Evolution of Ming Dynasty Perceptions of the Japanese." In *Sagacious Monks and Bloodthirsty Warriors: Chinese Views of Japan in the Ming-Qing Period*, edited by Joshua Fogel, 17–41. Norwalk, CT: EastBridge.

Index

Altan Khan, 13, 139
Amoy, 8, 10, 27, 36, 38, 48, 86, 90, 141, 143
Annan 安南. *See* Vietnam
antipiracy measures, 16, 30–31, 37, 43, 60–62, 68, 91, 92, 115, 134
aojia 澳甲, 111n6, 143
appeasement, 42, 67, 134, 144. *See also* pacification
Austin, Francis, 40

Bailing 白齡, 43, 127–128, 132, 134–136
Baldy Li. *See* Li Guangtou
baojia 保甲, 68n28, 91, 143
Batavia, 8, 27
Beihai 北海, 80
benevolent thief (*rendao* 仁盜), 83–84. *See also* noble robber
Black Banner Fleet, 129n32, 136. *See also* Guo Podai
black markets, 4, 9, 35, 47, 50, 63n19, 103, 105. *See also* shadow economy
Black Pig Sea (Wuzhuyang 烏豬洋), Battle of, 70
Blue Banner Fleet, 41–42, 119. *See also* Wushi Er
Bogue. *See* Humen

booty, 4, 8, 18, 25, 42, 47, 50, 63, 88, 103–106, 108, 111, 113, 119, 120–122, 127, 130, 143; division of, 4, 35, 50, 88, 105, 119, 121, 135; sale of, 4, 8, 19, 29, 47, 103–104, 106, 113. *See also* pirates, common fund

Cai Qian 蔡牽, 35, 36–37, 107–109, 115, 141–142
Cai Qian Ma 蔡牽媽, 5, 37, 46, 109
Cai Shanji 蔡善繼, 85
Cambodia, 6, 30, 101–102
cannibalism, 19, 24, 74, 108
Canton, 8, 19, 29, 30n3, 38, 40–43, 48–49, 75–78, 94–95, 103, 104–105, 120, 121n22, 127–128, 129n33, 134n49, 136, 143–145
Canton System, 30n3, 143
Captain China. *See* Li Dan
Champa, 101
Changguo 昌國, 89
Chaozhou 潮州, 8, 19, 26, 28–29, 48, 76n39, 98, 115n14
chastity (*jieyi* 節義), 100
Chen Rui 陳瑞, 63–64
Chen Shangchuan 陳上川, 26, 29–30
Chen Shunxi 陳舜系, 24, 152
Chen Tianbao 陳添保, 35, 105

Chenghai 澄海, 92
Chey Chettha IV, 102n23
clandestine trade. *See* shadow economy
cosmic revelations/portents, 96–98
Cui Zhi 崔芝, 25, 26, 83–84, 88

Damao 大猫, 15–16
Dan/Danmin 蛋民, 20–21, 26, 28–29, 79–81, 94–95, 109, 141, 144
Danzhou 儋州, 98, 120
delivery ticket (*jiaopiao* 交票), 89. *See also* protection racket
Deng Liangzhi 鄧良知, 86
Deng Yao 鄧耀, 26, 30, 96–97, 141
Dog Head Li. *See* Li Goutou
Donghai Ba 東海八, 38, 42, 110, 141–142
Dongning 東寧, 101–102
Dongxing 東興, 9
Duolang 多浪, 79–80
Dutch, 24–25, 26–28, 88, 90, 140–141; Dutch East India Company (VOC), 24, 27–28, 50, 88, 140, 144; privateering, 24, 25, 27, 50, 88, 140; Taiwan and, 25, 27–28, 88, 90, 140–141; Zheng Zhilong and, 26, 27, 50, 88, 140
dwarf bandits. See *wokou*

empire building, 19, 50–51
Empress of Heaven, vii, 31, 49, 123
Escobar, João de, 75
extortion, 4, 8, 11, 28, 38, 42, 48, 89, 113, 122, 129–131. *See also* protection racket

famines, 24, 27, 34, 42, 85, 98, 127, 133–134, 139, 142. *See also* natural disasters
Fan Chengmo 范承謨, 94
Fang Sanqiao 方三橋, 63
Fangcheng 防城, 96–97
forced coastal evacuation policy (*qianjieling* 遷界令). *See* Great Clearance

foreign pirates (*yifei* 夷匪), 35, 147
Fort Zeelandia, 28
friendly ports, 8, 10, 16, 47, 59, 63, 114
Fujian 福建, 5–6, 10, 16, 18–20, 23–25, 26, 27–29, 34–38, 42, 59–64, 66–67, 69–70, 74, 78, 83, 85–86, 89–94, 97–109, 115, 139–146
Fuqing 福清, 83, 89
Fuxing 福興, 60
Fuzhou 福州, 60, 107

galleys, 13, 95, 144
Gaspard, Nicholas. *See* Zheng Zhilong
gentry, 10, 15–17, 27, 58, 98–100, 114n13
Giang Binh. *See* Jiangping
Góis, Gil de, 75–78
Glasspoole, Richard, 39, 42, 126, 128, 142
Great Clearance, 29, 91–95, 97, 141, 144
green oil (*qingyou* 青油), 105n1
Gu Yanwu 顧炎武, 74
Guangdong 廣東, 6, 10, 16, 18–19, 24, 26, 28–30, 35, 38, 40–43, 64, 67, 69–70, 74, 86, 91–95, 98, 101–103, 110, 114–116, 119–120, 122, 124, 126–129, 133–135, 140, 141–146
Guangzhou 廣州. *See* Canton
Gulf of Tonkin, 6, 9, 20, 26, 29–30, 41–42, 79–81, 96–98, 101–102, 103–106, 119, 123, 127, 140, 141, 145
Guo Podai 郭婆帶, 38, 110, 127–128, 129n32, 136, 142
Guo Xuexian 郭學顯. *See* Guo Podai

Haicheng 海澄, 10, 24, 63n19. *See also* Yuegang
haifei 海匪. *See* sea bandits
Haifeng 海豐, 29, 86, 112
Haikang 海康, 80, 106
haikou 海寇. *See* sea rebels
Hainan 海南, 6, 96, 98–100, 104, 106
haini 海逆. *See* sea rebels
Hakata 博多, 16

Index

Hangzhou 杭州, 13, 61, 66, 99n12, 139
He Yuli 何玉理, 105–107
He Zongpei 何宗培, 128
Hepu 合浦, 9, 21, 80, 97, 120. *See also* Lianzhou
Hirado 平戶, 27, 47, 78n45, 84, 89
homosexuality, 40, 106, 118n18
Hong Dizhen 洪迪珍, 15, 140
Hong Kong 香港, 123–124, 129n31, 145
Hong merchants, 33n1, 127, 144
Hu Zongxian 胡宗憲, 17, 67, 140
Huang Jin 黃进, 102
Huang Mingchu 黃明初, 94
Huangpu 黄埔. *See* Whampoa
Huizhou 徽州 (Anhui 安徽), 18, 63–64
Huizhou 惠州 (Guangdong 廣東), 115n14, 123–124, 128
Humen 虎門, 76n39, 78, 127, 129, 136

Iida Koichiro, 56
illicit trade. *See* smuggling
Iquan, Nicholas. *See* Zheng Zhilong

Japan, 6–7, 13, 15–18, 21, 25, 26, 27, 47, 55–56, 58–61, 63–68, 77, 84, 89, 101, 139–140
Jiajing emperor 嘉靖帝, 13–14, 16, 21, 60, 63, 76n39, 139, 140
Jiangping 江坪, 9, 35, 47, 103, 105–106
Jianning 建寧, 60
Jiaqing emperor 嘉慶帝, 42, 105, 113–114, 119, 128, 135, 141
Jiazi 甲子, 38, 112–115
Jin Guyang 金古養, 110
Jin Shijie 金世傑, 63
Jinmen 金門. *See* Quemoy

Kangxi emperor 康熙帝, 30, 92, 94–95, 97, 100, 141
kidnapping, 4, 19, 25, 29, 38–42, 74, 103–104, 106, 112–113, 116, 118n19, 119–123, 126, 133, 141–142. *See also* ransom

Kitaura Kanjuro, 56
Korea, 6–7, 13n1, 139–140, 147
Koxinga. *See* Zheng Chenggong
Kyushu 九州, 16, 18, 55

Ladrones, 48, 116, 118–119, 126, 129–132, 145. *See also* pirates
Lantau 爛頭 (Dayushan 大嶼山), 124, 127n29, 129n31
Leftover Calabash (*Piaosheng* 瓢剩), 95
Leizhou 雷州, 19, 27, 30, 41–42, 79n48, 80, 104–106, 120, 140
Li Chaoqin 李朝欽, 100
Li Chongyu 李崇玉, 38, 47, 112–116
Li Dan 李旦, 25, 26, 27, 84
Li Goutou 李狗頭, 16
Li Guangtou 李光頭, 15–16
Li Rong 李榮, 26, 29, 94–95, 141
Li Xiangqing 李相清. *See* Jin Guyang
Li Yafa 李亞發, 115
Li Zhifang 李之芳, 93
Liang Bao 梁保. *See* Zongbing Bao
Liangshan 梁山. *See* Mount Liang
Lianzhou 廉州, 79n48, 80, 97–98, 104, 120–122. *See also* Hepu
Lienzhou 連州, 114
lijia 里甲, 80n49, 143
Lin Daoqian 林道乾, 19, 69
Lin Fubang 林輔邦, 94
Lin Guoxian 林國顯, 69
Lin Jian 林剪, 75
Lin Shuangwen 林爽文 Rebellion, 34
Lin Xiyuan 林希元, 19–20, 62, 74
Lin Yu 林昱, 59
Liu Xiang 劉香, 25, 26, 27, 83–84, 140
Ljungstedt, Anders, 8
Longmen 龍門, 29–30, 96–98, 101
Lord of the Imperial Surname (Guoxingye 國姓爺), 90, 141. *See also* Zheng Chenggong
Lufeng 陸豐, 112, 114
Luo Hanqing 羅漢卿, 80
Luzon, 19, 88n9

Macau (Aomen 澳門), 8–9, 19–20, 25, 29, 38, 39, 43, 48, 75–78, 84, 116, 118, 126, 136, 140, 145
McClary, John, 33n1
Mai Youjin 麥有金. *See* Wushi Er
Malacca, 8, 16, 78
Malacca Strait, 45, 51
Manchus, 23, 28–30, 84, 91, 92n13, 96, 109n4, 140, 146. *See also* Qing dynasty
Manila, 8, 25, 27, 39, 84, 88, 144
maritime trade, 4, 6–8, 14, 16, 18, 21, 24n1, 25, 29–33, 50, 59, 67, 84, 90, 91n12, 96, 101n22, 139, 141, 146
Mazu 媽祖. *See* Empress of Heaven
Melo, Luís de, 76–77
merchants, 4, 6, 8, 10, 15–18, 21, 27–29, 31, 47–50, 59, 65, 74, 76n38, 78–79, 83–84, 90, 96, 112, 115, 122
merchant-pirates, 15, 16, 19, 25, 26, 45, 65–66, 145. *See also* smuggler-pirates
Mercury (British ship), 127n29
Ming dynasty 明朝, 4–6, 8, 13–21, 23, 25, 27–30, 50, 55–57, 59, 66, 69, 73–75, 79–81, 83–84, 89–90, 96–97, 139–141, 145–146
Ming loyalists, 25, 28, 30, 90, 140–141, 145
Mo Guanfu 莫官扶, 35, 104–107
Mong Cai 芒街, 9, 21
Mount Liang, 66, 133
Murakami Zusho, 55
murder, 3–4, 39, 48, 58, 65, 70, 73, 76–77, 80, 94, 103, 105–107, 113, 115, 130–132. *See also* piracy, violence
My Tho, 30, 101

Nagasaki 長崎, 8, 78n45, 101
Nan'an 南安, 85
Nan'ao 南澳, 15, 18, 25, 69–73, 85, 140
Nanjing 南京, 13, 16, 28, 59, 66, 139, 141

natural disasters, 34, 42–43, 96–98. *See also* famines; typhoons
Nayancheng 那彥成, 38, 113, 115
Ningbo 寧波, 15, 58, 60, 64, 89, 91n12, 139
Ninghai 寧海, 63
noble robber, 5, 27, 30, 66, 84, 86, 100, 146. *See also* benevolent thief
Noshima 能島, 55

occasional piracy, 25, 33, 46, 101
ocean bandits, 6, 33, 35, 127–128, 147
overseas trade. *See* maritime trade

pacification (*zhaofu* 招撫), 80, 85n4, 86, 94, 97, 132, 137, 147. *See also* appeasement
Pang Shunyu 龐順遇, 103–104
Pangasinan, 88
Panyu 番禺, 95, 120
Patani, 15–16, 19
Pearl River Delta, 19, 24, 34, 42, 48, 94–95, 101, 105, 124, 127–128, 130n34, 133, 135, 141–142
pearl thieves (*zhuzei* 珠賊), 20–21, 79–81, 140, 145. *See also* Su Guansheng; Zhou Caixiong
Penghu 澎湖. *See* Pescadores
Pereira, Diogo, 76–79
Pescadores, 25, 43, 145
Philippines, 6–7, 19, 21, 25, 28, 55, 88, 141, 144
Pho Hien 舖憲, 9, 21
Pinto, Mendes, 19
piracy, as a job, 46, 118; banners and, 40, 95, 110–111; causes of, 10, 14–15, 23–24, 33–34, 133–134; Chinese terms for, 4–5, 144, 145, 147; decline of, 21, 30–31, 42–43; definitions, 4; importance of, 3, 45–51; petty, 10, 20, 33, 103–104; professional, 33, 35, 41, 46; punishments for, 28, 35, 43, 48, 59, 91, 105, 119–123, 128; seasonal

activity of, 15, 35, 65, 77; support for, 5, 10, 15, 27, 35, 38, 58, 62–68, 75, 91, 128–130; suppression of, 16, 21, 29, 37–38, 70, 95, 120; trade and, 4, 8–10, 15–16, 19, 27–28, 47, 75, 90, 110–112; victims of, 98–100, 103–107, 114–115, 121, 129–132; violence and, 28–29, 48, 69, 76, 104, 131; warfare and, 4, 23–24, 96
pirates, brutality of, 28–29, 48, 69, 78, 80, 98–99, 100, 104, 130–132; captives of, 13, 38, 46, 48, 106–109, 118; codes/pacts (*yue* 約), 38, 50, 110–112, 135–136; common fund, 4, 111, 119, 135; customs and lifestyles, 8, 118, 126; deification of, 5, 18, 46, 90; division of booty, 4, 119, 121, 135; fishers/fisherfolk as, 29, 35, 45, 56, 104–105; islands, 15–16, 22, 27, 28, 30, 42, 70, 129n31, 134; lairs/bases, 15, 27, 28, 30, 38, 42, 48, 70, 73, 86; popular culture and, 3, 5, 50; recruitment of, 105, 118, 120–121, 131; religious beliefs/practices, 49–50, 85, 123–125, 130; ships, 5, 18, 35, 40, 56, 63, 90, 95, 106–106, 110, 116–119, 126, 129; social backgrounds of, 5, 15, 45–46, 104–105, 113–114, 118, 120; weapons, 18, 28, 56, 58, 63, 84, 116–118, 130
political pirates, 28, 145
Portugal/Portuguese, 8, 15–16, 18–20, 39, 50, 62, 74–79, 84, 88, 129, 139, 140, 144, 145
privateer, 4, 19, 24, 28, 33, 50, 88, 145. *See also* Dutch, privateering
prize. *See* booty
prostitution, 8, 40
protection racket, 8, 18, 27, 37–38, 48, 88–89, 135. *See also* extortion
Putian 莆田, 89, 141

Qi Jiguang 戚繼光, 21, 69–70, 73, 140
Qianlong emperor 乾隆帝, 34n2, 141

Qing dynasty 清朝, 4, 6, 8, 10, 23, 28–31, 34–35, 37–38, 41–42, 50, 83–84, 90–92, 95–98, 101, 109n4, 111n6, 114n13, 115n15, 119, 140–142, 144–146. *See also* Manchus
Qinshe 欽舍, 101–102
Qinzhou 欽州, 9, 21, 30, 96–98
Qiu Hui 邱輝, 26, 28
Quemoy, 38, 62n17, 90, 146
Quang Nam, 101–102
Quanzhou 泉州, 10, 27, 37n3, 60–61, 85–86, 107–108

ransom, 3, 8, 29, 38, 39, 42, 106, 112n8, 116, 118–119, 121–122, 126, 129n33, 130–132, 141, 142. *See also* kidnapping
rape, 4, 104, 135–136. *See also* piracy, violence
Raoping 饒平, 69–70
Red Banner Fleet, 40, 116–117, 126, 135–137, 142. *See also* Zheng Yi Sao; Zhang Bao
Revolt of the Three Feudatories (1673–1681), 92n13, 97–98, 141, 146. *See also* Wu Sangui
Righteous Yang 楊義. *See* Yang Yandi
rivers and lakes (*jianghu* 江湖), 71, 83, 133, 144
robbery, 4, 21, 28, 94, 104, 113, 133–134
ronin 浪人, 13, 55, 146
row boats, 117, 126, 129, 132. *See also* galleys

safe conduct passes, 38, 48, 89, 111–112. *See also* protection racket
Saigon, 30, 101. *See also* My Tho
Sanpo 三婆. *See* Third Old Lady
Sato Shinen, 55
sea bandits, 4, 93, 144. *See also* pirates
sea bans (*haijin* 海禁), 4, 8, 10, 14–16, 18–19, 21n3, 23, 29–30, 59, 66n24, 67, 86, 91, 95, 139–140, 141, 145–146. *See also* Great Clearance

Index

sea rebels, 6, 23, 91, 97, 144. *See also* pirates
secret societies. *See* Triads
shadow economy, 3, 8–10, 15–16, 18–19, 47, 59, 96. *See also* black markets
Shandong 山東, 91–92, 144
Shang Kexi 尚可喜, 92, 94–95, 97n17
Shaoxing 紹興, 60, 63–64, 91n12
Shi Xianggu 石香姑. *See* Zheng Yi Sao
Shicheng 石城, 79–80, 106
Shuangyu 雙嶼, 15–16, 18–19, 50, 63–64, 66n24, 139
Shunzhi emperor 順治帝, 91, 92n13, 140
Siam. *See* Thailand
slaves, 13, 19, 25, 122
smuggling, 4, 8, 10, 13, 15–16, 18–19, 25, 26, 31, 47, 56–58, 59–64, 83, 86n6, 96, 123, 139, 145. *See also* shadow economy
smuggler-pirates. *See* merchant-pirates
Sō Sokyo. *See* Song Suqing
Society of Filial Sons, 114
sodomy. *See* homosexuality
Sonck, Martinus, 88
Song Suqing 宋素卿, 58
Songmen 松門, 59
South China Sea, 6–7, 9–10, 19, 23, 25, 27, 33, 45, 51, 84, 101n22, 141
Southeast Asia, 5–6, 8–9, 15–19, 25, 26, 28, 33, 45, 47, 51, 55, 59, 66, 74, 75n37, 101, 139, 144
Southern Pacification King (*Ping Nan Wang*平南王). *See* Shang Kexi
state building, 50–51
state sanctioned raiding. *See* privateering
Stinky Red Meat (Chou Hong Rou 臭紅肉). *See* Qiu Hui
Su Cheng 蘇成, 26, 29
Su Guansheng 蘇觀陞, 21, 79–81
Su Li 蘇利, 26, 29
Suixi 遂溪, 104–106, 120

Sun Quanmou 孫全謀, 131n38
Suzhou 蘇州, 13, 64, 91n12, 139

Tagawa Matsu 田川松, 89
Taizhou 台州, 59n12, 89
Tan Lin'gao 譚琳高, 94
Tanka. *See* Dan/Danmin
Taiwan 台灣, 5–6, 10, 19, 25, 26, 27–30, 34, 36–38, 47, 50, 84–85, 88, 90, 92, 96–98, 101, 140, 141
Tay Son Rebellion, 9, 34–35, 38, 41–42, 50, 105, 110, 141, 146–147
Thailand, 6–7, 19, 39, 101–102
Third Old Lady, 50, 123–125, 130
Tianhou 天后. *See* Empress of Heaven
Tianjin 天津, 91
Tokugawa 徳川, 21
Tong'an 同安, 36, 62, 107–108
Tonkin, 102
traders. *See* merchants
treason, 5, 58, 66, 91–92, 109n4
Triads, 37, 112, 114n10, 120
tributary system, 13–15, 39, 58n9, 60–61, 70n32, 97, 139, 146
Turner, John, 38, 39, 116–119, 142
typhoons 24, 34, 135. *See also* natural disasters

Veloso, Pêro, 78
Vietnam, 6–7, 9, 18–19, 21, 30, 34–35, 42, 47, 50, 69–70, 79–80, 96–98, 101–102, 103, 105–106, 110, 141, 143, 146, 147
VOC. *See* Dutch East India Company

wakō. *See wokou*
Wang Songchen 王崧辰, 107
Wang Tengkuei 王騰奎, 115
Wang Yin 王印, 95
Wang You 王猷, 86
Wang Zhi 王直/汪直, 15, 18, 55, 65–67, 139–140
Wang Zhijian 王之鑒, 30
Wang Zhihan 王之瀚, 30

Index

water fee (*baoshui* 報水), 89. *See also* protection racket
Weizhou 灣洲, 20, 42, 48, 79, 119–123
Wenzhou 溫州, 58, 59n12, 91n12, 109
Whampoa, 39, 118, 127
White Dragon Tail (Bailongwei 白龍尾), 104
White Lotus Rebellion, 34
wokou 倭寇, 6, 13, 15–16, 18–21, 25, 55–57, 58n9, 65–67, 139, 96, 139, 140, 144, 147
women, 5, 24, 29, 42, 46–47, 94, 120–121, 126; as pirates, 5, 37, 42, 46–47, 101, 109, 133, 135–137; as victims, 43, 46, 65, 80, 98–100, 118, 121, 130–131, 141; committing suicide, 100, 131; on board ships 5, 46; wives of pirates, 29, 37, 46, 109, 118, 121, 123, 126, 131, 136. *See also* Cai Qian Ma; Zheng Yi Sao
Wu Guifang 吳桂芳, 70
Wu Ping 吳平, 18–19, 69–71, 73, 140
Wu Ping's Sister, 18, 46, 71–73
Wu Qi 吳綺, 98
Wu Sangui 吳三桂, 92n13, 97, 146. *See also* Revolt of the Three Feudatories
Wu Shangde 吳尚德, 112
Wu Xiongguang 吳熊光, 119–121
Wu Zhiqing 吳知青. *See* Donghai Ba
Wu Zhipu 吳芝圃, 107–108
Wuchuan 吳川, 24, 103, 107
Wushi Er 烏石二, 38, 41–42, 45,110, 115, 119–120, 141–142
Wutu 烏兔, 79–81
Wuyu 浯嶼, 15, 69–70
Wuzhou 浯洲. *See also* Quemoy

Xiamen 廈門. *See* Amoy
Xian Biao 冼彪, 26, 29–30, 96, 98
Xian Yasheng 冼亞盛, 103–104
Xiangshan 香山, 93, 127, 136
Xin'an 新安, 24
Xinhui 新會, 104, 120, 127
Xiong Wencan 熊文燦, 86
Xu Dong 許棟, 15–18, 64, 139

Xu Er 許二. *See* Xu Dong
Xu Hai 徐海, 15, 65
Xu Xinsu 許心素, 86
Xu Yongtai 徐永泰, 76n39
Xu Chaoguang 許朝光, 69
Xuwen 徐聞, 106

Yan Jizu 顏繼祖, 86
Yan Siqi 顏思齊. *See* Yan Zhenquan
Yan Zhenquan 顏振泉, 25, 26, 27, 84–85, 88
Yang Er 楊二. *See* Yang Yandi
Yang San 楊三, 26, 30, 96–97
Yang Yandi 楊彥迪, 26, 29–30, 45, 96–102, 141
yangdao 洋盜. *See* ocean bandits
yangfei 洋匪. *See* sea bandits
Yangjiang 陽江, 70, 100
Yongan 永安, 80–81
Yu Dayou 俞大猷, 69–70, 78n46
Yu Yonghe 郁永河, 89–90
Yu Zigao 俞咨皋, 86
Yuan Yonglun 袁永綸, 123–124, 135
Yuegang 月港, 10, 63. *See also* Haicheng

Zeng Guobin 曾國賓, 80
Zeng Yiben 曾一本, 19, 69
zengchuan 繒船 (silk boat), 95n14
Zhang Bao 張保, 8–9, 40–43, 45, 49–50, 116, 123–125, 127–129, 132–133, 135–136, 142
Zhang Linbai 張麟白, 83
Zhangpu 漳浦, 34, 86
Zhangzhou 漳州, 27, 37, 58, 60–61, 64, 86
Zhao Pishi 趙劈石, 93
Zhao Qi 趙柒, 63–64
Zhaoan 诏安, 19, 38, 69, 115
Zhejiang 浙江, 6, 15–16, 20, 26, 35–37, 56n3, 57–61, 63–67, 83, 86, 89, 91, 109, 139, 140
Zheng Chenggong 鄭成功, 5, 25, 26, 28, 45–46, 50, 89–92, 96–97, 141, 144

Zheng Kezang 鄭克壓. *See* Qinshe
Zheng Jing 鄭經, 25, 26, 28–30, 50, 97–98, 101n21, 141
Zheng Laotong 鄭老童, 110
Zheng Liutang 鄭流唐. *See* Zheng Laotong
Zheng Ruozeng 鄭若曾, 15
Zheng Shangzhi 鄭尚知, 98
Zheng Shaozu 鄭紹祖, 85
Zheng Wenxian 鄭文顯. *See* Zhang Yi
Zheng Xiao 鄭曉, 56–58
Zheng Yi 鄭一, 35, 38, 40, 110, 115, 135, 141–142
Zheng Yi Sao 鄭一嫂, 5, 9, 40, 42–43, 46, 116, 127, 129n32, 133, 135–137, 142
Zheng Zhilong 鄭芝龍, 5, 25, 26, 27–28, 49–50, 83–86, 88–89, 140–141
Zhou Caixiong 周才雄, 21, 79–80, 140
Zhou Feixiong 周飛熊, 8, 38, 136
Zhou Qingyuan 周清源, 66
Zhou Yu 周玉, 26, 29, 94–95, 141
Zhu Fen 朱濆, 35, 37, 113, 115–116, 142
Zhu Gui 朱珪, 105
Zhu Jinshan 朱近山, 64
Zhu Qinxiang 朱欽相, 85
Zhu Wan 朱紈, 16–17, 60–64, 74, 139
Zhu Yifeng 朱一馮, 86
Zongbing Bao 總兵寶, 110, 115